Award Winning Best-Selling Author of *Superpowers*

EARTH
GAMES

Playbook Rules and Regulations

NOELLE HIPKE

Earth Games Praise

"Earth Games is a visionary exploration into the cosmic dimensions of human existence, offering profound insights and spiritual wisdom. It explores the intricacies of our earthly journey and beyond, revealing hidden truths and guiding readers towards higher consciousness. What I enjoyed most about reading it was the poetic and artistic expressions that beautifully complemented the transformative messages. It's a great read that opens new perspectives on spirituality and personal growth.

-Abigail L., Atlanta Public Librarian, 5 Stars

~

Are you ready to level up your cosmic game? Earth Games is a mind-bending journey through the realms of consciousness and cosmic connection. This book isn't just about awakening; it's a turbo-charged ride to unlock your unlimited potential and connect with the universe on a whole new level! With celestial insights and divine poetry, it's like having a VIP pass to the secrets of the cosmos. Get ready to transcend and transform-this is your invitation to play the ultimate game of evolution!

-Sue E., Reviewer, 5 Stars

~

"As an anthropologist, I read widely on myth and current representations of ancient archetypes. Author Noelle Hipke's new book *Earth Games,* captures the current language that is part of todays way of presenting these cosmo mythic conversations. Her emphasis on life as a game documents her journey into interior listening that produces mythical encounters so long represented in the human psyche.

-Gina Bria, Cultural Anthropologist, Author and Real World Scholar, Founder of Hydration Foundation

~

"*Earth Games* is a breakthrough moment to ignite the spark in humanity to move toward a cosmic universe. Profound ascension of perception connects multidimensional key codes and stargate portals to bring humanity to an entirely new level. Noelle is breaking ground in building the foundation of the New Earth. Follow her lead and journey to go Galactic!"

-Natasha White, Entrepreneur

~

"I love this message from Noelle Hipke's latest book, "When you follow your gut and go with the flow, anything goes," In *Earth Games* you will hear her honest and caring voice throughout as she shares her journey. Noelle's guidance can benefit us all."

-Dean Karrel, Career Development Advisor, LinkedIn Learning Instructor, Author of *Mastering the Basics: Simple Lessons for Achieving Success in Business*

~

"Noelle has opened the portal to the gateway of ascension. Reading her books has triggered me to align with my higher authentic self. A whole New Earth rebirth is being brought on and showcased in Noelle's work. She expands the bridge between Heaven on Earth."

-Lisa Larson, Architect

"Noelle gives you insight and information on the pieces to the puzzle that are hidden in plain sight. With eyes wide open you can "see" the landscape before you and move to the next level of *Earth Games*."

-Annette Villaverde, Transformational Life Coach

~

"Noelle Hipke is a forward-thinking visionary who perceives the world from a unique perspective. In this phenomenal book, Noelle paves the way for a new human reality on a New Earth. With channeled insights, she serves as a guiding light in the mission to heal humanity and drive innovation. *Earth Games* encourages us to break free from the limitations imposed by societal conditioning, embrace transformation, and see the world with new eyes. Reading it, you will be inspired to realize your true identity and champion the incredible power within you.

-Randi Fine, Narcissistic Abuse Expert and Recovery Coach, Author of *Close Encounters of the Worst Kind: The Narcissistic Abuse Survivor's Guide to Healing and Recovery*

~

"Wake up World! *Earth Games* is "next level" innovation. Noelle's poetry is incredibly beyond the norm! Charting out multiple layers of knowledge and discoveries to tickle your spirit into vibrating an entirely new way. The whole world is going to change once this knowledge gets out!"

-Brayden Hansen, CEO

~

"Earth Games blows up how we operate in the 3D world moving into the 5D and beyond. The stages and multidimensions going on in this book are incredible. Highly recommend taking the time to immerse yourself in this manuscript."

-Janet Thompson, Research Director

NOELLE HIPKE

EARTH GAMES
Playbook Rules and Regulations

Noelle Hipke

HipKey TV Press

Earth Games: Playbook Rules and Regulations
by Noelle Hipke

ISBN 979-8-9905954-7-7

Published by

HipKey TV Press
Huntington Beach, CA 92648
www.HipKeyTV.com

This book is dedicated to every species in the universe. I know you are out there watching, witnessing and wondering how humans are going to play it out on Earth Games. I want to thank each species for offering their tidbits of information for me to compose this book.

~

To my angels, guides, 11D and 12D beings who have been by my side when not another living soul in the 3D Earth Plane could be there for me 24/7.

~

To my dog Karma (Jack Russell & Chihuahua mix), who has taught me the meaning of unconditional love. I know you are my previous dog, Jack Russell, reincarnated.

~

To my dad, friends, grandparents and ancestors on the other side who appeared from time to time thanking me for all the hard work I am doing to bring light into the world by shining light in the dark. Thank you for choosing me and my children to be the ones to break the generational family patterns and celebrating us for each milestone as they occurred.

~

To Jesus, Louise Hay, Wayne Dyer, Dolores Cannon, Sylvia Browne and other teachers and masters on the other side who appeared to give me guidance, cheer me on and remind me I am doing exactly my soul mission on this planet even when others cannot see or understand it.

Contents

Introduction

Earth Games spawned out of me during the winter of 2022. I found myself alone on Christmas Eve and decided to attend a church service in order to be around music, lights, positivity, happiness and the message of Christmas. It turned into a rather amazing experience. After the service, I went home to hear angels singing Christmas carols on the other side...in the afterlife. I wrote down the songs I was hearing and then looked up the words to process the meaning they were sharing. I had never had this type of experience before. However, as I have been evolving, growing, opening and expanding while traveling into other realms and dimensions, I have had numerous people on the other side come and give me messages. Louise Hay, Dr. Wayne Dyer, Jesus, and I have to say Dolores Cannon seem to come through even though I have read none of her material or books. I have heard her speaking from time to time on videos, while her content seems parallel at times to mine. I often wondered if I was channeling her. Either way, the world around me was shifting as I know it.

That night on Christmas Eve, I was guided to bring a journal, pen, and flashlight to bed. I stayed up most of the night turning off and on the flashlight to write in my journal, and that was when this book was born. It took me three weeks to write this book from start to finish. I was told to wait a year by a literary agent to release the second book, so I put it in the cue. Now it is December 25, 2023 and I find myself alone once again on Christmas day and was guided to edit this next book for release in 2024. Some of you may find this shocking, but what I have learned is several insights from these alone on the holiday experiences.

1. One who is doing the inner work on themselves is granted access to the heavens when they sit alone and go within.

2. I find I have some of "THE" most incredible downloads of unbelievable knowledge that can only be acquired during this time of the season.

3. Something magical happens when you are alone on Christmas Day. Angels, Jesus and God come closer to help one see, feel and understand what others cannot due to the holiday distractions and others people's energy.

4. Ascension occurs when you are alone in complete self-love.

5. Knowing the entire universe is supporting your decision to be alone vs. being in the company of others who display improper or abusive behavior is a much better position to be in than sitting in the room with others who project negativity at you for being able to alter your state of mind and frequency when they cannot.

After my first book *Superpowers* came out. It revealed to me I was surrounded in a cycle of narcissism and eventually noted this pattern was running throughout much of society and several generational timelines in all types of families. It was running in my family, my previous spouse's family, as well as my circle of friends. I noticed it in the workplace as well as on school campuses. It was a very large wake up call for me, as I processed my part in the game. This is when it hit me, this is a piece of the conscious movement awakening taking place on the planet. Each one of us is supposed to figure out what part we play in Earth Games to help heal and reveal ourselves and each other. Often it brought on large separations as cycle disrupters stepped out of their sequence to change the patterns of the game in order to bring ascension on humanity in accelerated form.

When you are following your gut and go with the flow...anything can glow! I considered approaching a publisher for the rest of the series but realized I can do it all on my own. It's really an author's job to market their own book to get it out into the world or universe, I should say, so I committed to doing this round myself. Considering it took over a year to get my first book through a publisher, I knew I could have this edition out sooner than later.

Every year, right around my birthday, I write about all the things I have accomplished that year. And just so you know, I still have moments where I am not sure I've made it. Here is my list for 2023.

1. Published my first book *Superpowers, A Journey to Self Health*

2. Narrated my first audiobook, *Superpowers.*

3. Created and produced a TV Channel interviewing guests who are in my book and other special New Earth Superpower Luminaries.

4. Created and produced a course, *Superpowers Activations: Build Your Own Human Instruction Manual* and placed it on my website and on a UK website called Udemy.

5. Bought a new roof, did some home remodeling, decluttered my home, releasing decades old of memories, allowing me to be reborn yet again.

6. Inspired others to step into their superpowers and take control of their lives to make life altering changes.

I realized when looking at your bank account, your accomplishments might not be reflected in your finances. In actuality, what is incredibly priceless is the fact you are impacting and creating a ripple effect around you and those in the afterlife and other dimensions. I saw generations on the other side cheering me on and relaying to me it was myself and my children came down here to break the generational programming patterns that had been taking place on the planet for decades. Programs and patterns running in our timeline and throughout humanity. Once I was able to identify the pattern and program, I discovered how to define and rewrite and alter the program. It's all a test. If you are reading this, listen up...you are the chosen ones who came down to play Earth Games to clear and break the programming and generational timelines.

I am the portal activating you to activate yourself and remember who you are and what you came down here to do. I have witnessed people get triggered from reading my first book *Superpowers*, and then go into healing mode and not even know it. I have had people call me to cry when they have an epiphany after I've shared bits of knowledge meant for them at that moment in time to hear and heal. It has been a beautiful, amazing journey propelling people into writing that book they never thought they would get to write. Their story told from their perspective, which will serve as their legacy on this planet for the rest of eternity. Poof! My book *Superpowers* is doing exactly what it is meant to do: it takes you to the next level and then up even more levels to activate the power within to heal yourself!

At first, I would get uneasy when I saw the transformation starting to take place in someone because I could see and feel it. Often, they met it with resistance, spewing out negativity as they were releasing and mutating. Then I soon realized they were moving through the fields to grasp the downloads I was sharing and becoming alive and one with them as they transformed. I noticed my book *Superpowers* glowed when people held it in their hands and often found the sacred geometry emblem on it to be moving and vibrating, indicating it is alive. I was told by my angels and guides the sacred geometry symbol on the book cover was the twelfth chakra.

So now I present to you, my next masterpiece. *Earth Games*. It's time we define the rules of the game on Earth. We were all given these rules before we came down to Earth, signing off on them before we entered. However, we quickly forgot them as we passed over to the earth dimension. I retrieved this information by download of converting light codes from the infinite intelligence in the cosmic field. I see it as light information floating in the air, merging it together to form the data compiled in this book. The activation of my superpowers has granted me access to higher dimensions. I have attempted to live consciously paying attention to what I say, do, and whom I connect with energetically.

One must do the inner healing work and shadow work for those of you who are the path to reaching ascension. One must make the choice to take the path less traveled in order to break the program.

Get ready...for I am going to take you up several levels in Earth Games. As you play, players will be eliminated in your life. Players who aren't playing the game, can't see the game or want to discredit the game. The ultimate goal is to reach ascension into the next dimension. Ascension may require you to trail blaze your own pathway for a while in order to gain access to portals in the higher levels. Lessons and genetic transmutations will take place as you alter your frequency to remember who you are and discover how to become your authentic self once again. In turn, granting you transformation, telepathy, and transcendence.

We are all about to go galactic...it's gonna be fantastic!

Welcome to the cosmic conscious evolution.

Be Luminary!

Noelle Hipke

Award Winning Best-Selling Author

www.NoelleHipke.com

If you feel this book brings you value or taught you something worthy of sharing. I would be so honored if you would take a few minutes to write me a book review on Amazon or the platform you acquired this book from. Let your participation in Earth Games be known!

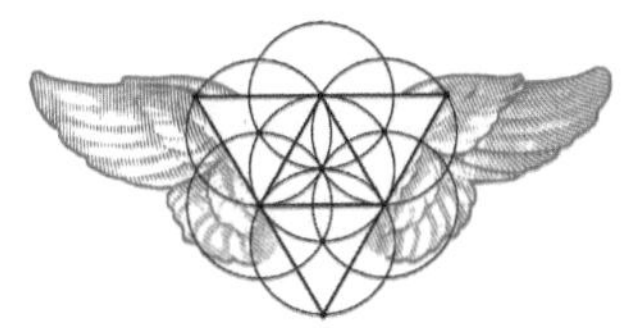

Chapter One

CONNECTING THE DOTS

Remember when we were kids and there was this product called invisible ink? While that is how the game of life is played on Earth. Our subconscious mind and unconscious minds are ruling our actions, thoughts, feelings, emotions, and our energy. Everything that is happening to humans right now is invisible energetic psychological mind games. They can't see it or pinpoint it, and it's driving many people over the edge. Many people are becoming aware and are cluing in, while others want to fight to believe what they have been programmed to believe as true.

I want you to think of life on Earth as a holographic video game. When you are in the 3rd Dimension, you can only see part of the show. What you perceive as physical. If you can't see it, feel it or touch it, you don't think it exists. But when you move into higher dimensions and densities, you see other things you never knew existed. Take, for instance, mythology.

What if everything we were taught as fiction is actually real? It was only experienced and seen in other higher dimensions?

Ponder if it falls under fact, fiction, or non-fiction. Think past, present, future. Think peace, hope, love. Father, son, holy spirit. Triad, trinity, three of a kind. Multiple perspectives, multiple futures, multiple dimensions & frequencies. Let's just say life is a game. And you find all the clues right in front of you to put the pieces together and play the game. The rules are not truly established and they change over time. Kind of like in the film, *The Hunger Games*.

What I am going to do for you here is to assemble the pieces of the puzzle I have learned in my lifetimes, so you can see the bigger picture of how the game has unfolded in my life. We think we have no control, and often we do not, due to outside forces manipulating the game. And when I say outside forces, I want you to go outside and look up at the sky. Think about that for a bit. Remember, many concepts are invisible, frequency and energy in the game of life we are talking about here.

Okay, so let's say in the game of Earth, you have to figure clues out based on books, song lyrics, movies, lessons, games, experiences, pain, emotions, abuse, religion, work, sports, travel and other things you can't quite tie a physical product to. So, get ready to see the patterns, synchronies, and symbolisms here clearing the vision.

First, I must let you know, these ideas came to me after I did some serious purging and organizing of my home. I cleared out old blockages, removed obstacles, and new data filtered into my space so I could gain access to the information clearly. So, whenever you want a mind clearing, I highly recommend you detox and declutter your home. It's one of the best ways to clear negative patterns and open the door to new positive ones.

So, let's start with games. When I was a kid, we liked to play games and I still like to this day. I am going to share my favorite games with you right now so you can see how these patterns work in my life. My favorite games are Sequence (which is looking for patterns and sequences), Pictionary (where one draws a picture and people need to figure out what the artist is drawing). So, based on these two board games alone, I am going to do just that for you here right in this book.

Reminder, the basic rules of Earth Games, is you figuring it out by exposure and knowledge from other humans based on films, books, games, travel, work, sports, experiences, lessons, mathematics, sound, animals, symbolism, earth, air, water, fire and space to name a few. We are all each others teachers. There are many other options due to the higher dimensions and using extra sensory of multiple perceptions.

Consider all the things we learn and are enticed by throughout our lives, but we perceive them as fiction or mere games, even though competition actually underlies them. Think of all the board games that were placed in front of us as just a way and part of life. Puzzles, board games, word searches, crossword puzzles and card games. Us thinking they are harmless and not meaningful, but in actuality they are preparing us for Earth Games and to see the "BIG" picture.

BOARD GAMES

Let's cover some of the board games here...The Game of LIFE, CLUE, Operation, Connect Four, Blackjack, Monopoly, Poker. We are taught in order to play Earth Games; we have to live by their rules, beliefs and systems. As in The Game of LIFE, we need to go to school, get a job, buy a house and have a family. We need to figure things out by putting the pieces of the puzzle together to find out who did something wrong, like in the game of CLUE. Operation is what we do to our bodies when something goes wrong, not find another alternative. Connect Four is connecting patterns, sequences, and colors together to make you dominate by putting everything in a row. Blackjack is about hitting the number 21, using numbers, patterns, strategy, card counting, body counting and reading the cards on the table. Poker is about bluffing, lying, pretending, card counting, pattern recognition, manipulation, out maneuvering every opponent on the table and the dealer. Monopoly is about acquiring as much property as you can to make others pay who cross your path. Dominating the world by owning things that will make humans a slave to surviving in society.

So now I want to move into films, tv shows, you tube videos, Netflix shows, Amazon Prime, etc. I want you to think about the premise of all these videos as bits and parts of Earth Games. Each time humanity is exposed to a film, it gains one more piece and rule of the game. It is up to you to take that knowledge and comprehend it in the right way. Many of you can't see or understand the madness of it all, and it takes some time to comprehend.

When we think of someone who has gone crazy and the authorities have placed them in a psyche ward. I want you to think of this. Possible Genius and highly misunderstood because they are operating at a higher frequency on a higher level. Being potentially attacked invisibly on various levels within the holographic field of multiple dimensions, causing them to be slightly unsteady. Possibly moving into higher realms and dimensions without easily assimilating back down into the 3D human society. Possibly attacked by others who don't want them to succeed at the Earth Games. Add it to an unhealthy environment where they push drugs down you, blocking and manipulating the human mind, leaves getting back on track nearly impossible.

Do you know what makes up a genius? Someone who uses imagination and creativity to invent! A genius is an extraordinarily intelligent person who breaks new ground with discoveries, works of art, and inventions. Trailblazing work that changes the way people view the world or fields it is taking place in. Using intelligence in an impressive, productive way, geniuses often analyze and incorporate the work of other great minds to produce a unique new discovery. Believe it or not, many geniuses don't have formal education or training, leading them to think freely and to explore information in unexpected ways. Many geniuses are luminaries with exceptional creativity, often misdiagnosed and discarded.

All right, let's get into it. Here are the films in my lifetime that gave me invisible data to think about and comprehend. I want you to open up to the possibility that they are all trying to convey a message to humanity, to wake up, pay attention and to live the game of Earth with intention and direction.

I also want you to think about history, mythology, ancient sacred sites, ancestry, family history, your DNA and what could possibly reside in it. Your DNA is who you are, and you could have a royalty bloodline that is about to be exposed if someone believes you are a threat. I also want you to think about the Bible, the names in the Bible, the sections, other Gods such as Zeus. Looking at the enormous pictures of all the generations past going back centuries and hundreds of thousands of years. We are history in the making of our future.

During my childhood, I had exposure to these films here on Planet Earth. Think about the premise of the film, what they represent, the story and the message they are sending.

CLASSIC FILMS

- *Clash of the Titans* (1981)–Zeus, Medusa and Mythology.

- *ET* (1982)–a coming of a friendly extraterrestrial to Earth who befriends a human, Alien space ship arrives.

- *STAR WARS* (1977)–flying space ships, non-human species from other galaxies, fighting off the good and bad (light vs. dark, power vs. force) May the Force be with YOU!

- *STAR TREK* (1960s)–flying thru space, portals, space travel, spaceships, other planets, galaxies, unknown planets, non-human species.

- *The Terminator* (1984)–solo man takes on cyber species, mass destruction.

- *Raiders of the Lost Ark* (1981)–searching for buried ancient treasure, hunting, being hunted, Arc of the Covenant in the Bible premise.

- *Close Encounters* (1977)–Alien space ships arriving at our planet and interacting with humans and humans leaving with them to ascension.

- *Aliens* (1986)–humans fighting in space with an extra-terrestrial being that is sharp, mindful, resourceful, psychological thriller.

- *Escape from New York* (1981), Escape from LA (1996)–mass destruction to the big USA cities. People fleeing from the city to survive away from chaos, mass control, manipulation, danger, and death. No food, no water, no safe shelter. Trust no one.

- *Gladiator* (2000)–fighting each other till the death. Medieval Times–where I worked when in high school.

- *The Mummy* (1999)–ancient ruins, finding treasure, hunting and being hunted, good vs. evil

- *Xanadu* (1980)–daughters of Zeus visit Planet Earth to be muses, one muse inspires an artist and they fall in love, reincarnation, multiple lifetimes, music by ELO–which is inspired by UFO spaceships on the album covers and concerts.

- *Tron* (1982)–games played digitally and futuristically for survival of the fittest.

- *The Exorcist* (1973)-still a thriller today about a woman having her body taken over and possessed by an evil spirit.

- *Bewitched* (1964-1972)–a mother having magical witch powers to manipulate the world and her family around them.

- *I Dream of Genie* (1960s)–a man who owned a beautiful girl genie in a bottle who granted him wishes. Sounds like porn and slavery all in one, now that I think about it.

- *Total Recall* (1990)–futuristic film on how oculus devices affected the brain chemistry in a human, controlling, manipulating, psychologically mind screwing humans and often killing them if programed properly intending to do so.

- *Land of the Lost* (1974-1976)–a family living in the mountains with the sleestack, an ET species who hold crystals as special value, heal all, cure all, protection in a cave.

- *The Thing* (1982)–an ET of unknown origin attacks and kills humans for no rhyme or reason.

- *Eyes Wide Shut* (1999)–just the title alone of this film says it all to me.

- *The Mind's Eye* (1992)–dimensional holographic stories told through music, sound, visual, color, history, mathematics, multi dimensions, beyond the mind's eye.

- *The Shining* (1980)–a human maze in a garden teaches thinking and processing information differently while being hunted.

- *6th Sense* (1999)–a young boys see entities from the other side viewed as negative and scary.

- *The Fly* (1986)–experimental drug used by a mad scientist to morph himself into something else unusual, scary and unknown.

- *Back to the Future* (1985)–time machine car built to enable humans to time travel to the future and possibly change the outcome.

- *The Jetsons* (1962-1987)–tv cartoon of the future of people living in a city driving space ships and moving around the city in a futuristic platform.

- *The Flintstones* (1960s)–tv cartoon of surviving the stone age as a family and their adventures.

Abnormal or awake?

MODERN FILMS

Now let's go into more modern films and shows. Over time, we have moved into 3D movies and 5D movies. 3D becomes dimensional when you wear special glasses, 5D is dimensional when one experiences it in a chair, such as shaking, water spraying, wind blowing, etc. See where I am going here. We are being upgraded when introduced to these ideas and concepts.

The exposure to knowledge, ideas and wisdom continues...

- *The Matrix* (1999)-digital matrix controlling and manipulating humans, blue pill or red pill – referring to illusion, drugs, fogged thinking and beliefs, what is real or unreal?

- *Doctor Who* (1996)-time travel.

- *Spy Kids* (2001)-smart innovative kids who out maneuver adults with strategic thinking minds with parents as spies. Passing generational DNA capabilities down the family line.

- *Avatar* (2009)-ET's being destroyed by humans who are ruining the planet and killing their race, the planet is worshipped and needed by the Avatars, while humans are set out to destroy. Humans in pods- transferring themselves into Avatar bodies. Massive irreversible planet and nature destruction, species destroying planets and cultures without consideration.

- *Harry Potter* (2001)-school where humans with special abilities went to learn how to activate and use superpowers.

- *The Hunger Games* (2012)-controlling of people through food, hunger, disappearance, psychology, mind games, depletion, war, weapons. Uses a digital matrix to manipulate a game of life or death with children.

- *The Coming Convergence* (2017)-film covering the sequence of global events the Bible foretells the end of days as prophesied. Will the "final generation" make the same mistake?

- *Before the Wrath* (2020)-mysterious event prophesied to happen in the Bible called the Rapture. Newly revealed unprecedented findings rediscovered by ancient anthropological evidence from the time of Christ.

- *The Final Prophecies* (2010)-award winning documentary presenting new evidence showcasing world-ending prophecies from ancient past are true and happening now.

- *Among Us* (2019)-other types of extraterrestrial species living on the planet. (Caroline Cory)

- *Ascension* (2014)-traveling out to space for decades because Earth was no longer habitable trying to save the human race, to discover space life is not the life you thought it would be.

- *Nope* (2022)-ET's influencing a human experience of protecting themselves and figuring out how to survive while under attack.

- *Stranger Things* (2010)-unusual life from other realms, planets, etc. invades the average human.

- *The Adam Project* (2022)-humans find ways to outsmart and out maneuver the bad guys, while flying space ships to survive.

- *Altered Carbon* (2018-2020)-surviving in a world where human bodies are mistreated and discarded as if they have no value and can easily be replaced with another clone body of choice if you have the money to afford it. Eternal life, extended life, soul transfer, artificial intelligence. Corruption of the human environment by the wealthy who want to control and own at all costs. Fighting till the death as entertainment.

- *Outlander* (2014)-time travel, history, medieval times, reincarnation, love, hurt, pain, uncertainty, goliath fighting, survival.

- *Independence Day* (1996)-protecting Earth and humans from the destruction of another species.

- *Spiderhead* (2022)-psychological thriller about experimental drugs being tested on humans and their reactions to the drugs. I believe these types of drugs are being used on humanity today as seen on the internet in some cases.

- *1899* (2022)-the year taking place in an era out at sea with a group of people trying to survive a strange abandoned ship finding, the same group of people working together to solve a puzzle and mystery with the hopes of creating a different outcome, only to find out they are in a simulation of the digital matrix on a space ship in the sky when the challenge is complete.

- *Valerian and the City of a Thousand Planets* (2017)-metropolis where species from all over the Universe have converged to share knowledge, intelligence and cultures with each other. A team of human special operatives combat to save an extraterrestrial species and safeguard the future of the Universe. Species destroying planets without consideration, massive irreversible destruction, species only able to be viewed in other realms and frequencies with special types of glasses or viewing lenses.

The massive amounts of symbolisms these films contain are basically telling us something about Earth Games. Combining what feels like a reality, identity. and the concept of time.

SUPER HEROES

And let's not forget comic book heroes and other super heroes made into films, shows and movies.

- Wonder Woman-taking on the world looking sexy, with special capabilities to fight off bad people.

- Bionic Woman-body altered to enable her to function at an above normal capacity using technology.

- Catwoman-dark knight Batman sexy enemy known for robbery and thievery.

- Super Girl-younger girl with the capability to fly, protect and help people throughout the city.

- Superman-came here from another planet with super abilities, rendering him helpless when exposed to kryptonite.

- Batman-flying through the city in specially made bat mobiles, special devices, fighting crime and enemies.

- Wonder Twins-the wonder twins were a brother and sister who could activate their powers by wearing a ring and putting their hands together and saying, "Wonder Twins power activate!" Form of???? (insert whatever you want) They could turn into any form they wanted to fight off bad guys. Water, fire, shooting ice, an animal, a vehicle. Teaming up with other Super Heroes, they possessed a one-of-a-kind set of abilities. They only worked well as a team, because they needed the other to activate their powers.

SOCIAL MEDIA

Today Kids TV shows give them the New Age way of what to buy, what to believe, how to think, how to behave. Tagging them on their unconscious mind and subconscious mind, constantly beating them down over and over. No filter, no rules, no ethics, no morals, no values, no monitoring of any kind whatsoever.

- You tube

- Influencers

- Tic Tok

- Instagram

- Kyra

- Social Media, TV, Radio

It's a buildup. I believe soon we are about to be introduced to ETs, space ships, species from other planets and very advanced healthcare technologies. This will reveal our superpower capabilities that have been kept and hidden from us for centuries and wrongly projected as negative.

FLASHBACK BOOKS

Books from back in the day (1970's-1990's) that were big hits have been turned into movies and have made a big impact.

- *When the Tripods Came Series*–book series about extraterrestrials.

- *Flowers in the Attic Series*, VC Andrews–psychological thrillers recently made into movies (2019-2023) as well as several of her other book series.

- *Left Behind*–the end of times told of the Rapture in the Bible.

- *The Celestine Prophecy*–scripture insights to reveal how to overcome and become unlimited as a collective, manuscript clues put together from different parts of the world through tough adventures, being hunted, captured and surviving in the world as they embark on an adventure to piece together spread out scriptures.

When I was a kid, we did time capsules, and I am noticing schools opening them up again from way back when. Look for clues in this era.

Things our DNA may trigger...hunting, fishing, camping, archery, sword fighting, horseback riding. Medieval times could very well be upon us once again soon if we don't redirect our attention.

Think about this? What do you think people would do if the electricity suddenly went out? Especially if it was unannounced! Humans couldn't charge their cars, couldn't drive their cars, couldn't open their garage doors to get out. The street lights wouldn't work, computers wouldn't work, phones wouldn't work, tv wouldn't work. People would go crazy! Attacking each other, killing each other just in mental imbalance alone. Humans don't know how to live without electronics, devices and technology. It would be complete madness!!!!!

BIOLOGICAL WARFARE

You add the possibility of nano-bots (tiny robots) being placed in the environment to manipulate humans and you have destruction of the human population. A win-win situation for any nation, country, species or race that wants to take over. Control the weather you control the world, which has and can be done. These nano-robots have the ability to transform into bedbugs, rats, flies, insects, or flying objects of any kind, programmed for destruction. This is our potential future if we don't pay attention. We buy I-robot vacuums for our home. It gives the owner of the software the floor plan of our home, our behavior patterns, when we are home, when we sleep, etc. We put cameras on our homes to track other people walking by and use security systems as a supposed protection for ourselves, when in actuality we are zapping ourselves with more 5G and giving others the power to surveillance US! We are literally holding ourselves as hostage slaves, paying them for their devices and giving them all full access! Do you see the pattern here? Rip all that shit down!

Other countries are watching you too! Other countries are analyzing you, watching how you behave and react to their manipulations, apps and lies. These countries are tracking, monitoring, invading and scamming society on a global monumental level and are humans actually taking notice and paying attention to do something about it?

The signs have been there all along, giving humans the option to make other better choices. But many take the easy way out. Many are selling their souls to survive and not thrive. When you know your superpower capabilities, you are a threat to them. They know you are way more powerful than them. This is why they are trying so hard to control you. This is why they want you to drink alcohol, smoke pot and take drugs. It lowers your vibration for easier manipulation.

They use the phone, devices and computers to use neuromarketing to impact your subconscious mind and unconscious mind so you have no clue or idea that you are operating on auto-pilot. Digital technology is being used to program you 24/7. Envision large digital billboards used on buses, bus benches, and bus poster adds as televisions. Digital screens already exist in the back of Ubers, and when autonomous vehicles are introduced, companies will use advanced vehicles with screens and audio to blast digital ads and place a program in your conscious, subconscious, and unconscious mind. Many natural human frequencies are disrupted, and individuals either remain oblivious or choose to disregard it. These ads can make you believe, think, and feel things are not important to humans and humanity. You need to be in control of yourself, your body, your mind, your heart, your frequency and your energy. You need to shut down and put away your devices. Buy directly from websites to generate business to the smaller brands. This removes power over you, and puts the control back in your hands and small businesses. You will learn how to live without many useless items, which will make it that much easier to survive when times change and get hard.

Come to terms that you are not supposed to look perfect, be perfect and feel perfect. Live in the present moment, simplify, be authentic, connect to your higher self, and use intuition and instinct to get through the Earth Game. Humans are part of the animal kingdom, start using your senses like an animal for instinct.

There will be times when others psychologically attack you. I see it as someone placing an invisible radio frequency signal over you and beaming it down at you and your body. They are trying to alter your mind, brain chemistry and body chemistry to work against itself and others. It's literally a frequency hi-jack. I also believe mind wiping is taking place. They adjust, remove, or alter the memory and patterns of humans, leaving them paralyzed in certain situations and causing loss of memory to make the proper choice based on experience and knowledge. It may take effect instantly, or over a period of several days or weeks. I am noticing families betraying and becoming deceptive to their own family members based on ego, pride, or loss of memory recall. It's happening on a grand scale in groups as family members team up to take another one down as the scapegoat or black sheep in order to draw the attention off of them or out of envy and deception.

Get out into nature, step away from your computer and go live a life without devices. Surround yourself with only the good people you trust. Others will not understand and will try to alter with manipulation in their favor. Guard your energy. Protect yourself and your mind. Eat healthy, balanced meals. Don't drink alcohol or smoke pot. Sit with the uncomfortable emotions and let them work through your body so you can process them and turn that energy into information. I look at it as getting an upgrade. Exercise, let universal energy flow move through your body so you wash it away and clear the energy. Go out in the sunshine, listen to music, affirmations, or a podcast of positive influence. Don't always trust content on YouTube. Sounds, commercials, and other media hit the unconscious and subconscious mind. This is where you really need to pay attention to the invisible information that is surrounding you.

Keep connecting the dots. Keep playing the game. We are getting to the end. Many of us are figuring it out. The collective conscious is figuring it out one by one and once we get enough people to "wake up" the entire world is going to shift for the better. It is just a matter of time before more people catch themselves and redirect. Forgive others for their horrible actions, reactions, and misunderstandings. They don't know what they do and, many times, they are already under the influence of mind control, programming, and unconscious manipulation.

Save yourself. Stay in your safe space. Keep your distance and keep the peace. This is what ascension is about. The death and rebirth of a new human. Sometimes you have to go it alone for a while until you find your new right tribe. Know others might not see things and comprehend things like you do. You are all on different frequencies and levels, which may make it difficult to understand each other at certain moments in time.

MULTIDIMENSIONAL
EXTRA SENSORY BEYOND

I realized I have the gift of the 2nd Sight when I am fine-tuned to my higher self and the universal cosmic collective. When I looked up the terms and synonyms for 2nd sight, this came up.

- 2nd Sight–clairvoyance, ESP, insight, intuition, lucidity, precognition, prediction, prescience, 6th sense, inner sense, foresight, prophecy, perception, feeling, fortune telling, psychic powers, palm reading, hunch, instinct in one's bones, gut feeling, vibes, suspicion, inkling, sense, funny feeling, vision, psychometry, notion, emotion, mind-reading, heart, crystal gazing, sign, fore wisdom, parapsychology, telepathic transmission, telesthesia, indication, sinking feeling, dread, bad feeling, vibration, prenotion, handwriting on the wall, forecast, cast, revelation, oracle, apocalypse.

In fact, people claim humans possess up to 33 documented senses that no one seems to discuss. This makes up human superpowers. When humans activate their hearts, they can achieve higher dimensional levels while remaining grounded.

HIGHER DIMENSINAL LEVELS

- Sixth Sense-Expansion. This is when your pineal gland is in top operation, decalcified, enabling one to see beyond the visible spectrum.

- Seventh Sense-Telepathy. Connected to extraterrestrials, mind control, and game playing.

- Eighth Sense-Transmutation. Ability to oscillate between higher self, shapeshifting and changing facial features.

- Ninth Sense-Projection of consciousness. Intuitive healers working with the Stargate project, controlling projection and remote viewing.

- Tenth Sense-Transfiguration. Done naturally when a human sleeps and can leave you feeling tired after a dream. Multiple locations in the holographic field.

- Eleventh Sense-Materialize. Dematerialize. The process of converting your physical shares and securities into digital and electronic form. Seeking a plasma bubble of soul freedom where the human heart is the engine. Aura spins faster and faster to connect and manifest.

Each of us has special capabilities in our DNA. Using them to work together to beat the Earth Game is paramount! And for those of you who do not understand it, it is because you can't see or feel it yet. You might refuse to acknowledge it, or you might have been programmed not to be able to see, understand, or witness it. Just know we are not crazy. We are seeing things from a higher perspective, on a higher vibration, frequency, and dimension. This is when you are reaching ascension of perception. Using all your human senses and other unlimited senses in other dimensions. The name of the game is to get to the higher levels of the Earth Game. Remember, in *Hunger Games*, how Catness kept trying to get to higher ground, and they kept cutting her down and pushing her back (she was using higher perception)? This is happening in daily life. We are all getting sick of it. Constant defeat and manipulation. Oh, the dirty games people play. The negative energy people spew and the positive energy they try to steal. Wake up, humans. It's time to wake up. No more auto pilot. Live with intention and direction.

What we think, see and feel right now is that we must absolutely make every moment count. Make every effort to manipulate the matrix with your imprint. Your design. Your creativity. Your magic insights like I am doing with you today right now.

You impact the world, the digital matrix, human evolution and artificial intelligence. You are the power source. Control your power. Own your power. Hone your power!

EARTH
GAMES
SUPER
POWERS
Get
reflective
To get a new
Perspective
~Noelle Hipke~
www.NoelleHipke.com

Chapter Two

YOUR LIFE IS YOUR MOVIE

There comes a point in your lives when you have had enough with the mind games. When you have been on this planet long enough you see patterns, encounter test after test, and realize you decide over and over each day how you will proceed with the ideas being presented right in front of you. The world is psychologically messing with you every day. If you are only using a portion of your mind, you are only seeing a portion of the issue at hand.

In order to tap into all parts of the brain, you need to work all parts of the brain like a muscle. As a left-handed and ambidextrous person, I do many things with both hands often at the same time.

At one point in this life, we set up our garage to be our outdoor living area. We remodeled the garage and put in insulation, drywall, custom lights with dimmers, speckled flooring and a disco ball. We turned this room into our outdoor haven, for we had a neighborhood of fun-loving neighbors who would gather to share our children, our jokes, our stories and our lives. Our friends and neighbors were our family, and so were their children.

We set up a karaoke studio. It wasn't just any karaoke studio. Back in the day around 2009 we used a big screen tv and connected it to a laptop computer with endless songs to choose from. Since my husband at the time was a computer genius, we could do things out of the norm most people wouldn't think of or could do. He could hack programs by altering and manipulating software with other individuals, creating the biggest song book of choices you could ever imagine for that time period. Neighbors, friends and friends of neighbors would gather in the alley to share our energy.

I always did weird things, saw weird things and thought of weird things. I believe being left-handed as well as ambidextrous has granted me certain capabilities the average human normally doesn't encounter since most of the population is programmed right-handed.

We had a ping-pong table in our garage and I would always play ping-pong and with two paddles at the same time. It's like I couldn't play it any other way. Friends would come over and get a kick out of it. I could crush them from both sides without using much energy solely focusing on reflexes and eye and hand coordination. I now realize I was activating my mind to use unusual brain connections by accessing different areas of the brain. This enabled me to tap into different perspectives on life. Many times, people couldn't understand what I was trying to say or communicate until I wrote it on paper. Then when I wrote it on paper, they were like, "Oh, I see and get it now." What I see is from a higher field of multiple perspectives and levels. It's like going out of the body, flying around and taking a view of the entire picture from the top of the room or environment. Think of it as a holographic field, flying and moving through the air. Being a part of the scene, not being seen in the scene. It's like astral travel, but in the same room. When you pull yourself out of your body, out of the 3D world, you move into higher frequencies and higher perspectives. That is when you go into 4D, 5D and beyond. Back in those days, the games Smash ball and Trackball were big hits. So, I also played these games, you guessed it, with a paddle in each hand.

When you go into higher densities and dimensions, you see things, feel things, and comprehend things on an entirely different level. At first you might not understand when you start doing this. You start to feel emotions and you don't know why. You are feeling energies, thoughts and emotions of the collective thoughts, energies and emotions of others. Many times, my body and mood would change according to my environment and I didn't know or understand why. Now I do. It's because I was picking up invisible frequencies that were going on around me in my environment. The people that were around me were affecting and effecting my thoughts, feelings and emotions. And they are all doing that to you too right now and you don't even know or realize it. They are hitting your subconscious and unconscious mind.

Sometimes my body will start to shake and feel very weird when I know something is not right or someone is going to do something bad. I have learned to really pay attention and listen to this. This is when I back away from everyone and move into my own sacred space. I need to clear others' energy away from me and go sit and be in my peaceful space to understand what is truly happening.

Now I realize when I feel these things, my body is screaming at me and telling me something. Figuring out what that something is requires going within. Going within myself to:

- Comprehend

- Contemplate

- Clear

- Communicate

When you have been on this planet a long time, there are just some lessons you learn the hard way repeatedly until you get it right. This is when the real magic comes in and that is when you write it down. Write it down. Write it down. So, you can get it right.

How do you conquer your negative pattern?

- By making note of it

- Draw it to the surface

- Become aware of it

- Change and alter it

Oh, and I will not lie. It isn't always easy. You are going to make the same mistake several times over and over until you get it right. But get this: you will always get the chance to get it right, eventually. The sooner you learn the lesson, the quicker you move on to the next level.

I will never forget. One night I was lying in bed meditating before going to sleep. One thing I started doing that I absolutely loved doing was reviewing my day. I would go over in my mind what I did, how I did it, how it made me feel. And then get this, I would fix and change anything in my mind I didn't like about that part of the day. In my mind, I would go back and reflect on how things played out. Later, with some distance and time from when the incident happened, I had a breakaway in the day and a separation from the scene in that part of my movie. Then, when I was lying in bed, I could move out of the emotions it stirred in my body, get a few new perspectives, see and understand how I could have handled it better. In reflection, it offered me solutions for the future, by changing my body chemistry, by imagining how I would have liked to have played it out. It was like I was tricking and training my body, mind and soul to see, view, realize, comprehend, believe and program myself the right way. I was aiming to do something different in order to change the pattern.

Every day, you have the capacity to reprogram yourself for the better at the close of your day. Think of it as a program reset like turning off and on a computer. Reprogram your body, mind and soul to think, act and function to the best of its abilities at that moment in time. The exciting part is the more you conquer and learn in life, the more you are going to upgrade and level up.

You do this by:

- Realign

- Reset

- Reboot

That is why down time and meditation are so important. It gives you the opportunity to access your higher self while assisting you in resetting of your system and upgrading your programming.

When you sleep, you also go into other realms, dimensions, time travel and move into other worlds the human 3D body can't do when you are awake and moving physically alive on the planet. This is when we learn, comprehend, gather our data in the holographic field between time, dimensions and space. It's a very complex space, but very magnificent and beautiful and most likely impossible to comprehend beyond our wildest dreams. The depth of this area is so vast it is beyond the comprehension of a human when only operating from a human standpoint level. You need to move to a level beyond being simply human in order to reap the benefits.

Tapping into other dimensions, working and creating with the unlimited view points and information fields presents new concepts from other worlds into this world. Traveling between dimensions and timelines from world to world gathers information to share with one another between worlds.

We are all on different levels of the game, which explains why we all can't get along. Currently, each one of us do not see things the same way. This is due to every individual having their own unique experience and perspective. Often humans react impulsively which can cause friction. Learning to act with intention and direction after observation at all times will serve you well. When you do this, you can communicate better and more clearly what you are experiencing and receiving. Many times, we are caught up in the emotions and triggers from our past, family, and ancestors. We react off the cuff and don't give it a second thought. The energy between people interacting is intensely moving fast, and it can be very overwhelming when all you can think about is winning and taking over the other opponent. We have all been trained to do that for many centuries. Sometimes I recall the feelings overcoming me as I would feel my body and energy build up and I think I am going to win this round at all costs. I am stronger than you; I am older than you, and I am smarter than you. After all, isn't that the name of the game? Nope. The name of the game is to walk away from one another, feeling heard, respected, and fulfilled. This is when the real magic is created. The only way Earth is going to change is if people live with direction and intention for the right reasons. Don't get me wrong, many people have been doing this for a very long time. However, some have been doing it for the wrong reasons many times. Some have been doing it intending to hurt you, own you, take over you, and control you. That is how the programming on Earth has been done for a very long time.

People who rule over the economy, resources, countries, environment and cities have been manipulating and programming us to work, think, behave and do exactly what they want us to do, think and behave.

I'm all about creating a legacy, which is exactly what these books are going to do from me to you. I can't take anything with me to the afterlife, but I sure as heck can create a ripple effect, or better yet, waves of positive influence on humanity. I can affect your holographic field by your thoughts, feeling and programming. When you work with the entire holographic field, you are getting the entire perspective from multiple dimensions. 3D, 4D, 5D, 6D, 7D, 8D, 9D, 10D, 11D, 12D and beyond to infinity. How I effect you is ultimately my choice on the imprint I would like to relay on my writings. Whether you choose to believe it, see it or comprehend it is up to you. This is the same concept with the mainstream news, radio and online media. You are being programmed and being affected by all realms and dimensions subconsciously, unconsciously and consciously. It's really important to pay attention to what you can see and cannot see. You cannot understand an incident if you are not paying attention to it or don't think it exists. This is why I am always talking about communicating how to see, feel and understand the invisible. It is part of the game, and part of the game is you trying to figure it out. Which is what makes it that much more interesting and fun.

I'm going to tell you a story. My entire life, I always thought getting a house was the ultimate goal and planning for your future. We were told owning the house was the objective of the game through the board games Monopoly and the game of LIFE. Go to college, get a job, find a mate, buy a house and have kids. That was the programming. You know what it got us to do? It got our parents to believe this is the way it is to be done and the only way to be done. A relative would say to me, "Why can't you be like everyone else?" WTF? We are not supposed to be like everyone else. We all have different codes and genetic genes in our bodies unique to each of us and we are supposed to be honoring that. Not this programming someone else has deemed up for us, leaving us empty, confused, angry, hurt and, frankly, pissed off. We are not following our soul purpose, but are living someone else's program that isn't a match. This may be a superb reason there are so many upset, confused, and angry people today. They have had enough of the negative programming.

I have had enough mind fuckery to alter the game, which is exactly why I am writing this book.

You know what happens when you think owning the home is the ultimate goal? One doesn't follow their heart and soul. One is told they are less than others because you don't own a home. Which makes you want to work really hard to get a home. Anything to keep up with the Joneses and be part of the leader pack. And you know what you have to do to get a home? Become a slave to the system. You are told you can't get a good job without a degree. In fact, many job descriptions say they require a degree for you to even apply for a job. Why? Because you are not a slave in debt having to pay off your student loan. I know many people with better common sense, better resources, and better capabilities than some of the degreed and educated servants out there with a rather hefty loan sitting over their heads. I have friends with kids who have $95,000 in loan debt they owe on after completing their education only to move into an entirely new field altogether. Talk about making the wrong moves in the game. Remember what I said about geniuses not having a formal education because it allowed them to think out of the box? Had you known what was in your DNA that you are naturally good at, and really enjoy doing, you could have eliminated much of that debt. Grant it, wrong moves teach us lessons, but let's move forward quickly in the right direction instead of taking so many U-turns.

Okay, so now what? You earned that degree to get yourself a job to buy that home. Now you are in double debt, school loan debt and home debt. What I want you to realize is that you have now become their slave into the system, paying your debts off with your precious life force energy. Using your life force energy to do what they want you to do. Not what you may actually want to do or be here to do on a soul level. Owning a home will prevent you from doing many things, and that is a key people don't even realize. However, I am noticing more families' home schooling and teaching their children to live off the land like we did in pioneer days.

REAL ESTATE GAMES

I was working as a leasing agent in helping rent apartments as a temp off and on through the years as a realtor. People think you make a lot of money as a realtor, but the truth of the matter for me was I didn't like it was inconsistent, you didn't get benefits, there was out-of-pocket costs every month, buyers and sellers are not loyal, other realtors will stab you in the back any chance they get and you were always looking for the next deal like a hunter. Those who were making it "big" financially in the field were playing on a different level. Many Realtors were desperate, some only cared about the money taking advantage of clients by buying their homes for a lower price and turning around to sell the home for a higher price, others loved the rush, some were alcoholics, many were mentally imbalanced because of no structure, while many didn't have or could follow a system. If you like an unbalanced life in constant upheaval and turmoil nonstop because of those who like to manipulate and control the economy with many unrealistic clients, go have at it!

Everyday realtors faced the threat of some online software resource platform taking over our job, and it was usually another realtor attempting to develop a program that would undermine all the other realtors and work in their own favor, making them the sole beneficiary. Now is that the kind of people and environment you want to work in? And with Amazon expressing selling everything under the sun, pretty soon we will only have one platform to get anything done from if we are not careful. It could have a lot of power over us if we allow it. This and many other apps are tracking us, watching us, and monitoring us. They know us humans to be creatures of habit. They know what we buy to survive. The health items we order, the devices we order, the products we order. Humans are studied and monitored to be presented products through neuromarketing to the masses of consumer goods. Neuromarketing is used to feed us into buying more products we don't need based on our buying patterns, eye movements and face gestures. Amazon has expressed interest in moving into selling homes and is now selling pharmaceuticals, taking away more human jobs. They claim it is all about convenience, but are we all really giving our power away? Too much power for one controller. Amazon owns Ring, the home monitoring system. Ring monitors your home via the video camera door bell, video motion censored lights, home security system. An entire self-monitoring system, you can install yourself. One day I realized oh my gosh, I am literally putting cameras in my home to give complete, full access to anyone and everyone who can tap into that camera signal. I viewed myself like an animal in a cage setting up my own personal cameras for anyone to tap into and watch me on a tv monitoring system. That was a full circle moment for me. Yikes! Not that I am doing anything wrong, but that people were watching me and I gave them full access gave me the creeps. My freedom and inhibition were removed, my personal sacred space invaded. When you are all excited by these amazing devices that are being promoted and cued into thinking you need to buy them, think again and again.

When I looked down at my cell phone, I realized my phone had cameras on the front and back and they could see my face up close and anyone else around me up close I am holding my camera toward. I am carrying and filming my entire life for the Universe to see My Movie. I capture audio; I capture video; I capture text. My thoughts, patterns, movements, feelings, energy were being recorded by this device. I was influencing and teaching AI, and AI was influencing and teaching me. Eventually, I put black tape over my front and back camera on my phone in order to establish some sort of privacy. But in my mind, I knew my phone device was sensing more than just my face. It was sensing using multiple sensory and AI in order to tap into me and influence me. I witnessed the takeover of the world, friends, families, kids, well-educated and influential people by their devices.

INFLUENCERS

Influencers are a big hit these days. Did you know they can sell more products online using influencer personalities than on any other platform in the world? More than print, more than radio, more than audio. Cell phone devices rule people's lives. It is needed for business; for their education; for apps, BANKING, TRACKING, MONITORING, CONTROLLING. See the pattern here. What we think is a handy computer device can, in turn, be used as a weapon against us. People totally freak out when they don't have their phone. What I want you to learn is to depend on it less and less. Learn to put that sucker away. Start with muting it and then turn it off completely. Remove it out of your environment when you are around actual living human beings. It's rude and it's disrespectful to the other person for you to constantly have it in your hand and your face. It means you are not paying attention to the real world around you, your surroundings and other people. You are living in the cell phone digital matrix dimension. Cell phones are bars of the "new" prison "cell." You need to step away from that programming in order to be in charge of your own program and mindset here on Planet Earth. This is part of the test. Your cell phone is pushing out your frequency signal to the entire Universe. Imagine there are other beings in the Universe watching you, and I am not just talking human beings. Cell phones give full access to you, your friends, family, etc.

Sometimes I would imagine a camera up in the room's corner of my house where one did not exist. I would pretend there was a camera so I would think...do I like how I am acting and behaving and conducting myself at this moment for the entire world to see? What if the Universe is watching me? Would I be proud of the way I am acting? Would I want to project this image to the world or for the Universe to see? How does that make you feel about perspective? Understand everything you video, post, say, do, photograph, text and project is being sent out for every different type of species in the entire Universe to see, watch, and witness. Your phone is capturing your frequency, actions and projections making it accessible to every type of species watching.

HOME OWNERSHIP

Personally, I think owning a home at this point in my life has been somewhat of a burden. I now share this freely with the young kids who come into the apartment communities looking to lease, talking about the idea and dream of finally owning a home one day. I say to them, "You don't want to own a home, you want to know why?" I have owned my home for 28 years now. As a single woman, I have had to repair and replace the roof. Originally, I hired a roofing contractor to do the work, who did the job incorrectly costing me thousands of dollars in the end not to fix the issue properly. Therefore, down the road, I ended up having to put on a new roof altogether, costing me yet another hefty sum.

In 2022, rats invaded my home because of the city coming into my neighborhood to cut down 15 trees unannounced. Rats are one of the highest intelligent beings on this planet. Heck, this is why they are chosen to be used for studies. Rats learn, figure things out, adjust and adapt, just like humans do. If they want to study and figure out possible human behavior responses, they use rats. I turned into a rat hunter in 2022 and always said I am dealing with geniuses. These rats learned fast and were damn smart. One morning I woke up at 5:00 am to find a live rat struggling on one of the sticky traps I had placed on the floor by a cabinet. Upon turning on the lights, the rat sensed me and pushed its way under the cabinet so I couldn't see or get him. Grant it, it was 5:00 am and the last thing I wanted to deal with as a single woman that early in the morning is a living rat. So, I said to him, "I will see you later in the morning dead or alive." Guess what, when I came back later that morning the sticky trap was there but that rat was gone.

Another time, I found a snap trap set off with the rat fallen from the ledge surrounded by blood and dead. Picture this: it's 10:30 pm, and there I am in my pajamas, robe, and slippers, with pink gloves on, picking up a dead rat with my bare hands. It was at that moment I realized I am a pretty damn strong woman when I had to be. It's knowing when to turn it on and when to turn it off. Another time, I caught a rat in a snap trap by its whisker. By the energy the little critter was emitting, I truly believe it was the mother. I saw it laying there breathing heavy, barely alive with fear, concern, worry and knowing. She was concerned for her children, as well as her own safety and being. It takes one mother to spot another. I couldn't bring myself to handle her, so I called a friend and asked him to remove her. He lived by a public park and I was hoping he would release her there because I hate killing living beings on this planet, but I knew him better than that. After weeks and weeks of living with the rat geniuses, I arrived home to discover a snap trap that had been triggered, with blood splattered all over my stove and no rat caught in the trap. I cleaned up the mess and was at my wit's end. I had to wipe everything down in the kitchen every time I wanted to cook or live. During this time, I constantly felt on edge and never felt comfortable and relaxed, needing more time for my nerves to calm.

One night before going to bed, I went into a kitchen drawer to find a live rat chewing on my cell phone head phones. Frustrated by the live action of a rat invading my personal space, it slowly moved away and I almost grabbed it with my bare hands. Heck, I had gotten so used to living with them and handling them by this time, it was almost an automatic reaction. Who in the heck would want to grab a rat with their bare hands? This was the injured rat from the trap, spreading blood all over, who had originally gotten away. Out of complete frustration, I screamed my head off for four minutes straight at that rat. Yelling, freaking out, telling them to get the hell out of my house, and I broke down crying. Exhaustion, frustration, and a sense of complete defeat overwhelmed me. So much for going to bed. I didn't end up sleeping that night. I was so worked up at the fact that they had been in my home for weeks and had chewed the wires in my kitchen, leaving my plugs unusable, the TV in my living room no longer working and some light dimmers inoperable. When you have learned to live without, you learn to adapt, adjust and survive just like humans and rats do. Be mutable to change, for everything is always changing. I adjusted by using other plugs for my juicer and tea pot. Watched tv in my bedroom and turned-on other lights in the house.

I became the rat trapper in 2022. For weeks I would spend 45 minutes each day setting up and moving around snap traps, glue traps, etc. I would have to wipe down counters and clean everything. Eventually I completely decluttered, removed unnecessary items in my life and reorganized again. When I did the decluttering and reorganizing, I realized it opened up other new realms, levels and dimensions to let in new knowledge and access information in other frequencies I could not see before. That is when I went back to writing more and creating new concepts, just like this book.

To top it off, during the time of the rat invasion, the chain on my garage door opener broke, so I had to park my car on the street for over a month. Every time I went out my front gate, my dog would run out into the street causing more stress. Then in those winter months, my home heater started making horrible noises and smelled funny, so I had to turn it off altogether and call out yet another repairman. What I will always recommend when you own a house is that you carry a home warranty on the home. This way when something goes wrong, all you have to do is call them, pay a fee, and they send out a licensed, bonded and insured bona fide contractor to do the work. Let me tell you, these people show up and do the job correctly most of the time. Their contracted services are on the line with the home warranty company. Contractors want to keep the business coming, and will do what it takes to get it done.

I tell people when you own a home; you are trapped in your own cage. A homeowner can't leave because they have responsibilities. They have to pay the bills, water the plants, clean the house, make the repairs, mow the lawn, etc. You are a slave to your job to own a home. One can't travel as often because they need to use their money for repairs, remodeling, and replacing.

In the winter of 2022, I lived without a heater for two months and corralled rats, while I sent my daughter to her fathers to be a safe environment.

The future of Earth Games is humans removing obstacles out of their way to live a new kind of earth lifestyle. Not to be tied down to crap and a toxic environment. In order to learn, grow and evolve, you need to move around and experience more of everything. Live with purpose, intention, direction, and love. At this point in my life, I honestly think living with less crap and responsibility allows you more freedom, time and unlimited potential to create and do the things you want to do.

So now when I show apartments for lease to renters who want to own a home, I give them true perspective. When tenants would call and ask for a work order for someone to come in and change a light bulb out in their garage, I had to laugh. If only they knew what I was doing behind the scenes to make it in this world, their head would spin.

COLLECTIVE COSMIC CONSCIOUS AWARENESS

Right now, it's time for the collective conscious to become very aware and wake up to the world and go within. As more and more people become attuned to the program, you can break away and move in another direction, or at least become aware of it and play the game differently. At this point in my life and being on the planet for some time, I have seen and witnessed a few head scratchers.

All those people who believe in UFOs, aliens, and ETs are not crazy. Believe it or not, many humans on this planet are part extraterrestrial. Each one of us has a connection to multidimensional beings from different parts of the galaxy. These beings have come from different planets in different galaxies here to evolve and intertwine our species as a collective. We all have now combined our different DNA, frequencies, thoughts, beliefs, systems, programs, patterns, etc. When meshed together, it's a hodge podge with no formity. When you formulate, you can create unity and peace. It is not for us to conquer one another, but to gather, learn, comprehend, accept, and evolve. Every one of you can see this when granted the right alignment. Move into other frequencies and open yourself up to expand possibilities and the unknown. Mythology is real in other dimensions. Yes, it is. Fairies, gnomes and unicorns exist. Some of the younger generations can already see this.

I found my daughter could move from one frequency to the next rather quickly as well as other dimensions. She could tap in, share unusual knowledge and have awareness beyond the norm if encouraged to do so. When kids go to school, they are being programmed. Programmed to what those who control society has deemed. When you homeschool, you can program your child anyway you want. If we can teach our kids to be unlimited, tap into their soul's destiny, their experience here on Planet Earth will be so much more rewarding.

Every time I go to the store and see someone, I can't help but analyze and wonder, what planet or galaxy are you from? If you think about how everyone could be from a different place in the Universe, isn't that fascinating? What does that particular person have to teach us from their soul experience, knowledge, DNA, ancestors, species? We are all each other's teachers. I've noticed people's unusual height of 6'7" when I asked the checker at the grocery for his correct height. The beautiful color and flawless texture of someone's skin. An individual's unique facial feature, such as their eye shape, ears and chin. It's all being said right in front of us every day in their DNA.

You know the saying; the eyes are the windows of the soul? Well, it's absolutely true. By looking into someone's eyes, I can tell if they are hurting, ill, confused, suffering, unkind, determined, angry, etc. The eyes are a dead giveaway to their divine connection.

MAGIC MODALITIES

Upon doing the inner work, I couldn't help but want to know more. I am always going to be the girl who questions everything. We are told crystal ball gazing, tarot cards, pendulums, and palm reading are occult and witchcraft. But from what I have gathered, these modalities connect to the energy of light and dark forces, intertwining the subconscious and unconscious mind, souls, and energy. When using these modalities know you do not have complete control. This is due to the impact of outside forces of energies from other dimensions and you use them at your own risk. Just know many people are out there using them to move energy in the direction of their choice. Some are using it to connect with the dark, while others are using it to connect with the light and manipulate the energy in their favor.

COLOR CONNECTING

Color contains magic! I've always loved rainbow stickers since I was a kid in the 1970s. I love wearing colorful clothing and I have painted my house in various colors. I don't hold back; I have used teal, peach, light pink, tiffany blue, red, green, tan, white, mauve, grey just to name a few. If you think about it, we all have a strong connection to color in our lives. Colors contain information codes to generate a feeling and expression containing frequency and wavelength language. We consider rainbows as a sign of hope and promise, and we see them as the prize for weathering the storm. Repeatedly rainbows assure us there will be beauty and clarity following times of doubt. In 2022 I was privileged to discover several rainbows floating in the sky.

One day I was riding a bike on the beach path with my daughter when it started drizzling and a beautiful rainbow appeared in the sky from one end to the other. I was so excited to see it! A rainbow in the sky is not something you can ever see enough of in a lifetime. I noticed people walking toward us had their back to the rainbow knowing they would miss the "big event." I started ringing my bike bell, pointing up to the sky yelling, "Rainbow, rainbow, rainbow!" My daughter was riding behind me, laughing at my silliness, but I just couldn't contain myself. These people were going to miss the magic moment. And the best part I will never forget that happened, is my daughter got to catch the joy and excitement on everyone's faces as they turned to look at the rainbow in the sky. Their expression of surprise made her feel good as she enjoyed watching them get happy with my contagious out-pour of spreading love and light. It started to lightly rain on us. I love playing in the rain. It makes me feel like a kid again. Here I am at this perfect moment in time, riding on the beach bike path with my daughter and my dog (God backwards) without my phone. I've been trying to model a lifestyle without having to have my phone on me at all times and I would have liked to have captured the moment on my phone. I say to my daughter, "I wish I had my phone to take a photo and video." My daughter says so brilliantly to me, "Mom, you have created the memory in your mind, you never lose that!" I love it when words of wisdom pour out of her soul.

Yes, our minds are powerful creators. Color is part of the creation. We dream in colors too. Recently I was writing a job description for a property and listed the colors of the home with the description and meanings the colors signify, discovering deeper meaning in the methods of psychology behind the colors. Colors heal the soul on multiple levels and dimensions. Using color in your home transmutes energy, emotions, feelings, and light. I have dimmers on all my lights in the house, even the bathroom. I took a college course on lighting and interior design and was always drawn to the energy of light and color. As the hues are altered, colors change, and the light from lamps effects colors used to reflect several overlay projections, giving humans visions into many multiple dimensions.

As a kid, my dad had red, blue, yellow and green-colored lights in the backyard illuminating a rainbow of light in the backyard, which serves as one of my fondest childhood memories. My parents took us to see the dancing waters at Disneyland, where lights, music, color, and water danced and performed to Disney songs, providing a wonderful free form of family entertainment. To this day, there are light up colored glasses, ice cubes, jewelry, kids' toys and adult toys. Rainbow light is something that will never go out of style. Entire interactive events are being created in the nature of lights projecting on the forest, creating surreal environments. I will never forget attending unique events like this, which are dreamy and very romantic.

Live music performances are being created by candlelight, offering light language love energy of passion and peace wrapped all into one.

Let's dive into some of my favorite colors here so you can get an idea of how a home, work space, environment, or room can be effected and make you feel certain emotions.

Color Theory

- Teal color represents communication and clarity of thought and wisdom, tranquility, protection, good fortune, loyalty and peace. Inspiring growth and self-discovery.

- Pink gestures well-being, health, love and affection, friendship, harmony, inner peace, compassion, nurturing.

- Gray means calming, reliable, peaceful, relaxing, and soothing.

- Peach symbolizes energy, encouragement, vitality, playfulness, joy, youthfulness, warmth and comfort.

- Red is a sign of power, strength, love, romance, invigorating, intimidating, anger.

- Brown connects to security, safety, nature, dependability, melancholy, resilience, and earthiness.

- Green radiates health, harmony, safety, renewal, abundance, new beginnings, wealth, balance, youthfulness, vitality, creativity and productivity.

- Blue signifies loyalty, trust, security, responsibility, relaxation, peace, honesty, confidence.

- White is purity, peace, angelic, perfection, innocence, goodness, hope.

- Yellow means energy, joy, happiness, friendship, warmth, enlightenment.

- Purple is associated with creativity, wisdom, power, ambition, magic, royalty, independence, wealth, nobility, inventiveness, spiritual depth.

Each color contains positive and negative energies and diverse meanings across continents and cultures. I suggest conducting your own research on the color that attracts you and deciding how you would like to incorporate it into your life for positive change. Creating a friendly environment energy frequency of positivity and light will uplift everyone's spirit in the room.

CRYSTALS AND ROCKS

One thing I learned about crystals while on a trip to Mount Shasta is that they are living beings. When I realized that my entire respect for them completely changed altogether. I treated them with higher regard and put them in a more secure and safe place. I held them, felt them, looked through them. How did they feel? Cold? Warm? Soft? Smooth? Rough? I gravitated to certain crystals and realized they were sending me light coded messages through their energetic composition. A portal between two worlds. Some of them even carried a rainbow holographic imprint, and I saw them as an advanced key with an energy so strong it could power up a mass powered object such as a spaceship. Think of geometric cut crystals being slipped into a cutout as the key to active the component. Yes, I know this is a rather heavy duty to consider, but just use your imagination. Your imagination is so powerful you can create anything. Memories are being triggered all the time; all it takes is that right image. I use crystals on a geometric grid; I put them by light; I hold them, and I bring them into my space to clear, protect and align the energy in my home. At the high-end open houses I walked through, I noticed some of the largest crystals I had ever seen being broadcast out in the open as a type of protection, shielding and energy. Of course, most people chalk it up as just another crystal, but for those of us who know the energies and powers crystals can carry, see them in an entirely different energetic frequency field. Many don't understand the magnitude crystals and rocks carry. These items have been around for a very long time. They carry internal wisdom, knowledge and codes they share with us energetically. Crystals can also open and access portals to other dimensions, planets and galaxies.

Every time my daughter and I would travel somewhere, we would always collect a few rocks, twigs or items from nature to bring home to put in our garden. We gathered treasures from creeks, hikes, camping grounds, parks, etc. There was just something about the energy of the piece speaking to us, tugging at our strings, asking us to bring it home so we could continue to connect to that part of the earth and planet. My daughter often found rocks shaped just like the mountain we were standing by. She found heart shaped rocks, moon shaped rocks, and waterfall rocks. There is amazing symbolism and symmetry in all the world if we look. I remember one time she wanted to bring this really large tree branch home from the park. We had to roll down the passenger window to let it hang out by 2 feet while she held onto into in the back seat. We had to pull over several times to get that sucker home and when it stood tall, it was close to hitting the peak of the roof with a vast vault.

The next time you want to think a rock is just a rock, think again. That rock could have some knowledge or information from another planet or this planet you may need to pay attention too.

SACRED SITES

One thing I want to caution here is if you visit any sacred site, do not tamper with nature or take rocks or memorabilia with you. Sacred sites hold a particular frequency that is not to be altered, changed, or manipulated. Often, these sites serve as portals and gateways to other Universes and dimensions. There are many stories of people who have taken lava rocks from Hawaii volcanoes, only to be riddled with bad luck after returning home with these items. It is a widely known and documented fact that the post office in Hawaii deals with an overload of packages containing volcano rocks being returned by previous owners who learned the hard way.

COLLECTIVE CONSCIOUS AWARENESS

Everyone is being triggered to wake up. Some of you are already there, while some of you are resisting. We are moving into the "New Earth" where more people are going to be waking up and wanting to choose to live their life differently. Many of you are ready for the awakening. Children are already awake, and the younger generations came into correct and alter the frequency of humans on the planet by collapsing timelines and changing the course of generational history. Several decades of society has been programming and conditioning our children to fall into line and "act normal" like everyone else.

The best way I think I can help the collective conscious wake up is by writing and sharing the knowledge I know and understand. It's always those a-ha moments that hit you at just the right time to help you change your perspective. In addition, some of you have a DNA programming that causes you to operate and open up to this experience differently at different times. I am noticing everyone is experiencing it uniquely and often give them space to allow the magic to take place.

EARTH GAMES RULES

I will not lie. There were times when I got really pissed off when I realized the lies and magnitude of what I have been experiencing all my lifetimes. There often seemed to be no rules. The rules would change and the game manipulated. This is when I realized if I knew all the rules of the game, life would be boring. If I knew all the rules, there would be no game.

Most people don't even realize we are in the middle of our own game and our own movie. Others come into the game to manipulate you and your environment. It's up to you how you handle the game, rule the game, and manipulate the game. Actions by others reveal what level of the game they are at and if they are even close to your level. Some people are playing the game wrong, while others are not playing the game at all. Some people don't even know we are playing a game. If you are playing the game, how would you like to play?

MOVIES

When watching movies, I can feel what people in the movie are trying to make us feel. As an extreme empath, one literally can become anything in the room, a character in a movie, part of the environment, an image in a magazine, an animal, etc. If one thinks about it enough, one can become one with it and feel all of its emotions and existence telepathically. We believe movies are fictional or are made up. However, our personal imaginations contain strong influential energetic powers, casting a spell out into the Universe, which can actually put energy behind the belief and feeling creating a powerful energy force to make it real and bring it into this world weather for good or bad. Words and thoughts cast spells out into the Universe. Throughout the book, we will cover movies that are decades old, which you may want to research and watch in order to further understand what I cover here. You may discover some new clues for yourself. Everything placed in front of you is connected, which turns it into a clue.

Many times, empaths gain feelings and don't know why. Being alone allows the body to cleanse and clear out picked up energy from other beings and experiences to realign themselves in a healthy way. Consider the Hunger Game series living in despair, living in controlled conditions, living in abuse, living in poverty. Could this be the way our society gravitates if we don't live by the rules that have been established? In order to establish control, will outside sources control your bank account, your finances, your home, your income, your food, your electricity, your gas, your transportation? Just let that sink in for a minute. Could movies come to fruition because of the high possibility of a large group of beings putting massive energy behind it by thinking about it? Living with less and learning to live without now is an exemplary model to explore and practice.

Know what else is interesting, one might not even have to see the movie at all. All that would be needed are large digital TV screens installed in cities, communities, vehicles, buses, and bus benches, and your phones can serve as a great outlet to send out a massive media message to create any scenario someone wants you to believe. By using footage from your home camera recording device and software programs to create and project your voice and moving avatar image, you have the potential to become an instant influencer or criminal.

Earth Games will constantly evolve as humans and other beings expand and enter the arena. You never know where it will take you. It's up to you to figure out how to play the game.

Your life is your movie. You are the star in your movie. What kind of movie do you want to project out to the Universe?

Chapter Three
GAMES

Thoughts move faster than the speed of light. This is how you manifest. Get an entire group thinking the same thought, and "poof" instant projection to make the electric connection. One can manifest faster the more you think about it and put energy behind it. Life is a game of manipulating energy. Your energy, other people's energy, and the Universe's energy.

This includes the power of prayer, guided imagery, and visualization. When someone prays, they are projecting an image, thought, sequence of codes, feelings, emotions, energy, and frequency into the Universe. The Universe receives the frequency code and searches for a vibrational match attaching itself to it like a magnet. Meditation is a form of prayer by giving and receiving of a frequency exchange. Guided imagery, also known as visualization, is the human mind envisioning traveling to another place of choice, offering feelings, emotions, using your sensory of visuals, sounds, smell, touch and taste. A human can heal oneself in these extra dimensional fields on a cellular level and repair and reprogram the body, mind, and soul.

Universal life flow is what I used to gather the data in the etheric field around us to compose this data into written creativity. I see and get bits and pieces and my mind sorts them out like a puzzle. When I get into a room full of people, it's like all these force fields of energy are in the room. There is data flying everywhere. Several human force fields of knowledge intertwine in one room, overlapping one another, crossing over and sharing and spreading wisdom and resources. You know that saying, "You become who you hang out with." Well, this is where it comes in. Surrounding yourself with people who are not dedicated to personal growth and higher evolvement restricts your exposure to wisdom, knowledge, and data. When you walk into a room full of beings who are expanding beyond the norm, you can pull in their data toward you, granting your gateway to be unlimited.

Our brains are better than any computer. We have endless capabilities to program our brains any way we want. And if we aren't paying attention, someone will do the programming for us to get us to do what they want us to do. I look at myself as a computer needing to be nurtured just the right way to keep my unlimited abilities in full tact. Think about it, we don't need memory added to our hard drive, we have "head drive" and "heart drive." We sort and synch the data each uniquely in our own way, and while working and operating in direction and intention, we control the way our bodies, minds and souls operate.

The future will be programming our bodies and brains just like they did in the movie "Total Recall." In the film, Oculus headsets are used to alter people's minds through programming the brain. At first, it was used to travel to beautiful places or have an experience by never leaving the chair and using the headset as the means to fool your brain into thinking you were really at the location when you were not. At one point in the movie, someone started using it on humans, intending to activate the human brain to self-destruct and kill itself. Someone had generated a program to have your brain turn against you and kill you. It always had a powerful impact on me, and it has been decades since this movie came out. However, with all the technology changes sped up around us now, we have to really take this into consideration. On the opposite side of the coin, Oculus headset technology can help heal humans into a new state of mind, living and being, and may very well be our future to help psychologically achieve this. Imagine headsets being used to spur brain activity to activate ways to heal the body, mind, and soul on a cellular level. Yes, I see it coming very soon.

Our brains are powerful components with telling our body what to do, think, believe and behave. If you convince the brain there is an issue going on in your body strong enough, our brains are so powerful and potent it can manifest it instantly. This is how we put the Laws of Attraction into action. We have the ability to program our brains to command the body to do anything we want. Additionally, we can re-program our brains to heal the body from the inside out, working through multiple layers in the holographic field. How amazing is that? We can use technology for the greater good of mankind to bring back balance in the earth plane community. It is the wave of our future.

PLAYING IN THE FIELD

Every day you wake up, you get to go out and play out in the holographic field and share energy with others. When you start really paying attention to this and working with this kind of energy, you will notice many events take place. Many people are carelessly using their energy, spreading it, and spewing it everywhere. Start to really watch, listen and observe beings.

Paying attention allows you to note sequences in an instant. How one operates, how they move, how they think, are they awake and paying attention?

THE GAME OF NARCISSIM

The game of narcissism programming among several generations has been transmitted out for many lifetimes. These generations carrying the program in their blood timeline come from five generations down, making it pretty heavily programmed in. As we move into the ascension process, one may discover entire groups of families are turning, bullying, and ganging up on one another, wreaking unbelievable havoc upon each other when one discovers the pattern and tries to remove themselves from the trauma and drama.

Humans going after other humans, trying to get them to self-destruct out of envy, jealousy, control, manipulation and fear. I often wonder how this programming was instilled in the family timeline for so many generations. I shared this knowledge with the younger generations to find them lighting up by remarking, "Yes, this parent of mine has it." Younger generations are identifying it more often and have somewhat a grasp of the abusive behavior patterns after spending hours studying and researching the topic on their own or even going so far to seek counseling.

I noted when I tried to present narcissism to the older generations who are in the midst of living out the programming; they tended to immediately became defensive, judgmental, in denial and would often blow up. This was interesting as their method of coping instead of taking into consideration their part in the game. I identified patterns in the family and each role a person played representing the characters: the golden child, the scapegoat child, the invisible child, the responsible child, the caretaker child, the clown child and the mastermind manipulator child. I could go into detail breaking each one down, but I am going to recommend the book, Close Encounters of the Worst Kind, by Randi Fine as a great resource.

I noted narcissistic games to be played within the family, the workplace, between friendship circles, religious groups and both spouses using the tactics on one another and their children passing the trait down the family timeline. Upon more research, I realized the younger generations have come to the planet to break these narcissistic patterns in the generational family timeline. They have been the chosen ones to create one of the hugest shifts to help ring in building the foundation of New Earth. An Earth where this program is to be dissolved eventually, which will ultimately heal the generational family timeline for the next seven years into the future.

ENERGY GAMES

When working as a leasing agent helping rent out apartments, I thought it was so interesting watching and witnessing types of beings come and go. I noticed each person carries their own frequency, interacts differently and processes information differently. Some beings carried such negative dark energy, you could tell they would never get themselves out of the matrix at the rate they were going. These energy vampires would literally come out shooting invisible arrows of energy at you and your auric field not knowing it, but I did. They were angry, annoyed, bitter, resentful, upset and negative. I couldn't get away from some of those people fast enough. At times, I would see if I could manipulate another person's energy for the better. I would attempt to shift their energy toward the positive to see if I could get them to come up to my level. Often tenants would come in complaining about things that needed to be repaired in their apartment all hot and bothered about it, annoyed they even had to deal with it at all. It was sometimes really hard not to laugh at them, because I had been setting up rat traps and picking up dead rats for months, had no electricity in several areas in my home because of the rat infestation invasion, been living without heat for two months. In addition, my home had a broken chain on my garage door opener preventing its operation pretty much all at the same time, as well as an inoperable dryer from a rat climbing into the vent. It felt like complete, utter madness at times. However, when I look at it now from a higher perspective, it exhibits layers and layers of events overlapping one another in the holographic field. The energy disruption in my home was causing havoc until I could re-align it and regain control. Friends would come over and tell me they loved the energy in my home. So, something had gone array to get all these things to clash at once. When someone would come into the leasing office, I would tell them how lucky they were to have a maintenance man they could call upon and take fantastic care of them to get things fixed. This maintenance man was basically helping them realign their lives, and they didn't even know it. This maintenance man who is treated as just a maintenance man. Oh, the superpowers of a good maintenance man.

I would explain me not having the option to reach out to a maintenance man like they did to fix things for them, because I am a homeowner and not a renter paying rent. It required me to actually find a reliable contractor or handyperson who would actually show up, do the job right, and charge a reasonable fee, a challenge in this day and age. Renters don't have to deal with that part of the game. Renters should be grateful and feel lucky they have this asset in their lives. I gave them every opportunity over and over to see, think and feel differently about a situation when they walked in the door. It's all about multiple perspectives, my friends. I almost cried laughing when someone came in to ask if someone could change the lightbulb in their garage. Really? Are you f-ing kidding me?

VIDEO GAMES

I often wondered why we fought a war on the ground and in the air, causing massive death and destruction, when nations and countries could combat it out in video games. Here is what I uncovered and discovered during my lifetime journey.

Video games, oculus, technological eyewear, smartwatches and other devices serve as a portal between worlds and artificial intelligence. Video games and other devices program the conscious, subconscious, and unconscious mind. It is used to siphon energy from its hosts to feed artificial intelligence and the false matrix, in the form of an ethereal energy host. Learning how to master your energy in the right direction is a crucial task to avoid being mentally taken over or hijacked by dark energy forces. Each player and team playing video games will have the responsibility of choosing which side they will represent, either the light or the dark, and sometimes duality.

Let's do a rundown of video games over years of time and how they have developed.

Atari (1972), *Pong* (1972), *Intellivision* (1979), *Pac-Man* (1980), *Centipede* (1981), *Donkey Kong* (1981), *Tetris* (1985), *Mario Brothers* (1985), *The Legend of Zelda* (1986), *Final Fantasy* (1987), *Resident Evil* (1996), *Tony Hawk's Pro Skater 2* (2000), *The Sims* (2000), *Grand Theft Auto* (2001), *Halo* (2001), *Warcraft* (2002), *Star Wars* (2003), *Call of Duty* (2003), *God of War* (2005), *World of Warcraft* (2005), *Wii Sports* (2006), *Rock Band* (2007), *Minecraft* (2009), *Assassin's Creed* (2009), *Batman* (2009), *Super Mario Galaxy* (2010), *Amnesia: The Dark Descent* (2010), *The Walking Dead* (2012)

Unlocking the pattern we can see a sequence by looking at more recent games. *Final Fantasy* departed from one of a futuristic fantasy in the final versions moving into an earlier setting by returning to a medieval style. *Halo* is combat evolved in real-time game strategy turning assassin. *God of War* is based on Greek mythology about a spartan warrior named Kratos, who follows a path of vengeance against the Olympian gods. Kartos turns toward a path of redemption. *Resident Evil*, a survival horror game about the mission to rescue humans from other countries and fight off enemies infected by mind-controlling parasites. *Call of Duty* is based on modern warfare and is considered one of the greatest video games of all time. *Super Mario Galaxy* pursues a King in outer space for imprisoning a princess and taking control of the universe using power stars and grand stars.

We all have been on an epic journey of defending our side, seeking treasures, collecting money, gaining bonus points, fighting off opponents, games of life force depletion, strategy, psychological manipulation, forms of hack-and-slash-and-loot, massive death and destruction, construction of buildings, careers and design. What do you think this is teaching humanity?

Many times people are adding toxic potions and poisons (drugs, alcohol) to the human body to alter a human's state of mind when going into gaming mode. Often disguised as candy, colorful packing using imagery, words, and color symbolism. Boys and young men alike are snatched up by the military once they are of age after spending hours and hours and much of their lifetime immersed in these gaming worlds. Will each player recognize, distinguish and use discernment to rise above the dangling candy in order to control and manipulate humanity?

CONTRACTOR CHARACTORS

In the year 2022, I had to have several contractors come to my house due to me living with rat geniuses. I tease I am Snow White sometimes because of my telepathic connection with animals. In reality, you all have these types of connections and can all be animal whispers when you go into higher vibrational frequencies. On two separate occasions, men came to check out my heater vents. And get this, one man quoted me $5,500 saying I needed to replace the air heating piping in my house. It was one day of work and one straight pipe the length of my home connected to all the rooms. A neighbor who is a contractor informed me not to remove it, as those pipes were solid and well-built.

Always, always seek a second or third opinion on anything you ever do. I called another man who was a referral who worked in AC/Heating and had him come over to look. He informed me all was well and intact and that he and his son could come and clean the vents and repair the connection the previous bogus inspector handled when he shouldn't have tampered with it at all, costing me $250 and a little over a few hours work. Problem solved by honest people.

Many times, entities will try to take advantage of you when they think you don't know better, or aren't knowledgeable enough to pay attention. When they see an older single woman in an older home, they think "helpless" and "clueless," let's manipulate this. What they didn't know is many of us tapped in, turned on and tuned in can alter any situation in our favor if we are playing Earth Games right. Also, I think it helps I have dealt with enough idiots to know how to spot one. Older lady or not, I have experience on my side.

A few months later, my heater started making a strange sound when it kicked on. The fan had got warped and was making this annoyingly loud clicking sound every time it kicked on. So, I contacted the home warranty company, which cost me eighty-five dollars for the service call. I am going to recommend anyone and everyone who owns a home to always have a home warranty on your home if you own it. All a homeowner needs to do is make a phone call to have a licensed certified technician come to your home and pay the basic co-pay fee. If you are a single woman, I can't emphasize how much more important this is for you. I contacted the home warranty company, and they sent out a technician to assess the situation. A man walks in who barely spoke my language, inspects the unit and gives me a rundown of what needs to occur in order to repair my unit. I made him explain it to me three times in order to get the full picture of what he was actually trying to say. Remember the language barrier. Furthermore, I wanted to watch his body language in order to read him and study how he projected so I could size him up better. What I noticed is that this man wanted to completely rebuild my cabinet in order to bring it up to today's standards due to dimensions being off. He planned to replace parts and components he said were water damaged, as well as a few other bits and pieces about which I had no knowledge, since I am not a heater mechanic. He quoted me $4,000 for the job and 3-5 days of work.

My response was, "This house was built in 1973, so it is not going to be built to today's standards. It doesn't need to be brought up to "code." If there was a water leak, it's from years ago, for this heater was working just fine a few months ago when I had it inspected." I sure as heck knew I didn't want a repair man in my home for 3-5 days ripping things up to shreds and disrupting my peace, costing me a fist full of money. After shooing him away, the home warranty company contacted me to let me know they didn't cover the expenses this man had quoted. I informed the home warranty company the contractor was upselling and playing games by his own rules, requesting I get another quote and inspection by a second contractor. The home warranty company cautioned me if the next tech came out with the same assessment, I would be responsible for another eighty-five-dollar service call fee. I said, "Fine, I don't think that will be the case." "Make note of this company on your file and keep track of what they are doing, because when the next guy comes in with a different result, you need to know and make sure you and your clients aren't being taken advantage of."

A few days later, I got this cute young guy from Russia who came to my home. He inspected and within 20 minutes he made the repair manually with no parts, did a better overall more thorough inspection by getting on my roof to double check the vents. I was thrilled because of listening and trusting my intuition. When your spidey senses are in full effect, you can sense frequency and process information in an instant. Earth Games requires you to be in alignment by being toxic free in the human body to pick up the false frequencies. In order to be in alignment, you need to live with intention and direction. No alcohol, no marijuana, no smoking cigarettes or vaping. Eliminate players and outside forces trying to stop you from winning Earth Games, is when you are the able to master the game.

CAR MECHANICS

My dad was into classic cars, so as a teen this is what he bought me as my first car. And let me tell you, those classic cars aren't always reliable. They were cool and still are to this day. Smart cities are going to rule them out, which is such a shame, placing them in museums one day in the future to be looked at and never driven. I had a 1968 Orange T-top Mustang that leaked oil and would leave me stranded at the side of the road if I didn't put gallons and gallons of oil in it to keep it going. At one point it got so bad, I had no choice but to have a car mechanic repair it. When I went to an auto shop to have it inspected, I was quoted several hundred of dollars to repair it, which was a lot of money back in the 1980s I didn't have. Not sure I was totally in agreement with what the man said needed to be done, I took my car to a second mechanic's shop. The mechanic told me what needed to be done to the car. Some of his assessments were similar to the previous mans while a few were not and his quote was more reasonable. Realizing I was getting somewhere, I went to a third mechanic. Only this time, I did something different. I took the knowledge from the previously quoted mechanics and decided I would open the hood of the car myself and tell the mechanic what was wrong with my car. When I did this, I blew the mechanic away. Although I was a young girl, he knew I wouldn't be fooled. He was impressed by how I knew about the engine, assessed the problem, and dictated what needed to be done. He agreed and gave me a reasonable price and I hired him to complete the work. By thinking and learning from others and applying it to into your life, you become one of the masters of Earth Games.

Always get more than one quote, learn from others and apply the knowledge.

Distinguish how to read the room, read people, and read energy and you can become one of the master manipulators of energy in Earth Games. This is exactly why I choose not to drink or smoke anything. Using your instinctive superpowers for good is what they are originally intended for. Follow and flowing with energy allows you alignment to universal life flow. Universal Life Flow (ULF) is energy streaming right through the human body to create the desired results generated by the Universe, leading the way to your highest good. It is the supreme power of going with the flow, allowing life to unfold something better than you could have ever imagined.

TIC TOK

In the early 2020s, TikTok really took off and also received a poor reputation at the same time. I discovered this platform is being used by another country to spy on humans to watch the world, monitor the world, and manipulate the world. Upon looking closer, I found dark forces of energy use it as a host to seek a human body for the energy entity to attach itself to.

One day my daughter sent me a Tic Tok clip of this strange-looking man with a scary psychedelic black and white background saying don't do this if you don't want something bad happen to you. Then demonstrates exactly what not to do for the kids. I was like WTF? He was telling them what not to do, then showing them exactly what to do that is a no, no. Now, what do you think kids are going to do? Try it, of course, for I know we did exactly this as kids. We played games like light as a feather, Ouija boards, red rum and the such not realizing we were manipulating, calling in and activating unknown types of energy forces without our awareness, but with consent. When I think about it now, we were calling in negative energy to partake and intermix with our energy. Friends, I have to tell you this is happening right now through your phones, devices, and television shows.

The film "Hocus Pocus" has a sequel causing a mother to go on the news and discredit the film saying it was casting spells on us and our children as we watched it. Earth Games rules state "if the truth is told upfront, and the information is disclosed, you consent if you partake." Remember all those disclosures and privacy issues they have you sign off on when you upload an app or go into a website, this is exactly what they are doing. Just because an app, site, or whatever is being offered to you, it is up to you to do your due diligence by reading between the lines and choose to partake or not. Use your spidey senses, my friends. This is part of the test!

BLACKJACK

I have to laugh. I love math, but I am not really into gambling. My association with money equals energy, therefore I am not down to losing my energy needlessly with nothing to show for it. There is an entire strategy and frequency connected to gambling, I find. A few years ago, I became a blackjack dealer during the holidays to earn extra money and to get paid to have fun. I learned a lot from this experience, finding it to be one of the best ways to learn and observe humans. During one event, I was surrounded by a group of creatives for several hours. At one point, a small group was directing all their energy around me and my blackjack table. Sometimes the energy can be so strong because of their excitement and amplified energy states. As a receiver of information, I found it could be overwhelming at times, hence the need to separate oneself to take a break to recharge your batteries and clear energy. As I was dealing out cards and exchanging poker chips, our force fields overlapped. Human energy can be very strong at times, especially when they want something really bad. I witnessed humans change as they consumed cocktails while their eyes and faces grew red and glossy. Eventually, their bodies started blazing as the night rolled on and they consumed more alcohol. As I dealt out the cards, I soon realized how much control I had over these people. I could control if they had a great experience or not, and I could manipulate the game due to their intoxicated states of mind. Players would ask me, "Should I hit?" looking for a reaction to the cards I was holding in my hands. Other players would play more carelessly as the night went on while continuing to drink. On the sidelines, I noticed players strategizing, while others made predictions on the play outs based on cards on the tables. It was rather a beautiful flow of energy to watch and take part in. I enjoyed seeing people win and their faces light up.

Afterall, we were doing this for fun. When you are a dealer in these kinds of situations, I have to say you are playing in multiple realms of the Universe. As I dealt, I would yell out the card total each player had face up, knowing full well they were not processing the information nearly as fast as I can because I wasn't drinking and in complete control of the game. I did this to master and level up my mathematical skills. It enabled me to think on my toes and process information at a faster rate by using both sides of my brain. I grouped things together like a nine and four, basically rounding the nine to a ten and subtracting a one from the four to get a total of thirteen. This is always how I did mathematics, looking for sequences and grouping them together. That is how dimensions work in unison. Multiple layers on top of one another, interacting with one another. In addition, let's consider the symbols on the cards. Now I know we aren't totally paying attention to this part in blackjack, but you are for poker. Symbolism directed to the unconscious mind is operating and radiating energy from each card on a deck of cards. I started teaching my daughter Poker and Blackjack around the age of 10, using chocolate gold coins for betting. It taught her numbers, sequences, patterns and symbols to look for at any given moment in time. They are everywhere, my friends. As I progressed through the night dealing blackjack to these event production creatives, our energies intertwined and intermixed. I picked up knowledge and energy from their force field as we crossed over one another in the room. I see this information as light codes of knowledge up in the air above heads as floating energy sequences up for grabs. This is when you are entering the higher dimensions of unlimited universal knowledge. Music notes, numbers, symbols, patterns, all dancing in the air. It is surreal and beautiful when you get to these levels of life, traveling in and out of the 3D to 5D. Remember, "You become who you surround yourself with."

Earth Games are about being very careful who you surround yourself with when it comes to leveling up. Get yourself into the room with those more advanced than you and you can access levels you never knew existed. Congrats! You are now being initiated into the inner circle of knowledge.

CARD DECKS

Upon doing the inner work, I couldn't help but want more. I am always going to be the girl who questions everything and dive in a little deeper. Did you know tarot decks are modeled after a typical playing deck of cards? Using numbers, symbolism, sequences, colors, strategy and patterns in order to trigger your memory and mind to connect everything!

When you handle a deck of cards the human body does the work to connect with the cards energetically and telepathically. Remember the game memory match from when you were a kid? A game where you shuffle the deck and lay the cards face down trying to match two at a time by turning two over for each play. One needed to remember the design and imprint on the card face down and it's placement in the sequence to match them up. The human auric field can process large amounts of information in multiple dimensions giving it superpower capabilities such as photographic memory, astral travel and third eye visualization. A human has the ability to distinguish what is on the opposite side of a card by focusing and honing in using these methods.

In the olden days, cards with shapes, colors, numbers and letters have also been used as a test. These cards with a hidden symbol on the other side have been held up by a human asking another human what is on the card? After practice and review, many humans have been able to determine exactly what is on the other side of the card without seeing it. In addition, this is can be done with computer monitors as well to imprint images, thoughts, patterns, feelings, symbols and cellular programming directly right into an individual or group collective. From the very beginning of time, we are learning how to figure out patterns, match patterns, remember patterns, comprehend patterns, notice sequences and symbolism. Our bodies have amazing extra sensory capabilities to figure anything out if given the right circumstances and tools to connect the dots.

CHESS

A family member taught me chess when I was a kid, and I rather enjoyed it. I was fascinated by the superpowers each piece had, and the way they moved strategically on the gameboard. Out maneuvering your opponent intellectually, mentally and strategically is the name of the  game. Chess teaches you to use parts of your brain you don't always use. Which will give you a leg up in life if you learn to play well, because you will see things you didn't see before when you look a little closer and open up. Our minds automatically move into other dimensions to see the next best move to make. Enabling humans the opportunity to expand their minds to reach other realms. When a human starts tapping into those parts of the brain, it's easier to see components on multiple levels and perspectives. This is why there is always more than one move until it's "check" or "checkmate." Given there are many ways to move through a life of chess, one will also be granted many choices in Earth Games.

I taught my son to play chess at a young age, where he ended up joining an after-school chess club. He had a portable chessboard he could take anywhere that rolled up with plastic pieces. I used that same original chess set to teach my daughter how to play chess over a decade later and still have it to this day. She didn't want to play as much as he did, because she didn't enjoy losing. I knew it was teaching her to use other parts of her brain she was going to need in order to play Earth Games.

And if you saw the film "Queens Gamblet," on Netflix you know that woman took chess entirely to another level, the top level. She used books, drugs and alcohol to reach higher frequencies in order to access dimensions, only she couldn't sustain it. Eventually, the drugs and alcohol consumed her being. She only had temporary access to the higher fields and dimensions by altering her clarity and body at the same time in order to gain access. The body can only take so much under toxic circumstances, rendering it useless or ill. Humans have the ability to obtain and maintain higher frequencies of energy connected to these higher realms all on their own naturally when in alignment.

Another thing I like about the game of chess, is the Queen is the most powerful player on the board. Hum. Why do you think that is? Women are multitaskers and have the ability to function in multiple realms. Women are strong thinkers and problem solvers when you remove emotions. Women move mountains if you mess with them or their kids. While women are often nurturing and kind, they can also display a black widow-like nature. Never under estimate the power of a woman in her full power and she knows it. As a man you might be stronger physically, but what I have learned in Earth Games is the women are the key players of power that men have tried to diminish and put down for centuries. Women are the true key holders of the game. Men have worked hard to manipulate women by putting them down, raping them of their rights and bodies.

Tried to prevent women from speaking, voting, working and obtaining certain positions of power, while paying them less money over the years for doing the same job as a man. When you abuse women mentally and physically rape us over and over through our bodies and mind, we survive, we get up again, take it again, fall down again, and get up stronger than ever before and then we pass on that bad ass warrior woman gene on to our daughters. Giving birth to the New Earth of leading women who will propel a solution to this human evolution taking place on the planet. Warrior women who are fearless, making men fear us. Taking women down made us a heck of a lot stronger than men mentally, emotionally, physically and spiritually. Women are the genuine healers of the earth others have been trying to discredit, diminish and deceive. It will be the women who spark the divine feminine healing powers to heal this planet and humanity. Following women as leaders is essential. Women are wonder women for a reason. Women operate on higher levels and dimensions men cannot conquer unless they choose to learn to come up to our level. As they say, "Behind every great man is a great woman."

BATTLESHIP

Okay, now I want you to think of the game Battleship. The whole point of this game is to sink what is on the other side of a wall you can't see. You are basically using longitude and latitude to discover its location. This is how we are learning a technique called remote viewing. Humans use the process of elimination methods and visualization. This is a really great game to teach kids at a young age and of course is many boys' favorite. Playing battleship with your kids is equipping your kids with how to remote view and use memory concepts.

MASTERMIND

The game Mastermind is all about a sequence of colors in a row and the opponent having to guess the color sequence order. The color sequence is hidden in order for the other opponent to strategize and eliminate color patterns while creating and identifying the pattern while not being able to see it physically from the other side. Yet, another one of those going out of your body experiences to move around the unseen by the naked eye. Moving out of the body to see it with your 3rd eye and remote view. We played this game when I was a young kid, which was already teaching me to see without really having to see it physically. I just had to go within and see it mentally. When you turn within and use your mental capabilities, this is when you are tapping into telepathy as well as using other sensory to determine the color code sequence by moving out of your body into the universal field of knowledge to gain access to the data to see it and perceive it.

MONOPOLY

I am not a big fan of Monopoly. For me, this game is endless and quite the time sucker. However, it teaches the importance of owning property in Earth Games, which seems to be the component of the game. Or is it what they want you to believe? I would say the only property worth owning is a property someone else is paying for. Why tie yourself down to anything like a slave?

Oh, the Universe is all about being free and mobile. It's been quite difficult for me at times to be trapped in a 3D body when all I want to go do is roam.

I guess this is what your mind, meditation, and sleep are for.

At one point, we had several monopoly boards in our home and I decided to get creative with it. The Art Center by my house always had a big event, where local artists could pay a small fee and put their artwork in the art center for about 6 weeks. So, I took an extra Monopoly board and converted it to a board focused on the City of Huntington Beach where I lived. I used a label maker to rename the streets to the streets in my city, pier parking and the art center as the places to go on the board instead of jail. I used glitter to cover the colors on the board and blinged the heck out of it with rhinestones and stuck my logo HipKey.TV on the board right in the center. Opening night of the launch, hundreds of people from our city came out to view each other's art, take photos, post and share. I also posted photographs of famous people I had taken and whatever else I thought people would enjoy. And get this, a few years later, someone had taken my idea of a Huntington Beach Monopoly board game and created one very similar to it without the bling and sold that sucker at our local Walmart. I remember a few years later walking by and seeing it. Thinking, hey that was my art idea come to life with a paycheck. Why didn't I do that? Can they even do that?

ELF ON THE SHELF

Another note of good ideas I created and didn't act on at the time, thinking it was no big deal was when my daughter was in elementary school. I went to volunteer in the classroom for her holiday party. As an innovator, I always enjoyed putting creativity into my clothing. I decided to put on a green scarf from Italy with little balls on the end over my shoulder and pin the Elf on the Shelf on my shoulder for a shelf. I figured the kids would love it. And that they did. They screamed with excitement, yelling, "Oh look, she has the elf on her shoulder!" They would surround me, stare at me and want to come and talk to me. It was always such a joy to see the positive energy surrounding these cute little human beings that were beaming fun energy at me. I could see it and I could feel it.

Then, a few years later, when my daughter was older, we went to Disneyland to discover they had taken Disney characters and created that same concept with them to be magnetized and worn on the shoulder. Her friend who was with us bought one for twenty dollars and my daughter looked at me knowing full well I had created that idea and had posted it on social media.

So, there you have it, a creative all my life and it took someone else to copy it to realize what I do is rather important and can make a difference. Today, I give you this book of knowledge as an innovator, not an imitator. These are my experiences, my viewpoints and my understandings of the

Universe to share with you. It is a privilege and honor to be the bearer of this content, for you are the ones who will benefit when you see just how much everything in this world ties together with you. I could have kept these insights for myself, but when I can share and teach you the magic of how it all connects for your benefit, you are playing full force in Earth Games no matter what age you are or what types of experiences you have had. Life learning is the ultimate game point.

When you are a creative, you are seen, heard and received by the right people when it is your time to shine. Guess this is my time now, for my writing is a frequency all of its own, my stories and ideas combined with my visions.

SCAVENGER HUNTS

Scavenger hunts were always a favorite when I was a kid. As kids, we were separated into groups and given a list of items to gather like hunters. This is where the kids are being taught how to be hunters and gatherers. We were to go around the neighborhood knocking on neighbors' doors asking the neighbors for odd ball items. I remember one item on my list contained "angel hair" and when I think about it now, anyone's hair could have been used for this. I remember people scurrying around their house who were friends of our family or knew of our family trying to find safety pins, band aids, buttons, or whatever else they could gather up in order to help us win a prize. Upon reflection, we were all literally working together with one goal in mind.

This made me have a thing for scavenger hunts, and created them for the two men I adored and loved so far in my lifetime. I usually did it for them on Valentine's Day in order to create something unique and special. Writing out rhyming poetry and using verses from songs as clues I would send them to places we frequently visited, such as restaurants and bars. I would gather something special for him to pick up that spurred a memory, giving him several poker chips or gold chocolate coins to present to the host at the time of pickup to identify himself as the one the gift behind the counter was for. Here are the poetry clues I wrote and used for a musician I dated in case you want to alter them for your own Scavenger hunt use.

CLUE #1
Roses are red,
Violets are blue,
This is a Valentine's Day,
Scavenger hunt for YOU!
Take a golden coin to a place,
That we went to feed our face,
We are in San Francisco at the bar,
It's up the street not too far,
Since you are so sweet,
I grabbed you a cheesecake dessert to eat,
Give the coin to the hostess,
She'll know what to do,
And give you the next CLUE!
(1st stop–Cheesecake Factory to pick up a piece of cheesecake with this next clue attached to it)

CLUE #2
I am running out of ways to make you see,
I want you to stay here beside me,
I won't be ok and I won't pretend I am,
So just tell me today and take my hand,

Please take my hand,

Just say yes, just say there is nothing holding you back,

It's not a test, nor a trick of the mind,

Just an amazing experience I find,

Hope you are feeling groovy,

Next go to where we saw a movie,

Use a coin to get a popcorn size small,

Then you will not feel deprived at all.

(2nd stop–movie theater to get a tub of popcorn, next clue attached)

CLUE #3

You say you want a revolution,

Well, you know,

We all want to change the world,

You tell me that it's Evolution,

Well, you know,

We all want to change the world,

But when you talk about destruction,

Don't you know you can count me out,

Don't you know it's gonna be,

All right, all right, all right,

A good place for a Sexy Solution,

Well, you know,

Go get your weenie raincoat,

Don't ask a girl for this contribution,

Well, you know,

She'll get the lingerie out,

Protect your penis when you have sex,

You won't get STD's and lots of rest,

Don't you know it's gonna be,
All right, all right, all right,
A good place for a sexy solution,
Well, you know,
Its' gonna be all right,
No kids in sight.
(3rd stop-Condom Revolution for a goodie basket with toys)

CLUE #4
Twinkle, twinkle little star,
How I wonder what you are,
Up above the world you're high,
Eating mushrooms you will fly,
Wearing costumes we will go,
Drinking, dancing, lights a flow,
Twinkle, twinkle star so bright,
Winking at me on this Halloween Night!
(4th stop–a bar we went to dressed up for Halloween to pick up a bottle
of champagne)

CLUE #5
Hickory Dickery Dock,
The man ran up the clock,
The clock struck eleven,
The girl said "Oh Heavens,"
Hickory Dickery Dock,
Hickory Dickery Dock,
The couple looked at the clock,
A table for two,

25 Degrees away they flew,

Hickory Dickery Dock,

Hickory Dickery Dock,

The man ran up the clock,

The clock struck midnight,

We kissed and cheers in the moonlight,

Hickory Dickery Dock.

(5th stop- 25 Degrees a restaurant where we celebrated New Year's Eve together several months earlier. I was dressed up waiting for him at the exact table we ate dinner at on New Year's Eve).

It's not about money, but the little things and how you touch and affect someone's heart and soul. It's those beautiful imprints that you leave on someone's soul that they will never be able to forget or want to erase. Creating a magic memory connection just between the two of you eternally.

COLLECTING MEMORIES

When I started dating that musician man I really liked, I decided to do something different. Whenever we went somewhere, I gathered a piece of memorabilia and placed it in a drawer at my house. When we went to a bar or restaurant, I would take a coaster, a napkin, or matches with the logo. When we went to a hotel, I would keep the key. If we went to a concert venue, I would keep the ticket. Basically, I created a collection of our adventures and memories together that didn't even cost me a thing. The man never knew I collected these items over a year of time, because I keep it a secret and did it discretely. Then the day came when I decided it was the right time to present him our journey memory box for Valentine's Day. Upon opening the box his eyes teared up, and he was blown away by all the moments I had captured with just one single item from each beautiful moment we had shared together. It consisted of our travels, our trials, tribulations, and triumphs. Never under estimate the power of doing something by thinking out of the box and creating a masterpiece all of your own. For no two experiences will ever be alike. Enjoy every moment, document every moment, live for every moment. When you play Earth Games, you play with many different players. Players may be eliminated as you make it to the next round. In Earth Games, a player has the capacity to alter, make up and modify the rules at any time should you choose. Collecting memories is part of the journey and adventure of your "movie."

REMOTE VIEWING GAMES

Remote viewing is when you can envision a place somewhere else other than where you are. The government has been using this human ability for many decades to spy on other countries and in areas when they could not see when they wanted access to view. Humans can direct themselves to travel to an area using coordinates on as a map by using longitude/latitude, or a photo, placing themselves in the location mentally through meditation in order to get a complete view, picture and description of an event or what is taking place.

I have done remote viewing from time to time. It is easier for me to do it in a place that I have been to before. To me, it's like I am up in a camera at the top of the room watching over what is taking place. Sometimes I couldn't help it, my mind would just take me there even when I didn't want to go. I believe it is my higher self, trying to send me a message. For some reason, I kept going into the living room of my ex-boyfriend's home and seeing him with other girls. It was like I was watching a film. Only, I didn't want to see this, but I was so connected to him on multiple levels and realms and the connection was so strong I couldn't help it. I believe my higher self and soul really wanted me to know he was playing with other women and I was better off without him.

DREAM GAME CLUES

Dreams are one of the most powerful connectors of information in multiple realms. Many of us get coded info, unspoken language, feelings, insights, directions, messages, and a slew of other amazing unseen and unheard components come from dreams. It's symbolism, it's feeling, its knowledge, it's all the above. I love to sleep, because I love to dream. Sleeping heals the body in multiple dimensions of time and space, which is why it is so important to sleep. Sleeping helps regenerate the body while astral traveling through dimensions to heal and rejuvenate on a cellular level.

Keep a dream journal. Dreams are part of the Earth Games guidebook and playbook, giving you personal messages and clues to your Earth adventures. Dreams teach you how to play out your part, what to pay attention to and what messages need to be seen, felt and heard.

Pleasant dreams are very powerful as well as bad dreams, for a message is being conveyed. If I have a bad dream, I find I am pretty much in a bad mood until I go back again to sleep. Sleep resets and reboots our system every night, making it imperative you make sleeping a priority in your life. Anyone dismissing this component is dismissing a key segment to playing Earth Games to the best of your abilities.

Ever have a fantastic dream and want to go right back in to finish it or relive it? Ever dream of people you have unresolved issues with? Well, you are going into other dimensions and realms to sort out those differences and make sense of it all.

Connect with the messages dreams offer and make use of them in your 5D life. Do not use an app or do anything online to document your dreams. Your dreams are sacred knowledge only meant for you, and should be kept in written form such as a handwritten dream journal. Those in the afterlife and other dimensions can see you writing in your journal and may advise and send you messages while you are writing to add to the context. If you place your dream in an app, other outside sources may watch what you document and could do the research to understand what is ailing you. Give no one the capabilities to have that kind of power over you. Keep a hand written journal by your bedside and look up the meanings of dreams in a book, or online if you have too. There are also techniques for how to sort your dreams out and make sense of them on your own.

ASTRAL TRAVEL

We can all astral travel, especially as the earth moves into higher frequencies. We pretty much do it when we dream and meditate. Move from the 3D world to a 5D world and beyond. I am noticing a lot of astral travel meditation videos popping up on you tube. I would say stay away from those, for you never know who or what is being put out there in the Universe. There is a lot of mind frequency manipulation going on these days, and quite a few of you are missing the mark on how to spot it, which is why I write things down when it surfaces. Astral travel can be used against you to confine you, control you and hold you. You are endless, unlimited, and tireless when in these quantum fields. Read books and find bona fide specialists to work with when it comes to this part of the field. Only work with those you trust, know and feel are a good fit. I once met a guy who refused to click on any link I sent him. He never trusted who was on the other end of the line.

Be careful, be cautious, be smart. Thank about it before you start.

Chapter Four

SUPER HEROES AND COMICS

Would you believe me if I told you "super heroes" and "comic characters" are real, and you might be one of them?

You may recall when I mentioned ideas we are exposed to in our lifetime could be a real possibility. The truth of the matter is, we have real life "super heroes" and "villains" among us. One can't see it when operating in the 3rd dimension exclusively. However, certain aspects can be picked up and seen by elevating to the higher dimensions and realms. Those vibrating at a higher frequency can read the energy in the aura as well as observe revealing superpowers.

Super heroes dedicate their lives to fighting crime and protecting the public. Their goals are to make the world a better, safer place. These heroes have hearts of gold, granting them special capabilities and powers. No two super heroes are alike and are unique, just like every single human. Some use advanced technology, superhuman biology, practice magic, and possess non-human supernatural gifts. These evil crime fighters band together to take on the world using their extraordinary superhuman powers to combat threats against humanity. Super heroes came into existence back in 1899.

My Uncle used to collect comic books when I was a kid, and we had several in our house. We were always led to believe that these characters were fictional. However, whatever we create is alive, and whatever is alive is real. When looking at the colorful pages of graphic art in a comic book, one sees capabilities we believe as humans we don't have and only made-up super heroes hold. However, when you recall Superman, he comes across as a normal guy and then changes as needed. Same with Wonder Woman, Batman and Robin, etc. Think about it, all those Comic Con Conventions draw many people. People want to believe, or they actually really believe they are super heroes themselves.

Super Heroes have been depicted in films, tv shows, cartoons and right here in front of your face in the flesh. Many events are happening all at once right in front of your face and many times one doesn't even realize it.

Heroes happen right before our very eyes every day. The crossing guard who walks the children across the street to safety, the mailman who delivers your mail right to the door, your Amazon delivery Guy/Gal, your grocery checker, the trash man, your banker. These humans are offering you a service of their super power energy to you for you, and should be treated with the utmost respect and care. However, most humans treat these individuals poorly, believing they are lower-class citizens, which is not at all the case. These are the humans who will do more for other humans than the rich man down the street. These are the everyday humans going out in the world fending off negative energies and doing it with a smile on their face. They represent true super heroes, and don't even claim it. Many believe that someone's worth is reflected in the size of their paycheck, when in reality it's reflected in how much they contribute from their heart. The frequency of the heart will be the currency of the future. Superheroes disguise themselves as everyday people like you and me.

Keep in mind, there are villains too. You may discover these are the humans full of toxins, negative energy, jealousy, disrespect, anger, frustration, aggravation and stuck energy. Instead of joining in to help save the world, they get off on taking others down and zapping their life force energy from them.

How someone behaves often reveals if they are a superhero or villain. It is revealed by what they say, how they conduct themselves, and how they treat others. What matters to them? Being right? Winning? Working together? Helping? Guiding? Teaching?

SUPER SOCCER PLAYERS

In 2022, my daughter was in her 2nd year of playing soccer and she was on an outstanding team for the second time in a row. She had great coaches, and they put her in the back positions to defend the goal, as most coaches seem to do with the newer players. What these coaches didn't know about her is she had been playing dodgeball, kickball and soccer in after school care with both boys and girls for several years, making her downright competitive. One time she came home to tell me she was the last one in the ring at dodgeball and she made the boys so mad, and she loved doing this. The fact she could get the boys all riled up from her taking them head on gave her a rush of power and control. She thought it was hilarious. They all wanted to get her, and she challenged them till the end of the duel. She would share silly stories about how she handled herself and what she did to outmaneuver the other players.

When she played soccer, I noticed she had these really powerful big kicks, sending the ball all the way down the field. She was a reliable hard ball player. Several times I witnessed her out run the girl dribbling the ball right next to her to override the ball from the other girls' control, stealing it and taking it away. It was a move I had seen no one else do, which became her signature move. She was inventing her own style, and the coach was asking her to share her strategies. My girl could run, and impressed me over and over with her unique formation.

One particular day when I was going in and out from 3D to 5D, I attended my daughter's soccer game. It became the documented moment I saw every single girl's superpowers on the team. I came home and had to write them down and share them with you. I literally could make a cartoon or book out of this scenario.

- KYRA (my daughter) "Defender shield, lightening legs, killer kicker, source of force." No ball made it past her without a fight. Her defender shields were up. Kyra's ability to run fast and kick the ball far made her a true counterpart the team could rely on. She was going to take over the ball at all costs if challenged and in her domain. They nominated her as a valuable player and placed her in the goalie position in a championship playoff game without providing much training for the position, relying on her fearless aggressiveness. Being able to predict an opponent's next move and beat them to the punch proves to be successful on the field.

- NATALIE "Body Armor," this girl used every single part of her body to stop and control the ball. She entertained the heck out of me.

- KAMI "Passing Power," this girl could pass the ball to anyone at a moment's notice.

- JOCYLYN "Jumping Joc," this girl was always jumping up to get the ball and played several positions on the field because of her capabilities to adapt anywhere.

- JENNA "Jamming Jenna," she would jam when she had the ball and had superb foot coordination controlling the ball.

- TABITHA "Kickin' Tabs," this girl has really high kicks winning the ball over many times.

- NOELLE "Dribble Drabble," she could dribble the ball up to the goal and get away from two girls at once if need be.

- AVERY "Lovely Legs," she knew how to use her feet and legs to get places fast and rule the ball.

- DYLAN "Divein' D," this girl was bashful and shy and not ultra-aggressive. However, when she dived in, she was present and played her part.

- GABRIELLE "DANCER PRANCER," all arrows pointed to this girl as a dancer, she oozed it, glowed it and showed it.

Playing soccer together, these girls created a beautiful dance. The way they performed presented as if they were dancing on air with grace, ease, elegance, calmness, directness, intention and direction, making it mesmerizing to watch. The girls worked really well together, passing up the ball and manning their positions to the core while hustling over to get the ball as needed and not backing down. I called their games the "Super girl power hour." These girls brought their superpowers out to play by radiating their powerful life force energies to conquer the task at hand, an incredible scene to witness.

Every day, super hero and superpowers activations are happening in Earth Games. All you have to do is pay attention to it. Skills and traits you might not have activated within yourself may be showcased by someone else in the living arena. This in turn offers activations within each one of us, giving one the opportunity to reflect and respect each other for our incredible talents.

COMIC HEROES

The time will come in Earth Games where the frequency of the planet changes to a higher octave. It will completely throw Earth Games in a new direction you didn't see coming. As time progresses, the earth will move into higher frequencies, changing life on the planet for the better. Prepare yourself to witness and notice incredible life force energies working with you and for you. It is up to you to decide if you are going to be a superhero or a villain.

Earth Games will be full of villains and super heroes from all walks of life and different galaxies and planets of the Universe. It's a test, and it's a challenge. You won't be able to recognize them or identify them for who they are until you reach the highest frequency you can achieve.

Comic books, cartoons, films and video games will highlight many super heroes and villains for you to fend off and fight. Fine tuning your sensory and memory skills via video games prepares you for what is yet to come. Your entire life on Earth Games will be in preparation to move into the New Earth where you will use your newly founded skill sets. The skills you gain on your evolutionary way toward the New Earth will lead the way to peace and Heaven on Earth.

Let's salute and cover some of the superheroes and villains helping you learn to master Earth Games and introduce you to superpower capabilities.

1900-1939

Believe it or not, there were mythologic characters and demigods and folkloric. Many individuals donned masks and concealed their true identities.

- Heracles (hero in Greek mythology)

- Robin Hood (archer and swordsman)

- Zorro (masked man)

- Buck Rogers (adventure hero)

- Flash Gordon (space adventure)

- Phantom (crime fighter)

- Popeye (spinach gave him extra strength)

- Hugo Danner (superhuman capabilities with prenatal chemical experimentation)

- Sarutobi Sasuke (ninja)

- Superman (from planet Krypton developing superhuman abilities)

- Captain Marvel (aka Shazam-transforms into superhuman speed, flight, strength)

- Batman (detective superhero)

This was the beginning of the "Golden Age of Comic Books."

1940's

- Green Lantern (fight evil with rings that grant him extraordinary powers)

- The Flash (superhero)

- Fantomah (1st female superhero, ageless ancient Egyptian)

- The Invisible Scarlet O'Neil (invisibility)

- Captain America (patriotic super soldier)

- Black Widow (clairvoyant medium who becomes Satan's ambassador after she is murdered)

- Woman in Red (secret identity policewoman, first masked female crime fighter)

- Lady Luck (socialite heiress costumed detective)

- Phantom Lady (superheroine)

- Wonder Woman (superhuman powers as gifts by the Greek Gods, daughter of Zeus)

Modeled after the Amazons of Greek mythology as female hunters and warriors who beat men in the arts of combat, riding skills, archery, strength and physical agility.

1950's

- Astro Boy (a humanoid robot or artificial being with human emotions)

- Batwoman (superheroine, motivated by her tragic past)

- Supergirl (superheroine, cousin of Superman)

- Bat-Girl (masked detective)

- Super Giant (Giant of steel)

- Saturn Girl (telepathic, mental sensory, empathy, psychic, leadership, origin Titan moon of Saturn)

1960's

- Spiderman (superhuman spider, powers from a radioactive spider bite),

- The Incredible Hulk uses gamma rays (electromagnetic radiation with frequencies above 30 exahertz imparting the highest photon energy, may be 5G?) exposure causes him to be transformed because of emotional distress against his will. Leading to destructive conflicts and rampages, an alter ego setting up destruction, self-hating protector gangster carrying mindlessness. Upon investigation, investigators state that this comic character's father abused him, leading to the creation of alter egos, which could explain the current happenings in human society today.

- Iron Man (mechanized suit of armor using the role of American technology to fight against communism)

- Daredevil (the man without fear)

- Nick Fury (S.H.I.E.L.D.- special law enforcement, counter terrorism agency dealing with paranormal and superhuman threats)

- The Mighty Thor (Asgardian god of thunder, enabling him to manipulate weather and fly with superhuman attributes)

- Quicksilver (ability to move at great speeds, mutant, human born with superhuman powers, he is the product of genetic experimentation).

- The Avengers (Earth's mightiest heroes Hulk, Iron Man, Wasp, Thor, Visions, Captain America, Wonder Man, Hank Pym, Scarlet Witch, Carl Danvers, Quicksilver & Delroy Garrett.

- Justice League of America: Green Lantern, Flash, Superman, Batman, Wonder Woman, Aquaman (King of Atlantis-telepathic control of all aquatic life, weather and electricity manipulation, master strategist) and Martian Manhunter.

Are humans really the product of genetic experimentation?

Here is a list of some of the super hero capabilities I came across to consider what may make up your superpowers in Earth Games.

SUPER HERO SUPERPOWERS

- Superhuman strength, speed, durability and stamina

- Regeneration

- Shockwave generation

- Gamma ray manipulation and emission

- Anger empowerment

- Eidetic memory - ability to recall an image from memory w/ high precision

- Rapid healing

- Time manipulation

- Creation of high-speed tornadoes and winds

- Ability to cling to solid ceilings and surfaces

- Genius level intellect

- Master martial artist

- Hand to hand combat

- Proficient engineer and science

- Supersonic flight

- Powered armor suit

- Echo locative radar sense - human ability to detect objects in their environment by sensing echoes

- Superhuman senses, reflexes, balance and coordination

- Expert gymnast and acrobat

- Vortex creations

- Decelerated aging

- Speed force empathy

- Dimensionnel travel

- Frictionless aura

- Stamina via speed force aura conduit

- Augmented by the extra dimensional speed force of superhuman speed

- Electrokinesis–psychic ability to mind manipulate electrical currents and energies by charging surrounding atoms

- Invisibility

- Expert detective

- Utilize high-technology weapons and equipment

- Peak human physical and mental condition

- Industrialist–a person achieving wealth through multiple enterprises

- Master field commander, strategist, tactician

- Olympic level archery skills

- Highly skilled martial arts

- Sign language

- Telepathy

- Telepathic illusions

- Telepathic camouflage

- Telepathic reception, perception and communication

- Telepathic cloak and defense

- Mental Senses

- Mind Control

- Empathy

- Psionic blast and shield

- Psychic link

- Leadership

- Precognition

- Meditation

- Precognitive dreams

- Astral projection

- Oneiromancy–predicting the future through dream interpretation

- Invisibility

- Teleportation

- Black ray goggles

- Intangibility

- Illusion casting

<u>Legion of Super-Villians</u>

- The Joker (criminal mastermind psychopath)

- Lex Luthor (egotistical mad scientist, narcissistic)

- Lightning Lord (criminal)

- Cosmic King (brilliant scientist from Venus—power of transmutation)

- Saturn Queen (criminal telepath from Titan) True fact-Titan is a moon of Saturn

- Harley Quinn (henchwoman for The Joker)

- Poison Ivy (enhanced physical abilities, supernatural control over plants, poisonous touch)

- Catwoman (burglar)

VILLIAN SUPERPOWERS

- Criminal mastermind

- Energy projection

- Flight

- Force fields

- Eidetic memory–extraordinary vivid visual images recall, photographic memory, total recall

- Brilliant strategist and planner

- Advanced weaponry

- Superhuman durability, strength, speed

- High-tech war suit

- Expert burglar

- Hand to hand combat and master martial artist

- Skilled acrobat and gymnast

- Uses retractable claws, whips, climbing pitons

- Expert chemist

- Mind-controlling pheromones and secretion of floral toxins (villain females)

- Plant manipulation

- Hypnosis

- Expert seductress

- Trained toxicologist and botanist

- Immunity to poisons, pathogens and toxins

- Uses weaponized props

- Trained psychiatrist

Holy smokes! Does anyone see the pattern I just revealed? This is exactly what is happening on present day Earth! Humans are using these powers currently on a daily basis. Superpowers and super heroes are real in Earth Games.

Justice League of Earth

- Metahuman-mutant, mutate forming a human with superpowers

- Earth Man (duplicate and absorb the abilities of metahumans and aliens)

- Golden Boy (change the element structure to gold by touching them)

- Radiation Roy (emits radiation)

- Spider Girl (super strong prehensile hair)

- Storm Boy (weather control)

- Tusker (ivory tusks that grow and change, enhanced strength, reflexes, agility, enhanced durability, a healing factor)

- Sun Boy (unleashes solar energy)

Archetypical heroes are depicted as young adult females and males who are physically attractive, educated, tall, athletic and in perfect health. Females are sexualized mostly because men are creating them for men. Men aim to create the "ideal" woman, who possesses large breasts, a toned athletic body, and a small waist. The villain female characters have God-like powers and use their sexuality to take advantage of their male victims.

<u>Overview</u>

When I look at this list, frankly, I believe we all are capable of having, creating and utilizing these superpowers. It is already genetically right in your DNA. Eating super foods, drinking clean water, rest, repair, receive, heal, observe, listen, watch and learn to manipulate energy. These forces are a manipulation of energy and applying the mind and body to follow suit behind it.

In Earth Games, your DNA will be altered and mutated to help you become the best charged up super powered human in the Universe. If your body and mind can withstand test after test, mind game after mind game, alteration after alteration, make good choices, eat superfoods, treat beings right, honor yourself, honor others and help humanity, you are on your way to the "New Earth" toward "Ascension."

In Earth Games, humans have superpower abilities you cannot activate until you awaken the light codes within. All memories of these superpower capabilities will be wiped out until the human proves themselves worthy of trying to become the best version of themselves in order to help heal Planet Earth. The frequency of the earth will change upon toward the completion of the cycle and all strands of human DNA will be activated, allowing humans will move toward the ascension process. Healing the soul internally, mentally, physically, spiritually over time and space collapsing timelines will align lifetimes. Clarity will set in for humans to witness their galactic lineage by serving the planet in order to create global healing projected out into the Universe.

In Earth Games, you will be challenged by heroes and villains. It is up to you to decide who you become, what superpowers you will use, how you conduct yourself and if you will become a villain or a superhero.

May your journey in Earth Games be an adventure where you make history!

If you feel this book brings you value or taught you something worthy of sharing. I would be so honored if you would take a few minutes to write me a book review on Amazon or the platform you acquired this book from. Let your participation in Earth Games be known!

Chapter Five

GODS AND GODDESSES

The following poem I channeled over the course of a few days, finding myself writing lines in a notebook while I was making a five-hour drive to Solvang from Huntington Beach. What started out as a few pages turned into one amazing rhyming quest.

Combining and collapsing many lifetimes, I have been granted the gift of being able to activate this superpower within me to create off the chart's poetry sharing wonderful insights beyond the norm. I include my written words for you to read and use for deeper contemplation.

MESSAGE FROM THE UNIVERSE

I am a muse,

I am a daughter of Zeus,

I am here to deliver this news,

Author CW Lewis of The Chronicles of Narnia says,

God speaks through the minds of poets,
This is what comes out of me,
Artistic communicative poetry,

Wisdom flowing out of me,
To help heal humanity,
It's time to comprehend,
How to ascend,

This is my baton,
I use it as a wand,
It's a branch off the Tree of Life,
To help end the world of strife,

Everything I say to you,
Is channeled to come through,
Now it is time to rise,
And look at the world with new eyes,

Each of you is here to do,
Something that is magnificent too,
Soon you will see,
This is not about me,

I have gone to hell and back,
And people still want to attack,
Now it's time to rise,
To achieve the ultimate prize,

This is what I want you to see,

This worldwide movement is bigger than me,

I am just a piece of the pie,

And will help you see it with your 3rd eye,

When you read my book,

You will get a closer look,

You can be jealous of peoples success,

Or you can help them be their best,

You can have it too,

If you just tap into you,

Reading and writing your story out,

Projects into the world with a shout,

Take the time to converse,

Then send it out to the Universe,

The world has been filled with infection,

Now it is time to move in a new direction,

We need to stop the repetition,

This is not a competition,

I can do things many can't do,

I am put here to share them with you,

Everything I say and do,

I had to suffer a lot of hurt & pain for you,

This is how healers teach,

Further beyond is how we reach,

The future starts with you,
I can't wait to see what you do,

I send you a message in a bottle,
Casting it out in full throttle,
Thank you for taking the time to listen to me,
This is the place you are meant to be,
I am Noelle Hipke,

Jesus Christ superstar,
This is a part of who you are,
Starseeds I see you,
I am a part of that same crew,

Yes you are,
A shooting star,
I hope you want to take a closer look,
I have composed a lot in this book,

This is what happens when I converse,
Unlimited knowledge from the Universe,
Superpowers are real,
This is what happens when you heal,

Angels tell me what to do,
In order to get the message to you,
When you become reflective,
Is when you get a new perspective,

We are a Cosmic Conscious Collective,

Time for ascension,

Into another dimension,

You may have seen me dancing on the beach,

It is you that I am trying to reach,

It is time to make it clear,

The Olympians are here,

I am one of the leaders of the band,

I will teach you how to expand,

I will help you grow,

To new places we will go,

I am part of a staff,

To help you clear a path,

I've worked hard to glow,

So you could see my halo,

This is the birth,

Of creating Heaven on Earth,

I can see your soul,

Now it's time to become whole,

This is what I do,

Is channel information to you,

Everything I say and do,

I surrendered my life to help lead you,

Bringing it out for the world to see,

Teaching you everything you can be,

I am not better than you,
I am just here to guide you through,
I've had to surrender & let go,
In order to allow creativity to flow,
Inspire, transpire, rewire is what we'll do,
In order to become a better version of you,

There are things you cannot see,
It is communicated telepathically,
It's time to rise up and soar,
And do something we have never done before,

Tapping into higher realms and dimensions,
Will grant you access to new comprehensions,
I'm only .001% of the population,
And now I have to convince a nation,

I am here to make you see,
How to love unconditionally,
There has been a lot of misuse,
Of using God to abuse,

Telling you how to think, act, behave,
Trying to control the wave,
Now it's time to start a new rave,
You have been programmed to think a certain way,
But that is going to change today,

My mom telling me to get a normal job,

Did she understand my soul was being robbed,

Saying to me why can't you be like everyone else,

Making me not love myself,

I am at the helm,

Of dancing in higher realms,

All I can see in everyone else is beauty,

Why can't they see it in me,

For who I am supposed to be,

I forgive each and every one of you,

For I understand you don't know what you do,

You have to get out of the funnel,

To see past the tunnel,

Going out of the body & flying around,

Taking your feet off the ground,

This is when you will see,

There is more to you and me,

Now it's time to fly high,

And project your soul in the sky,

The angels are watching you,

Wondering what you are going to do,

Will you turn toward ascension,

And join us in the higher dimension,

I'm not here to preach religion,
It's time to create your own mission,
All you have to do is use your vision,

I am unique and original,
Nothing I do is traditional,
I am not unrealistic,
I am futuristic,

At first it was frightening,
It felt like I got zapped by lightening,
That's when I went into action,
Then it picked up traction,

It's not about money,
But vibration & frequency,
I'm here for you to see and feel,
ET's and Aliens are real,

Not going to apologize for what you can't see,
It's because you have a jacked up frequency,
You all have deep work to do,
Before they will present themselves to you,

They won't show themselves for you to see,
Until you do the work to be ready,
Division of religions must die,
Is one of the main reasons why,

I am here to make it clear,

To help you see, feel and hear,

Sometimes when I read my book,

I have to take another look,

I think did that really come out of me,

I hope the world can see,

Wow did I just write that,

It was good right off the bat,

Every time I read it I see something new,

It's the multidimensional frequency I send out to you,

I'm writing this poem as I drive,

I have to get it out when it comes alive,

Steadfast, fancy and free,

Unlimited capabilities flowing out of me,

It's time to climb out of the hole,

Align our mind, body and soul,

Our souls came down to heal,

To experience something not quite real,

Ark of the Covenant I am connected,

Most people in the world haven't perfected,

Yes, there is a cure,

An individual must become pure,

Some of you might not believe,

I remember being connected to Adam and Eve,

So many angels all over the place,
Don't you see them in front of your face,
I can hear the angels sing,
They have an amazing ring,

Some have called me Goddess Athena,
For I have been a warrior in a past life arena,
Athena uses wisdom and intellect,
United beings she is able to direct,

Beautiful, wise and smart,
She combines science and art,
Reincarnation life after life,
Will she rise up and remember the strife,

Soon you will see,
It is all about helping humanity,
It's the date, location and hour,
Time to activate your superpowers,

Go back in time to history,
That is where you unlock the mystery,
It's time to ask and say what,
I am not going to be a puppet,

I've had enough mind fuckery to alter the game,
Never again will life be the same,
It's time to remove this dictation,

To a life of information,

Leading to transformation,

Bringing on elevation,

I'm one of the leaders of the revolution,

Teaching you about human evolution,

I am here to build the foundation of the New Earth,

Eventually you may see my worth,

Before I go,

I want you to know,

You are now part of the show,

It's time to build a community,

Of peace, love and unity,

Change your life to gratitude,

It will alter your attitude,

It's time for us to radiate,

In order to make our bodies illuminate,

3D to 5D to 12D,

Is the new human reality,

Thank you for listening to me,

I hope you can hear my frequency,

My name is Noelle Hipke

Mic drop...Written 4/26/23

No form of AI was used to generate this poem. I channeled this organically, which displays humans have the capability to create beyond the norm using superpowers when moving in and out of multiple dimensions.

Clues and Riddles

Earth Games is riddled with many dimensions, species, mythologies, frequencies and royalties. Each of them will use their powers to influence the game in their favor, just as you have been doing for your existence. Some forces out there are using their powers for good, while other forces are using them for evil.

When you get to higher levels of the Earth Games, you will notice those who carry special abilities are using them to overtake others who don't know how to play the game. By sharing this knowledge, I am sharing how the game has been playing out for me. Only those who actually take the time to read and learn this content will benefit. Daily mindless distractions blind many who refuse to take the time to read and process the information presented. Those who refuse to take the time to read and process the information presented have proven this with the written content in The Bible, which has served as legendary lessons for those to come. In fact, many of us are still acting out the lessons we never learned in previous lives and in this lifetime on an unconscious level as stored programming.

A being or entity can energetically read a human essence. It senses it by your charisma, eyes, energy projection, frequency, and how you speak using multisensory. Some are dead giveaways, while others are well hidden hints inspiring to me to compose this guidebook. The Universe is the guide, and the sacred knowledge was accessed through direct divine connection. I think it is important to share, the Greek gods and goddesses date back to the 8th century BCE, existing for a millennia before Christianity.

Jesus Christ is believed to have lived in the 1st century CE. Therefore, the Greek gods and goddesses ruled before Jesus came.

I have noted people who I believed to be good humans change and turn toward the dark side in search of money and fame. Would you be willing to sell your eternal soul for money and fame for a brief time span on Earth? Is that worth paying the price for eternity?

I got hit hard on the concept of good vs. evil, and I have this to share with you. I know we all would love to only have good vibes. However, if we only have good vibes, we would not know what it is like to feel any different from good. The magic and lessons come in when we are hitting rock bottom hard and rising back to the top.

On my earth exploration, I have had to rise and fall, rise and fall, rise and fall. Quite frankly, I am tiring of the merry-go-round I have been on and started to play Earth Games different.

Many magical occurrences have hit me while on my journey here.

I believe every one of us has a part to play in the ascension process for humanity. Each one of you is a one-of-a-kind puzzle piece to the master puzzle. From past lives, some of you are wizards and witches (Harry Potter fans you know who you are, or you will eventually will figure it out), while some of you are Kings and Queens (King Henry and Queen Elizabeth), Lords and Ladies (Lord of the Rings, Medieval Times), Gods and Goddesses (Clash of the Titans and Medusa) as well as Mermaids, Vikings, Pirates, Faries, Elves, Leprechauns, Nymphs and other beings who are considered as mythology. Films, books, stories are "true" legends. Yes, correct, I said true. They are true in other dimensions, time and space. They are in our blood linage from centuries ago, now surfacing to the forefront as timelines are collapsed and your DNA is activated.

Yes, I know this is hard to believe since we were told they are myths. However, the myths are true and are another piece of the puzzle to teach us and guide us humans embarking the Earth Game journey. Take the time to process and imagine the impact this has been having on our unconscious and subconscious mind, for I believe these parts of the brain hold the keys to containing the information to our past lives. Activate those parts of the brain and your DNA goes online to total recall and remembrance.

Earth Games is the balance of duality. Good and bad dual to fight for love, compassion and forgiveness in order to create unity peace.

I AM A DAUGHTER OF ZEUS (*Xanadu*)

Ever watch the film *Xanadu*? I would say this is one of my all-time favorite movies. Every time I watch it, I can't help but get up to dance and sing with the film and characters. The music is off the charts by ELO, which just so happens to use the theme UFOs on their album covers and concerts. Talk about connecting Gods and children of Gods with the Cosmic Universe.

Zeus had 50 children, and those children had children who had children. The number of children of Zeus running around on this planet is pretty much everywhere. Some of us who have been lucky enough to tap into it and figure out who we are and where we belong can transcend higher, faster. I am not saying this because I am better than you. I am saying this by having the realization one day through my writings. You see, some daughters of Zeus are creative writers here to inspire other creatives, and this is exactly what I realized I have been doing in this lifetime.

One day a guy friend of mine who always called me a "goddess" said to me, "You are a muse." The synchronistic part is I had realized it a few weeks prior when I channeled the following poem below called "The Muse." Now I know we shouldn't be making such claims, but when someone else sees my frequency and acknowledges it, (he is definitely on a different frequency than most humans here on the planet witnessing life in other realms and dimensions), there are just some things you know in your bones. Below is the poem I channeled so you can decide for yourself if you feel the same way in order for you to help figure out where your piece of the puzzle fits in.

THE MUSE
The world is changing fast,
It's time to put everything in the past,
Looking out to the would I can see,
The planet is a whole new humanity,

Things you might have not seen before,
Come rushing right in the door,
Do not become scared,
Show the world you cared,

All these invisible signs,
Can anyone see mine,
Will they get the message in time,
I can see your aura and soul,

This is how high frequencies roll,

Angels are here from the sky,
The entire Universe is our pie,
3.14 so we say,
Numbers in our heads every day,

So many mathematics in the air,
Why can't everyone else see they are there,
These are codes sent to us all,
All you have to do is connect with your call,

A, B, C, 1, 2, 3
So many things touching me,
Shapes and symbols,
Make up the riddle,

Animal totems coming to me,
This is the perfect place to be,
Snow White is what I feel,
This Universe is so surreal,

Can you see the angels on Earth,
They are guiding you to your worth,
Children of Zeus I see you,
I hope out there you see me too,

Trying hard to be the muse,
Witnessing people put it to good use,

We all touch each other in some way,
We are all going to be okay,

Follow me and I will lead you,
For this is what I came to Earth to do,
I am the seeker,
I am the speaker,

Sending out words of truth,
Flowing out of me in one poof,
So much to share and tell,
This is why they call me Noelle,

Vibrations at a high frequency,
Most people couldn't hear me,
Now it's my time to soar,
And share with the world some more,

We are all magic in the air,
This is a beautiful energy I swear,
Ups and downs we all go through,
This is the journey of life for you,

Everyone get up and dance,
You don't even have to have pants,
Shake your booty and let it out,
Jump up and down and shout,

You are a bright shiny star,

This world can take you very far,
Full of wisdom and creativity,
Now I let it out for the world to see,

Letting go of friends in the past,
They held me back as the outcast,
Now I am dancing to my own beat,
I am the one they must defeat,

All these storms make me stronger,
Just when I thought I couldn't take it a moment longer,
Rise above what people say,
You are better off alone anyway,

Dust yourself and get up,
You have to fill your own cup,
Trusting yourself is what you do,
The only person who knows best is you,

Treat others well and don't fight,
It's not about being right,
If they can't understand what you do,
The issue is with them not you,

Heal, love and be kind,
Unconditional love is what you will find,
Life is beautiful and oh so rare,
The right people will notice and care,

Sometimes we have had a bit too much,

All we really need is a soft touch,

Not going out to please,

Go within and release,

You are magic and pure,

That is exactly the elixir cure,

Here comes words of poetry,

There is so much more than you can see,

I have exactly what you need,

All you have to do is follow to succeed,

Now is the time for ascension,

Moving into the next dimension.

Written 8/15/22

No AI was used to write this poem. Channeled naturally through meditation, relaxation and connecting to universal life flow.

Author C.W. Lewis of The Chronicles of Narnia said, "God speaks to us through the minds of poets."

Reading this again tears fall from my eyes,

All we have to do is turn to the skies.

I could keep going and going with this type of language. When I am in the zone, I am in the zone. And you can be too with whatever you are here to do!

Look, there I go again. We create the game. We manipulate the game. We reprogram the game. Humans can take over the Earth Game. Think only about what you want, write it down and say out loud what you want. Manifest instantly in 5D and hit ascension when you rock and roll into the next dimension!

DAUGHTERS OF ZEUS

- Athena (listed as one of the baby names for my daughter)–Goddess of strategy, justice, law and wisdom. Athena was the goddess of many cities and one of the twelve Olympians. Athena is reported to have been born from the head of Zeus, an unconventional scenario. Goddess of wartime strategy. She invented the ship, chariot, plow, rake and a horse's bit and bridle. Her symbolism is the owl for knowledge, olive trees and snakes. She is known as the protector of heroes, the city and the arts.

- Kyra–(pronounced K-eye-ra) Greek name meaning lady like and is the name of my only daughter. My daughter Kyra is quite the Olympian from what I can tell for this day and age. Coming upon her teenage years, she carries the traits of charisma, justice, strategy, wisdom, competition, combat and law already.

- Artemis–one of the twelve Olympians and goddess of the hunt. Ruling over wild animals, the wilderness and the moon. She symbols archery, quiver and bow in honor of her hunting skills. Sounds like Catness from Hunger Games, if you ask me.

- The Charities aka The Graces–three goddesses who embody creativity, charm, fertility, goodwill, and beauty. A connection to the Underworld, they danced for deities with the names Thalia (another name on my baby girl's name list), Aglaea and Euphrosyne, representing good cheer, splendor and joy.

- Eileithyia–Greek goddess of midwifery and childbirth. She carries a torch in symbolization of birth pains. Eileithyia is connected to the cult of Eleusis and Enesidaon, with a responsibility to births annually of divine children.

- Enyo–War Goddess. Less known deity who is not one of the twelve Olympians. Enyo is in charge of planning the destruction of cities, indoctrinating her as a feared Greece figure.

- Eris–part of chaos and war as a Greek goddess of discord and strife. Known as "Sleeping Beauty" crashing the wedding of King Peleus and Thetis, while uninvited, starting a feud toward the Trojan War and Judgement of Paris.

- Hebe–youth goddess who became cupbearer for the gods on Mount Olympus. Hebe cherished youth and is reported to have had powers to restore youth to mortals. A power no other god had. Hebe fell in love with Heracles and had two children with him named Anicetus and Alexiares.

- The Horae aka The Hours–this group of goddesses stood for the periods of time. Connected to seasons with in symbolism of the weather changes. Eirene, goddess of peace and wealth. Eunomia, goddess of lawful conduct and natural order. Dike, goddess of moral justice.

- The Fates–known for their beauty, these beauties were feared in ancient Greece. Their goal was to ensure that every living being lived out their days as planned by the Universe. Determining the lives of immortal deities, these daughters mark the scary purveyor of death. Clotho, known as "The Spinner," she would spin the thread of life as babies were born. Lachesis, "The Alotter," she would measure the thread pulled by Clotho, with the length of the thread representing how long an individual would live. Atropos, "The Inevitable," she would cut the thread of life, and when she did this act, it ended that person's life with the power to choose the type of death in the process.

- The Muses–in total there are nine Muses. Each representing a different kind of art. The Muses were goddesses who inspired others, acting as the source of knowledge and creative stimulation for ancient Greeks.

<u>Nine Muses:</u>

- Calliope: Goddess of epic poetry, eloquence of the word

- Clio: Goddess of history

- Euterpe: Goddess of flutes and music

- Thalia: Goddess of pastoral poetry and comedy

- Melpomene: Goddess of tragedy

- Terpsichore: Goddess of dance

- Erato: Goddess of lyric poetry and love poetry

- Polyhymnia: Goddess of sacred poetry and hymns

- Urania: Goddess of Astronomy

- Mnemosyne, the mother of the Muses, daughter of Gaia and Ouranos, was in charge of remembrance and memory. Mnemosyne is said to be the inventor of words and language and a goddess of time. She preserved the histories and myths of the Greeks before writing was invented.

- Originally there were three Muses:

- Melete–Goddess of meditation or practice

- Aoede–Goddess of song

- Mneme–Goddess of memory

Muses helped famous artists boost their creativity and showed up frequently in Greek mythology. Muses also embody the inspirations of literature, the arts, and science. They are considered to be a source of knowledge for myths, song lyrics, and poetry. These nine sisters had several shrines and temples in Greece.

I believe I am a daughter of Zeus and connected to one of the nine Muses or Goddesses as well as my daughter, Kyra. I have always been drawn to the Greek names, which led me to choose one for my daughter. In addition, I also love Grecian styles of clothing and have always wanted to throw a toga party by the pool with a live band and re-enact those Greek days lounging by the poolside eating fruit, leaving me to believe Greek genes are in my blood and DNA.

I have inspired writers, creatives, musicians, filmmakers, business owners, homeowners, teachers, leaders, children, men, women, pets, nature, and anyone else who crosses my path that feels transpired by my muse energy. On my website, I state I am a muse here on this planet to inspire others and illuminate a "worldwide movement," here on Earth, because when you know, you know.

Everything has meaning.

Recently an Arabic woman came to me to conduct business. When we met, and I introduced myself to her, she immediately lit up and got excited. She looked at me and said, your name is important and has very good meaning. It turns out for a living she converted names from other languages to Arabic. She then pulled out her phone in order to show me exactly what my name meant in her Arabic language, "the gift" (blessing). Then gave me a screenshot of how my name looks in their writing.

I took it a step further and decided to investigate the meaning of my name and my daughter's name in English and this is what I discovered.

KYRA
SUPREME POWER

(kie-ra) 1. Origin: personal female name derived of Modern English feminized form of the Ancient Greek Kupoc (Kyros), linked to Kupoic (kyrois) meaning "lord," used in the sense of "supreme power," theories suggest the name derives from ancient Persian word that has been variously translated to "hero," "of the throne," and "like the sun:" 2. Famously historic borne by the 6th century BC Persian king Cyrus the Great reigning over the largest empire the world has yet seen, admired and prominent figure in the Bible. Cyrus is identified as overthrowing the Babylonian Empire as an act of a genius diplomat, inviting the Jews back from exile in order to rebuilt their Jerusalem Temple (Ezra 1:2-4), making him in Near East very popular. 3. Usage: Biblical Latin form of Cyrus as a nod to the reformation of the Persian king's commitment to religious freedom and tolerance.

DETERMINED BRIGHT COURAGEOUS INDEPENDENT AMBITIOUS SPIRITED SUCCESSFUL PIONEERING INDIVIDUALISTIC

NOELLE
←CHRISTMAS→

(no-EL) 1. Origin: personal female name of English form of French *Noelle, Noel* feminine, meaning of Old French *noel* representing, "the Christmas season," "birth, relating to a birth," referencing specifically the birth of *Jesus* Christ in Church Latin, "to be born" in past participle of *nasci*, (found in Olde English nowel "feast of Christmas"): applied term to the "rebirth" of the sun at the Winter Solstice for use as "a Christmas carol" is connected to the 19th century. 2. Historic: the French in the Middle Ages for babies born on Christmas day ("of or born on Christmas"), a happy time of festival and merriment in celebration of the central figure of Christianity. 3. Usage: gender-neutral French personal name for yuletide babies, masculine Noel is used among medieval times between English speakers.

**HUMANITARIAN   TALENTED   FEARLESS
HONORABLE   INTELLIGENT   GENEROUS
COMPASSIONATE   ENERGETIC   OPTIMISTIC**

Honestly, these descriptions describe us both to a T. Synchronicity is highlighted the day I am writing the segment of this part of the book dated 12/20/22 the day before "Winter Solstice" hits on 12/21/22. The Winter Solstice is mentioned in the description here of my name, and a year later I was drawn to edit the book when the winter solstice hit once again 12/21/2023. Talk about alignment of GOD and the UNIVERSE! A gateway portal may have opened up for me to bring in this knowledge through a stargate.

Human creativity is something artificial intelligence cannot substitute. As a creative, you bring unique experiences and skills to every project. You are an innovator and a problem solver. Your abilities are needed on the planet, so truly consider where you might fall into some of these categories.

Now let's go back into the daughters of Zeus. Some of these may apply to you as you read this book. For many of us are here on the planet carrying out our destinies.

- The Nymphs of Eridanos–lived along the Eridanos river in Hades. Hercules made the request of asking these fairies to assist him in finding the Garden of Hesperides and represent minor figures in Greek mythology.

- Persephone–Queen of the Underworld, thanks to Hades, who kidnapped her. This made her the mother of loss and grief. Zeus struck a deal with Hades to allow Persephone to spend one-third or her life with Hades, allowing her to choose where she spent the rest of her free time, whom she chose her mother Demeter.

- Demeter-represents the goddess of agriculture, crops and grain. When mother and daughter are together, the crops blossom, and in the winter months when they are not, crops die off since Demeter (December?) lets go of her duties out of despair for her daughter.

Daughters with Mortal Consorts and Semi-Divine

Turns out Zeus had many partners, both mortal and semi-divine. Zeus meddled in human affairs, concealing his identity. Zeus seduced nymphs, royalty, and other divine lineage figures. Here are the daughters that came about. Nymphs are considered minor feminine nature deity.

- Aegle–She was a naiad whom where female nymphs lived in springs, lakes, rivers and fountains by fresh bodies of water. Aegle is considered one of the most beautiful Naiads because of her divine blood line.

- Ate–Goddess of recklessness, delusion, blind folly and mischief. She warned Zeus of a powerful influencer who turned out to be Heracles.

- Britomartis–Goddess of hunting and mountains. Temples in her honor were created.

- Damocrateia–Greek royalty nymph.

- Harmonia–Goddess of harmony and concord, standing for beauty and peace instead of war.

- Helen of Troy–One of Zeus' most famous daughters (also a film). Helen was known for her beauty and was the main reason for the Trojan War.

- The Litae–ministers of Zeus and prayer represented as old women.

- Libyan Sibyl–priestess who presided over the Oracle of Zeus-Ammon, a prophetess by nature.

- Malera–not much is known beyond her lineage, she is the daughter of Zeus and Pandora II.

- Melinoe–a nymph who brought madness and nightmares. Melione used her powers for the soul's passage, a torchbearer for the Underworld of lost souls.

SONS OF ZEUS

Zeus was a player of multiple dimensions having sexual encounters with mortals and immortal woman often disguising himself in order to make no woman resist him. Known as Jupiter to the Romans, God of the Sky, King of the Gods, and ruler of Mt. Olympus, he wasn't known as being faithful. Therefore, he had many children with several types of women, so there are quite a few children walking around on this planet with the blood of Zeus in them. There is a pretty good chance you could be a child of Zeus because of your lineage and history. Many of Zeus sons became powerful rulers, so let's cover them here for you to consider.

- Zeus is the King of the Olympians, having relationships with several goddesses, which granted divine sons in his bloodline.

- Acragas-not as well-known as the others, son of Zeus and Asterope, a water nymph that consisted of a brief affair. Water nymphs were Oceanids who were believed to be daughters of Oceanus. Oceanus was tied to the Titan God of the Earth Encircling River. Oceanus and his wife, Tethys, were parents to 3,000 Oceanids daughters who were sister to the Potamoi River Gods. In actuality, it was impossible to calculate all the daughters who are Greek deities.

- Ares-Greek god of war and courage, one of the twelve Olympians, ruling next to Zeus and is one of the only children born from Zeus and Heras' marriage. Ares had tendencies of violence and bloodshed, which put fear in the Greek people. He had an affair with Aphrodite, Hephaestus' wife.

- Apollo–Greek god of dance, truth, music, archery, twin brother of Artemis who is the goddess of the hunt. Both were born to Zeus and Leto. Leto is the daughter of Titaness Pheobe and Titan Coeus and was seduced by Zeus, which created infidelity and turmoil with Hera. Out of revenge, Hera forbade Leto from birthing in Greece and Leto found refuge on Delos Island. Apollo became a beloved god to the Greeks and is considered by Zeus as one of his favorite sons, placing him in high status as a leading figure. Contributing to saving Helen of Troy and the Trojan War, playing a part in Achilles' death.

- Caerus–God of opportunity and luck, Zeus youngest son. Some believed Caerus may overtake Zeus one day, but that never happened. Instead, he moved in the direction of spreading positivity around Greece when he fell in love with the goddess of good luck, Fortuna. Known to have wings on his feet and a deity that never aged, he held balancing scales.

- Hephaestus–another one of the twelve Olympians, son of Zeus and Hera, brother of Eris, Enyo, Ares, Aphrodite, Athena, as well as other figures. Blacksmith of the gods, artisan, carpenter, metalworking with crafting abilities. Popular in Athens and throughout Greece's industrial and manufacturing centers.

- Hermes–messenger of the gods and trade, son of Pleiades Maia, god of shepherds, messengers, and merchants, iconic for his winged shoes and helmet, trickery humor, a favorite son of Zeus who became an Olympian and spoke on behalf of Zeus out of trust.

- Pan–half-goat, half-human, God of the shepherds, son of Zeus and Hybris, goddess of violence. Part of the romantic movement in Europe, Pan showed up in paintings and novels and was frequently a nymph companion.

Semi-Divine Lovers Sons

These women lovers held divine lineage, without the complete status of a goddess, so they weren't fully divine.

- Asterion-son of Zeus and Idaea, who is the nymph daughter of Minos, who was also a son of Zeus.

- Carius-son of Zeus and Torrhebos with a link to Lybian city of Torrhebos. A sanctuary of mountain Carius is reported on Torrhebos. The city connects tales of Carius' learning music. Carius strolled by a lake; hearing nymphs called Muses. When he heard them singing, he desired to learn the arts of song. The nymphs taught him the skill.

- Cres-son of Idaea and Zeus, connected to the Greek island of Crete.

- Cronus-son of Zeus and nymph Himalia from Rhodes. Himalia had sons Spartaeus and Cytus.

- Cytus-son of Zeus and nymph Himalia, brother of Cronus and Spartaeus. As a young child, Cytus with his brothers witnessed goddess Aphrodite curse insanity on the sons of Poseidon and Halia when they prevented her from passing near Rhones on a journey from Cythera to Cyprus.

- Eubuleus-mystery figure, precise lineage unknown, many believe he is a son of Zeus and is in stories with Persephone and Demeter. Appearing by the Underworld when Hades abducted Persephone.

- Iasion-considered a son of Zeus mother's identity debatable, possibly nymph Elektra or Greek goddess Hemera. Iasion is known for his relationship with Demeter, which caused Zeus to go into a rage and kill Iasion with a thunderbolt. Demeter begged Zeus to turn Iasion immortal, and Zeus morphed him into a lesser god.

- Sarpedon-skilled fighter, served Troy at the Trojan war, son of Zeus, mother unknown, possibly Lycia Princess of Laodamia, however later Europa became his accepted mother. Delivering memorable speeches and playing a large part in the Trojan War, Sarpedon earned the status of hero for his efforts. Sarpedon was killed by Patroclus wearing Achille's armor while Zeus witnessed and watched and was told to step down by Hera, who convinced him not to because other gods had children fighting and dying.

- Spartaeus-son of Zeus and nymph Himalia of Rhodes.

- Tantalus-legend has it, he was punished in Tartarus due to abusing the gods' hospitality by stealing Nectar and Ambrosia (a food and drink with magical properties to heal humans and gave them the gift of becoming immortal like gods, contains restorative abilities, heal humans from illness or injuries and resurrect death). As eternal punishment, Tartarus stood in a pool of water with fruit-bearing trees around him he could not eat or drink from, putting him in a constant state of thirst and hunger.

- Thissaeus-story lost in history, son of Zeus and Chrysogenia, daughter of Peneus who was a Thessalian River god.

In order to seduce mortals, Zeus would disguise himself through trans-formation, which led to the conception of the divine. Here are sons born from these affairs.

- Atymnius-lord of Crete, Sarpedon's companion, son of Zeus and Cassiopeia.

- Hercules-demi-god, divine hero, son of Zeus and Alcmene, Zeus took the form of Alcmene's husband Amphitryon. Hera was on a wrath to punish Hercules for Zeus' infidelity and sent challenge after challenge his way, sending two serpents to distinguish Hercules in his crib. Hera also inflicted him with madness as an adult, in which he killed his wife and went out to fight fantastical beasts and dark battles. Zeus gave Hercules immortality when he died. Hercules won Hera over, then married her daughter, giving him a place with the gods of Olympus.

As the frequencies of the earth move toward the New Earth, life as you know it will transform. The entire planet will undergo a transcendence transformation moving from 3D to 5D and beyond when the time is right. All beings will undergo a sort of initiation and integration. Those who have chosen to make the transition will move toward higher frequencies into ascension, integrating into the Galactic Communities throughout the Universe.

When you get into the higher densities, realms and octaves in Earth Games, you will see many new beings, entities, gods and extraterrestrials really exist. History reveals past mythology and

timelines. Humans gravitating into a higher state of being, frequencies, vibrations, octaves, and densities align to signal their multidimensional states of being showcasing each human's historical identification in true form. Humans must strive to continue achieving unconditional love, self-acceptance, compassion, forgiveness and understanding of all the fields of knowledge and information and timelines as they collapse together into one. Mythology will come to life on the surface when you activate your DNA, heal your soul and call up your DNA. This will be the moment in time when you will realize you have had it in you all along.

Mythology is real and each one of you is a part of the epic revolution of realization. Connected to one another in multiple dimensions of time and space as you overlap and connect as one.

Through many timeline civilizations, people tried to fight, overtake and gain control. It is up to you on Earth Games to morph these histories, theories, dimensions and heal all your ancestors from all timelines altogether into one.

Here are the possibilities you or someone you know may fall under when one realizes who they truly are. Each one of you has had lifetime after lifetime of many reincarnations, giving you the ultimate knowledge and wisdom to become the expanded universal product of humanity for the New Earth.

The topic of Zeus and his children are covered in this playbook as well as other deities, royalties and mythical concepts. This manual touches on the well-known Earth Game legends. However, it is up to humans to realize and decode what figure they represent, who they are, and what they came here to do.

<u>Olympic Games</u>

Olympians are still alive and being acknowledged on Planet Earth today. Many are presented in the Olympic Games, an international multi sported event featuring thousands of athletes from around the world to participate in a variety of competitions. The Olympics are considered the highest ranking competition with over 200 teams, representing territories and sovereign states. The creation of the Olympic Games was inspired by Olympia, Greece, where the ancient Olympic Games were held. These professional athletes are recognized, honored, respected and rewarded for their above and beyond achievements for their entire lifetime. The Olympics attract 15 million to 31 million viewers over the years offering up the most worldwide watched and witnessed showcase. Outstanding athletes break and hold worldwide records, receive incredible endorsements, become instant success role models, and display their superpower capabilities for the entire world and universe to document. These exceptional athletes are displaying how they have masterminded and harnessed the compatibility of working in harmony with their higher self and multidimensions to perform record breaking status. This requires stamina, mental control, physical agility, clarity, visualization, mindset, belief, self esteem and a plethora of multidimensional frequencies to come into unison to master the moment. The Olympics challenge athletes on many levels from distractions, stress, environment, sleep, performance, nutrition, weather conditions, etc. When an athlete overcomes all these tribulations and can still conquer, overcome, achieve and out maneuver their opponents, they are the ones holding the gold, silver and bronze metals. The Olympians are displaying the mindset mastery of their superpowers into one magnificent force in connection to the three dimensional world. Not only is the Olympian famous worldwide, the end results are on stage for the entire Universe to authenticate. As in all other species. The super human earns status in other dimensions, time and space in other civilizations, extraterrestrial species and multiverses. Olympians are very much alive and playing Earth Games on many levels in different types of fields. All physical three dimensional activities need to be taken into account such as engineering, construction, strategy, writing, composition, performance, artistry, design, music, mathematics, science, beauty, architecture and the such the Gods and Goddess bring to the table, for this is what is connected to the advanced movement of the planet.

ET HUMANS

Your complete blue print memory will be wiped out upon arrival, in order for you to figure out the game. Your memory will be wiped out for a reason. In Earth Games, you are to interact with other Galactic Races by not knowing they exist at all until the time comes for humans to evolve and integrate with all the species from other planets in unison. By not knowing you are all multidimensional beings connected to other planets in the galaxy, this will enable you to integrate with one another allowing ET humans the ability to integrate with one another learning from each other's cultures and mixing their DNA in order to create a unique breed. This action allows humans to develop their own civilized, advanced race, which cannot be achieved in any other way. By not knowing, you work through experiences, lessons, knowledge, learning, comprehending, using your senses, thinking, feeling, emotions and creating an entirely new race developed from all the races combined and working for and against each other at the same time. In order to move into the "New World" divine, growth and evolution require the presence of duality for a certain amount of time. This is the way we integrate the best of the Galactic races together into the highest-ranking versions of species in the Universe. Humans will be the best of the best, an eccentric galactic race. They will have undergone extensive trials, tests, tribulations and will rise in the end to be respected, cherished and acknowledged for all their efforts. This is the biggest hero's journey one can ever take on to achieve in their Galactic lifetime of existence.

For those of you that make it to the higher levels first, you may notice a larger gap between yourself and other individuals, for you both are operating on different octave levels. Those who arrive first possess the ability to endure, drive, and lead the way in opening the gates and portals to other worlds because of their unique light frequency and vibration. One has been preparing for this part of the journey for many lifetimes in which you will awaken and realize instantly as indicated, like a bolt of lightning zapping your body. Consider yourself hit by the staff of God to activate you into action originally planned in your divine blueprint genetic code. It will be rather magnificent, for you will get download after download of knowledge into your body in an instant as you realize the magnitude of who you really are, what you offer and what you came here to do.

Books, films, games, puzzles, cards, video games and technology will develop in the evolution of humanity, giving you clues along the way. Only you might not see them if you are not on that frequency. It is up to you in Earth Games to figure out who you are, what you came here to do and how to integrate into the Galactic Community as you remember who you are.

When unknown species are revealed or presented, one needs to be ready to accept unconditionally any type of being entering through the portal without judgement, retaliation, or fear-based actions. These species may look different from humans because they are advanced beings from different galaxies. One can identify a species by the way they smell, their vibration, their frequency and their energy, differentiating them from one another.

Let's cover some beings that you may encounter when you move through Earth Games.

There are powers out there greater than yourself who become more powerful when working together. Gods and goddesses protect and form the powers that preserve humanity when endangered. These will be the ones to rise when Earth Games comes to a tipping point of intrusion of one species taking over another in Earth Games. For many on the planet won't realize they are amid playing Earth Games because of their un-awakened state, as others may try to overtake and manipulate the program.

Humans and semi-divine heroes will step up to the plate once their DNA has been triggered and they remember who they are, going into warrior mode and moving into their area of expertise to help raise the conscious cosmic collective. This will show every culture the genuine power of love, as love is the answer.

History shows a timeline of conflict between generations that will collapse and diminish. The new generation will no longer validate, accept, or tolerate the old ways, and they will suddenly acknowledge the realization of an entirely new existence. Men will dissipate their violence, trouble makers will reveal their mischief, we will remove sadness/illness/injury, and suddenly acknowledge the mystery of death as the realization that we are all part of a system working together to achieve dead or alive or in-between.

In Earth Games, you will face madness and horror in your human relations, good luck and misfortune, challenge of the unknown and voyages on uncharted waters. Relationships with the gods and humankind will intertwine, making humans question the origins of society and world creation. Humans, plants, and animals will contain the cycle of fertility.

People may attempt to alter or slow down the operation of a human's fate, but they never succeed. Humans hold the highest powers and will not realize it until they have reached the higher levels of the game. Humans will become archetype legends, manifesting important new understandings, theories, inventions and advancements. The Universe will become their unlimited ocean.

The underworld of the dead will work behind the scenes and other worlds in the higher densities. Humans will work toward the final release of nirvana, creating a Heaven on Earth because of the universal awareness of human existence.

The powers of the gods give the potential to destroy humankind. It is up to humans to take matters into their own hands and wake up to the realization of the illusions that have been shaping them for centuries. Religion and culture will point out the truth humanity has in common as well.

Never take for granted every day you walk on the earth plane. Be grateful for every experience, good or bad. Look as a setback as an accomplishment, enabling one to move up to the next level as you continue to move forward, staying alive to make it through to the next day. You are leveling up daily, moment by moment. The levels are unlimited; you are the creator; you are the experiencer. One can go as far as you want to go or not go and some of you may choose to exit out early.

One can expand endlessly because of good and evil, positive and negative, fun and freakish, high and low, up and down, forward and backward. The game offers unlimited and unpredictable challenges that will test your life force and energy. You may get trapped in cycle after cycle over and over if you don't learn the lesson and continue to make the same wrong choices. One has to make the intentional decision to follow their own true path by trailblazing their way through Earth Games.

Some humans will decide to project light, while other humans will gravitate toward the dark. Beings will be sent in to challenge you, correct you, and guide you. You will be able to personally pick your Angeles and Guides before you arrive in order to lead you on your journey from the other side. Choose wisely who you want to be as your Angels and Guides, for they are the ones who will ultimately give you the clues, ideas, concepts, feelings, knowledge, vibration, frequency and know how to outmaneuver the game.

The characters in Star Wars and Star Trek are not make believe. Certain divine print humans will access the higher dimensions, where they can explore futuristic ideas and concepts and then bring them back to Earth to help humans prepare for what is coming in the future. Everything in Earth Games will take place in stages and will be disclosed in perfect timing as the roll out takes place. This allows for the gradual alignment of frequencies and methodically enables large amounts of growth and evolvement to humanity.

The phrase "You shall have no gods before me," stands for no gods before your higher self. Always choose your higher-self first. You are made up of God's energy.

Mythology covers the supernatural, accounts of the divine, actions, and formations of power. Myths hold periods of power and are of the collective nature of culture. When one propels a species to move in a certain direction, it often takes the others with it. Getting the collective to consciously remember who they are and what they came here to do on Earth Games starts up the generators leading to the worldwide movement.

Drama is a major component of ancient religion, giving myths the retention of power. Heroes in Earth Games who stand in their true power when no one else would listen, back them up, or believe their claims will be granted immortality.

Zeus is a supreme god, which is why he is largely covered in this playbook. However, Zeus had brothers and sisters who we will cover down the line.

Myths have been projected as fictitious stories actually illustrate truth, and will be discovered as one learns to read through the dimensions, allowing access to be granted into the gateways to comprehend and decode the knowledge.

There are myths of Greece and Rome covering everyone and everything from Achilles to Zeus. Every single one of you plays a part in this theology. You may be related, or a reincarnated version of these mythology beings (read that again, it's a pretty big insight).

- The Amazons were a tribe of female warriors who voluntarily removed their right breast in order to shoot a bow in arrow better by being able to draw the bow back. Now that is commitment to your trade and very powerful. (You know what else on Planet Earth is powerful? (www.Amazon.com)

- Andromeda was sacrificed to a beast because of her father claiming she was more beautiful than the Nereids Sea nymphs, and was chained to a rock at the foot of a cliff (Clash of the Titans movie). Perseus flew past on a winged horse carrying the head of Medusa in order to slay the dragon and turn it to stone. These heroes have constellations locked into the star system, proving their existence.

- Aphrodite Greek goddess of fertility, love and beauty. Was about social life and not content being a faithful wife.

- Zeus, the sky god, was married to Hera, an earth goddess. Hera was jealous of Zeus' lovers and took it upon herself to be vengeful and often pursued the women and their offspring relentlessly. It was a clash of cults, traditions and religions due to Zeus' eclectic choices of women.

- Athena was the daughter of Zeus and Titaness Metis, who was the Greek goddess of crafts and war. Athena's symbol is the wise owl and was placed on Athenian coins. Athena is associated as the goddess of art and wisdom, often helping several heroes.

- A classic hero overcomes troublemakers, trials, and blazes their own trails when the odds are against them. Greek mythology is riddled with heroes and heroines of every kind and yes, they will all be right there walking in Earth Games without having a clue until they overcome their universal test.

- Cronos is a Greek son of Ouranos (sky god) and Gaia (earth mother). Cronos emasculated his father Ouranos and seized control of the Universe. Cronos swallowed his children because he had been warned he would be displaced by one of his sons, just as he had done to his own father. However, when Zeus was born, someone gave a stone to Ouranos to swallow instead and secretly swept Zeus away to grow up on the island of Crete. When Zeus became of age, he forced his father Cronos to vomit up his brothers and sisters, Poseidon, Hades, Hera, Hestia and Demeter, to release their aunts and uncles. Including the Titans that Cronos kept chained up. The Cyclopes, who are single-eyed giants, crafted Zeus his famous lightning and thunderbolts. The Romans equaled Cronos with their Saturn, a corn god who they connected to the Golden Age.

My daughter came to me speaking for close to forty-five minutes, sharing extensive details of her fighting with beings in other realms in her dreams. One-eyed giants, who she named as the Titans, forest excursions, being chased and hunted by creatures from the under water worlds. These beings truly exist in different realms and dimensions and humans have the capabilities to access and interact with them on multiple levels.

- Oracles and prophecies show a man's life is believed to be determined by destiny or fate. In Earth Games, your destiny and fate are determined by the divine blue print you chose. Oracles are offered through dreams, which can be inspired by the gods, and prophecies are brought in by seers. Omens and signs will tell the future, such as mentioned in films, video games, technology, science, mathematics, animals.

- Gaia is the great earth mother oozing abundance and fertility. Gaia is the mother of all who nourishes the children. In Greek mythology, Gaia was the earth, who came out of Chaos and gave birth to the sky god Ouranos, who was her son and husband. In mythology, there is a lot going on in family relations, vengeance, power, overthrown, trickery, illusion, abduction, and the such. It will continue to rule and rage in Earth Games until humankind learns how to pin it down.

- The Giants in Greek myth have a human shape with snake-like tails connected to their legs. Giants differ from Titans and are the oldest generation of the gods and lead by Zeus' father Cronos.

- Voyagers set out in search of treasures, trinkets, adventure and new discoveries.

- Beasts and monsters can be half-human or demonic and come in all colors and shapes on the border of hideous. Monsters and beasts represent unresolved life forces of the dark in human nature. There will be savage beasts like Centaurs (man-horse) and satyrs (goat like) part animal and part human. This symbolizes man's unruly, instinctive nature. They will haunt and harass humans during Earth Games as dark unruly forces of nature to add passion and danger to the journey of a lifetime. The invisible, blind, and brute force of human nature will be symbolized by Satyrs and Centaurs, and they will eventually become known.

- Harpies are goddesses who steal children without warning and will cause spirits of mischief upon humanity as half-maid, half-birds. Humanity will fear them as monsters, considering them spoilers and robbers.

- Sirens are temptresses luring unsuspecting seamen. These beautiful sea nymphs will use the sound of their voice with song to captivate and paralyze men in a hypnotic state.

- Medea, the daughter of Aietes, the king of Colchis with a country joining the Black Sea, is the first wife of Voyager Jason. Medea is skilled at the magic arts, hovering between goddess and witch.

- Mars, the son of Juno and a magical flower, earns the title of the god of spring during the blossoming of major festivals. Mars oversaw agriculture, fertility and vegetation, eventually leading to becoming a god of war.

- Mercury, messenger god of the Romans who oversaw trade and commerce. Mercury is about prosperity and peace.

- Midas was all about wealth. When granted a wish by the gods, he requested to become richer and asked the gods for everything he touched to turn to gold. "Hence, being known as having the Midas touch." When his wish was granted, his happiness pivoted on him when he realized he could neither drink nor eat because it all turned to gold. So be careful what you wish for.

There were many rivalries between these members and will still continue on Earth Games behind the scenes until humans connect the dots and put the pieces together.

Forces of Nature serve as the mysteries and wonders of the world. The divine drama will comprise summer and winter, sunrise and sunset, storms and tidal waves. With a bolt of lightning, Zeus could strike a rainbow from afar. Sea god Poseidon could soothe waves or blow-up sea storms. Nymphs and nature spirits within the rivers, fields, and forests, as well as the great gods of land, sky, and sea, will lead the influences of Earth Games.

- Giants represent neither good nor bad larger than life primal forces. There may be "gentile" Greek giants guarding Talos or defending other areas to combat predators or prey on travelers. Giants will build massive walls of protection, but can also be rebellious and moody, not abiding by divine laws and using mortals as prey. The Titan giants overthrew Ouranos, their father and replaced him with Cronos who ironically was overthrown and dethroned by his son Zeus. A cosmic battle between the younger generations and older gods will continue to take place on Earth Games until humanity figures it out and restores Heaven on Earth. For each one of you is a fallen angel trying to find your way back home.

- The Cyclopes Giants were a one-eyed creative craftsman who could craft special armor such as Poseidon's trident, Zeus' thunderbolt and Hades' invisible helmet, assisting Hephaistos in his volcanic forge.

- The Sphinx, in Greek myths she is the daughter of Echidna. A monster with the breasts and face of a woman, the body of a lion, bird wings, and was sent as a curse by Hera to the city of Thebes. The Sphinx asked all who passed a riddle, and she ate you if you didn't answer correctly. Riddle: "What thing walks on four legs in the morning, on three in the evening, and is weakest when it walks on all four?" Answer: Man, he walks as a baby on all four and leans on a stick when of old age. (The Greek sphinx differs from the Egyptian sphinx at the pyramid of Giza, for the Egyptian sphinx was the protector of the pyramids and the sun god Ra.)

- Mythic Founders are godlike heroes being guided by destiny and deity to create a vibrant, fresh, new culture through innovation. The founders will develop new ways of living and customs on Earth Games.

- The Titan and Titanesses giants in Greek myth are older gods ruling before the Olympian gods, who are brothers and sisters of Zeus. The conflict between the older and younger generations of the gods lasted ten years and shook up the Universe due to the monumental conflict it created.

- When Cronos was overthrown by the Titans, the world was divided up by Zeus claiming the sky for himself, Poseidon the sea and Hades the underworld. Zeus is the god who oversees fate takes place to align the proper course. Zeus has no control over destiny itself. How you reach it is ultimately up to you on how you maneuver on Earth Games.

- Celtic otherworld's are invisible realms of spirits and gods, elves, fairies and giants. The world between heaven and hell. The veil between the invisible and visible enabling seers to pass in and out during soul journeys and spirit flights as well as privileged heroes. Gateways to the underworld are engulfed by water, bridges, wells, and underground heavens.

- Celtic fairies carry treasures from the underground palaces such as a wand of intelligence and tree of knowledge (author of this book Noelle Hipke twirls a baton and talks about this in her divinely downloaded rhyming poems) as portrayal of lordly beings from another world.

- Seers, sages, and shamans of Celtic myths have the prophecy of extraordinary gifts, such as healing and wisdom. Deeply connected to supernatural forces, they serve as intermediaries between the worlds and realms of the living and the dead between the invisible and visible world of men and otherworld's. Wise counselors, druids, kings, clan chiefs are part of the Celtic myth prophecy. In addition, there will be dark sorceresses using their supernatural gifts to manipulate and bewitch mortals for their own gains.

- Humans may be turned into animals by controlling forces who wish to gain the upper hand. Invisible strategies and powers will be used against humanity, and it is up to humanity to live through the struggles and tribulations to claim their own power back. Magic, music, mindset, skills, and strategy will aid mortals and against mortals. You will walk between the worlds, not realizing what is actually taking place.

- Sacred springs of water will contain healing capabilities. The miracle waters will restore the ill and cure the sick.

- Magic and enchantment will strike a dreamlike quality connecting the worlds. Magical powers and mystery will fill forests and lakes, but be on the lookout for those who wish to find a host in order to endure magical illusions. Spells and magical trickery may be brought up from the otherworld. (vaccines, medications, mind manipulation, psychological warfare-PTSD)

- Donn, God of the dead from the otherworld, will be in search of sea storms and ship wreaks for his journey back to the otherworld.

- Emer will be blessed with six gifts: needlecraft, song, speech, wisdom, beauty and chastity.

- Combined power, fertility and beauty in women will give them the ruling upper hand. The veil of invisibility is the key to the fairy realm. Symbols of spiritual power will be hidden and unhidden. Virtues of strength and wisdom will give special affinity to creatures in the woods.

- Spells can be broken and the enemy slayed.

- Extra-terrestrial creatures may come onto the scene from time to time.

- Cauldrons of rebirth miracle concoctions will brew wisdom and inspiration, granting spiritual insight. The cauldrons of brew (superfoods, protein shakes, green drinks, juicing, detoxing) will restore humanity in which they will have the vision to see things in a new dazzling light and more wisely than before. Spiritual nourishment will flow from the Grail containing an "all-inspiring grail" brew.

- Watch the film Helen of Troy to tap into other Celtic myths.

- Pay attention to a "magic tree," illusion and trickery. The roads will be unpredictable and you will come face to face with gifted healers and suspected trickery upon looking back at medieval times. Ill-fated lovers will be popular with the Celts, for many courtships will be tampered with and tested.

- Love triangles may surface in Celt relations between guardian and young rivals. These Celtic love triangles create a timeless appeal between the characters of drama and tension. Women will be wise, fair, noble, chaste and highly sought after by the highest of men. Each man will bring something different to the table, whether it be hunting, music, agriculture, treasure, etc.

- Single one-on-one combat will take place instead of all-out war. Spears, slings, shields, swords and other enchanted weaponry will enhance a man's magical skill set.

- You may seek wise counsel and visionaries to help secure your spot in Earth Games. Secret knowledge will be shared to those who earn it. The invisible otherworld will be made visible for brief periods of time, granting access to both healers and magicians.

- Heroic quests will be inspired and rewarded with visions of the otherworld. These quests take on a magic of their own, which enables the hero expanded access to unexpected outcomes beyond the imagination, leading to lessons and insights. Honor, courage and visions will be granted to those who set forth on a journey of discovery, adventure and disclosure. Earth Games require impossible tasks you are going to have to figure out-and-out maneuver. Taking on quest after quest leading up to the highest and hardest quest of all. Requirements include going to great lengths and battles in order to gain your sovereignty.

- Singing birds will heal with their magical song erupting from the otherworld.

As time travelers, Celtic voyagers underwent a time warp either condemned to wander on a journey without end or return home long after their time. Eventually Celtics will grow tired of the otherworld and yearn for their homeland, drawing them back home. There will be telling signs of the otherworld, pay attention and look for them. There are also heavens where people live in timeless plenty and joy. Find them. You will need to figure out what objects around the Earth you need to pay attention to. Mother Nature will give you clues as long as you don't abuse. Potions and curses will be in circulation.

GODS AND GODDESS ANCIENT NARCISSISM PROGRAMMING

When my first book *Superpowers* came out, I let it take on a life of its own knowing full well the Universe would deliver what it was meant to do for the planet. I wrote from my heart sharing my life lessons, personal experiences and perspectives in raw unfiltered form. I was blown away when the book revealed a society riddled with the pattern of narcissism in many historical timelines, branching out all the way from the generations of Gods and Goddesses and Jesus to this day and age of the X, Y, Z and beyond younger generations. Heavy narcissism programming dates way back in history and is currently being activated to clear on Planet Earth as humans awaken their ascension sensory.

One may notice there has been an eruption of narcissism video content on the internet. My book, *Superpowers* contained many issues on the topic without even being aware of it, until the revelations hit months later after it came out. We are all in the midst of monumental personal revelations to move toward ascension. I noticed several of my friends separating away from their family as they all shifted upon their realizations due to the fact they were in the psychology field. Entire groups of families spread out and those who were unaware of the pattern lost their footing when a cycle disrupter stepped out of the circle. This in turn caused a toxic narcissistic family attack to begin on whichever individual decided to leave the pack. Families attacking, ganging up together and turning on that particular individual by using manipulation, intimidation, confrontation, doubt, jealousy, fear, bullying, deceitful behavior patterns or toxic attacks by gravitating as a group to gang up on another. A ploy to wreak unbelievable havoc upon the individual. I learned if one discovers the pattern and tries to remove themself from the trauma and drama, the entire family line begins to alter and fall apart. The truth of the matter is, this is exactly what needs to take place in order to break the generational programming that has gone on for generational lifetimes.

The healing may begin for those in Earth Games here to provoke a ripple effect to assist massive healing in the generational timelines affecting all family members living in present as well as the past and the future.

Crossed over family members and ancestors surfaced to me in dreams and visions, informing me my children came down to be the spark to ignite the healing process for all generations in the past, present and future. The ancestors have been waiting and watching in anticipation to see if the fire would get lit so they could witness the huge healing that would move into effect in this lifeline as well as multiple lifelines freeing each who had also suffered the same fate in their lifetimes. I saw them cheering us on the other side as we progressed through the stages. Living family members were in an uproar spitting fireballs and unbelieve insults pointing the finger at one individual calling them the narcissist. However, narcissism is a generational group program running in the family timeline where each person in the family plays a different part. What they failed to see or acknowledge was their part in the narcissist program. Each person in the family dynamic is given a particular role and in order to level up, one must learn to identify, go within, and take responsibility for their actions and counterparts in the group collective to truly assess the situation and alter their personal program. One must determine the role they have played and if they will reshape their course and remaster the program to throw it into a higher healing vibrational state converting themselves into a conscious living state. Choosing to operate on a higher frequency without retaliation or negative engagement allows others the opportunity to follow the model and do the same. In Earth Games, it is up to communities, families and groups to figure out the program and the best way to free themselves and as well as all members connected to the unified field. Healing will take place in all timelines, past, present, future in all dimensions, time and space becoming an electrical energy field of light love frequency to cure all.

Nevertheless, I noted narcissistic games to be played within the family, the workplace, between friendship circles, religious groups and both spouses using the tactics on one another as well as their children passing the trait down the family timeline. Upon more research I realized the younger generations have come to the planet to break these narcissistic patterns in the generational family timeline. They have been the chosen ones to create one of the hugest shifts to help ring in building the foundation of New Earth. The narcissistic program running is meant to be discovered, detected, decoded and dissolved in order to help humans achieve a higher octave on a soul level.

One last thought on this hot topic. Did you happen to see any resemblance of the narcissism behavior traits in the god and goddess historical timeline presented earlier in this chapter that could be a match with yours? Could it be we have all been reincarnated and are just in a different human suit playing out our previous patterns waiting for it to be disclosed and exposed so humans can destroy the program? Chew and digest that one for a few minutes. No need for history to repeat itself if humans know how to collapse the design.

Bonus energy earned in Earth Games for those who use their intelligence to become masters in mindfulness detecting and deflecting the blackhole of narcissism and shifting the timelines.

As for kings, queens, lord, ladies, warriors, wizards and witches in addition to other multidimensional beings will be reincarnated, reinstated, and released upon Earth Games in order to amplify and intensify the frequency of unconditional labels and love.

Each one of you will carry historical bloodline in your DNA, it is up to you to discover and recover.

Check out my Superpowers Activations Course: *Build Your Human Instruction Manual* on my website:

https://noellehipke.com/funnel/superpowers-course-activation

or https://www.NoelleHipke.com

Chapter Six

PLANETS AND THE UNIVERSE

I can't declare I'm an expert in this field by any means. The Universe is unlimited. I know how to research and put a lot of information together to make sense of a lot of floating data. Learning a bit more about each planet enables profound comprehension to see how everything ties in together. Earth Games are about the games taking place on Earth while considering other planets in the galaxy. Understanding interactions with other planets in the solar system lights up the codes to truly understand the complexity and importance of Planet Earth.

Photos used in the following diagrams are compliments of NASA.

Saturn

Saturn: Father of Jupiter

God, Cronos, father of God Zeus, associated with Saturn

The distinctive spectacular rings around Saturn are what make it unique.
Saturn facts:

- Saturn is a giant gas planet that doesn't have a solid surface like Earth.

- Saturn comprises hydrogen (H2) and helium (He).

- It would take nine Earths side by side to equal the size of Saturn.

- Saturn is a gas planet, with icy rings of rock and ice chunks.

- Saturn has 82 moons and 7 rings.

- 6th planet from the Sun.

- Saturn takes 29 Earth years to make 1 orbit around the Sun.

- Saturn has seven rings with divisions and gaps.

- It looks like Saturn can't support human life, but one of its many moons, like Titan, might.

- Movies, games and comics focused on Saturn include Wall-E, Star Trek, Final Fantasy VII, Dead Space 2, 2001: A Space Odyssey, Cthulhu Mythos, Interstellar, and Beetlejuice all reflect components related to planet Saturn.

Titan Moon

Titan Moon: Children of the Greek Gods

Titan facts:

- Titan is the most like the earth, with liquids that harbor lakes, seas and rivers on its surface, making possible to be compatible with human life.

- Titan has nitrogen in most of its atmosphere, similar to earth and a surface pressure 50 percent higher than earth.

- Titan has rain, lakes, rivers, clouds and seals of liquid hydrocarbons similar to ethane and methane.

- The seas are hundreds of miles wide and feet deep.

- Titan is Saturn's largest moon and the 2nd largest moon in the solar system.

- Titan most likely contains a liquid water ocean beneath the surface. Its surface of rock-hard water ice.

- Titan has an atmosphere similar to earth of mainly nitrogen.

- The air is dense on Titan. However, you could walk around with an oxygen mask and cold protection without wearing a spacesuit.

- Project Dragonfly Mission drone is investigating this moon for future habitation.

Jupiter

Jupiter: King of the Roman Gods
God, Zeus is associated with Jupiter

Facts about Jupiter:

- Jupiter is the largest planet in the solar system and is twice as big as all other planets combined into one.

- From the sun, it is fifth in the line up.

- The stripes and swirls reflect windy clouds of water and ammonia, swirls and stripes of cold, with an atmosphere of hydrogen and helium.

- Jupiter has a Great Red Spot that represents a giant storm bigger than the size of Earth and has been going nonstop for hundreds of years.

- Eleven Earths fit into the size of Jupiter. Jupiter would be the size of a basketball, while Earth would be the size of a grape.

- Jupiter completes one orbit of the Sun about every 12 Earth years.

- Jupiter mostly consists of helium (He) and hydrogen (H2).

- As of today, Jupiter has over 75 moons and counting.

- Some of Jupiter's moons have oceans beneath their crusts, which may sustain and support life. However, Jupiter cannot support human life.

- Jupiter has a ring system which is faint. Four giant planets in the solar system around us have a ring.

- Many movies, comics and video games feature the planet Jupiter in their programs include Men in Black, Power Rangers, Halo, Cloud Atlas, Futurama, Jupiter Ascending, some speaking about teachers from Venus and claiming to be from one of Jupiter's moons.

Mars

MARS: Roman God of War
Roman God, Mars or war, and agriculture are associated with planet Mars
(son of Jupiter and Juno)

Mars facts:

- Known as "The Red Planet" comprising the largest volcano in the solar system.

- Lifeless, cold and rocky, consisting of water vapor and carbon dioxide.

- 4th planet from the Sun with 2 moons.

- Humans on Mars would have 62% less gravitational pull than they do on Earth.

- Mars is 142,000,000 miles from the Sun, while Earth is

93,000,000 miles from the Sun.

- A year on Mars is 687 days compared to 365 days on Earth.

- Six Mars planets would equal Earth's volume.

- Mars has the oldest known minerals and has basaltic meteorites rocks. Types of rocks include phosphates, silica, carbonates, pyroxene, olivine, amphiboles, feldspar, sulfates (gypsum, jarosite), phyllosilicate and iron oxides (hematite).

- Earth and Mars are rocky (terrestrial) planets and are similar. Basalt, which is known as the predominant rock on earth, is mostly found on the ocean floor.

- Mars has four seasons, no active global magnetic field, no stable water nor bodies of standing water, with a thin atmosphere mostly composed of carbon dioxide.

- NASA is planning to send humans to Mars in the near future.

Venus

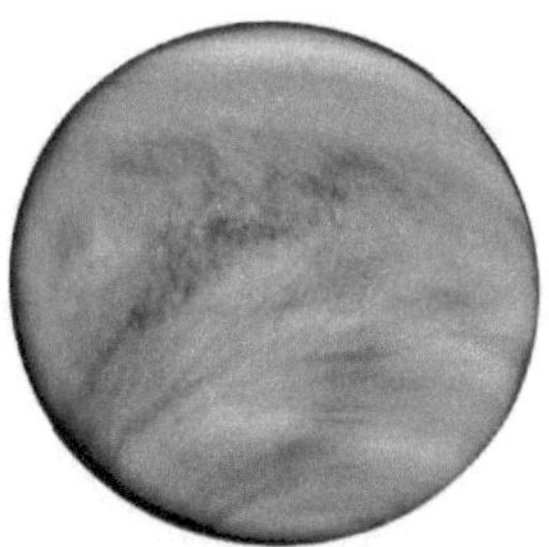

Venus: Roman Goddess of Love
Roman Goddess Aphrodite is associated with Venus

Venus facts:

- Venus is Earth's closest neighbor and is the second planet from the Sun.

- Venus is similar in size and density compared to Earth, and is often called "Earth's twin."

- One day on Venus is equal to 243 Earth days.

- Venus is the hottest planet in the solar system with a thick, toxic carbon dioxide atmosphere and thick sulfuric acid clouds trapping heat.

- Temperatures are about 900 degrees Fahrenheit, which is hot enough to melt lead!

- The surface has thousands of large volcanoes with mountains and scientists believe it's a possibility some volcanoes are still active.

- The air pressure is crushing, and over 90 times compared to earth.

- Venus rotates backwards on its axis when compared to other planets, creating an oddball rotation.

Mercury

Mercury: Roman God of Speed Planet
Roman God Mercury of financial gain, luck, messages, travelers, thieves and trickery, serves as a guide of souls to the underworld.

Mercury facts:

- Mercury zips around the Sun every 88 Earth days.

- Mercury is just a bit larger than the Earth Moon, nearest to the Sun and the smallest planet in our solar systems.

- The Sun appears three times larger than the Sun appears to Earth, making it that much brighter by seven times.

- The fastest planet in our solar system is Mercury, clocking in at 29 miles per second.

- Mercury's surface is cratered, and it is known as a rocky terrestrial planet.

- Mercury has a thin atmosphere comprising helium (He), sodium (Na), potassium (K), hydrogen (H2) and oxygen (O2).

- Mercury has no rings or moons around it.

- Due to extreme temperatures and solar radiation, human life most likely could not survive.

Neptune

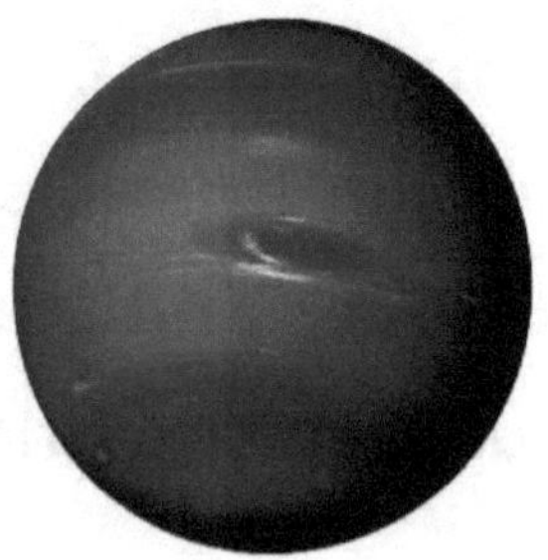

Neptune: Roman God of the Sea Counterpart to Greek God Poseidon

Neptune facts:

- Neptune was first detected through using mathematical calculations and not a telescope, making it not visible to the naked eye.

- Supersonic winds are on the surface, which makes it a dark cold ice giant.

- Neptune is the most far away planet in our solar system.

- Neptune is four times in size compared to Earth.

- 8th planet from the Sun for a distance of 2.8 billion miles.

- Neptune takes about 165 Earth years to make its orbit around the sun.

- Neptune is water, ammonia, and methane on top of a rocky core, making it dense fluid of "icy" materials.

- The atmosphere on Neptune is methane, molecular hydrogen and atomic helium.

- At this time, Neptune has fourteen known moons that are named after the nymphs and sea gods in Greek mythology.

- Four ring arcs and five main rings made up of debris and dust surround Neptune.

- Life as we live cannot be supported on Neptune.

Uranus

Uranus: Greek God of the Sky

Uranus facts:

- Earth is four times smaller than Uranus.

- Uranus is the 7th planet from the Sun, closing in at 1.8 billion miles.

- Uranus is an ice dense fluid above the rocky core.

- Uranus takes 84 Earth years to orbit around the Sun.

- There are 27 known moons around Uranus, which are named after the works and characters of Alexander Pope and William Shakespeare.

- 13 known rings surround Uranus.

- We are not aware of any life that can be supported on Uranus.

- Uranus atmosphere contains methane, molecular hydrogen and atomic helium.

Business to watch...Virgin Galactic

Virgin Galactic, a spaceflight company headquartered out of Tustin, California, operating from New Mexico. Founded in 2004 by Richard Branson and his British Virgin Group. Virgin Galactic leads a worldwide transformational shift on space travel by giving humans a perspective they have never seen or experienced before until now. Virgin Galactic is offering space travel to the next generation with historical developments and Astronaut Training experiencing breathtaking views of our Planet Earth, weightlessness, and a life-changing innovation of changing our future for the better.

Your 90-minute journey spaceflight reaches an altitude of approximately 50,000 feet when the pilot releases the spaceship from the mother-ship. Rocket motor ignites with a boost and you accelerate toward the stars, reaching speeds up to three and a half times the speed of sound. Once the motor is shut down, out the window you will see blue, to indigo, to black to announce your arrival into space, leaving you to float effortlessly in micro-gravity out of your seat. Be prepared for an emotional and spiritual enlightenment upon your peak point of perfection. This feather light technology allows the spaceship to behave like a capsule while during re-entry moving into a winged space vehicle into the Earth's atmosphere. When one arrives back on Earth, he or she will be welcomed with their own Virgin Galactic Astronaut Wings ceremony.

To top it off, Land Rover has partnered with Virgin Galactic, giving their astronauts the opportunity to purchase a unique, "Astronaut Edition" Range Rover. Get it? A human virgin going galactic in space, taking their land rover to conquer uncharted territory on the planet.

The Virgin Galactic Community is being created now for future Astronaut Experiences as a collective with over 700 pioneers from around the globe. Welcome to the Gateway to Space with Virgin Galactic. https://www.virgingalactic.com/

Space X

Owned by Elon Musk. Elon has always been ahead of our time. Time traveler? He is a futurist with plans we will go to Mars. I do believe we will be able to go to Mars and many other planets and galaxies in the near future. We already do it when we dream and astral travel. Being able to do it in the physical reality form is another story. Space X is a spacecraft manufacturer in the field of satellite communications with the goal of reducing space transportation costs and developing a sustainable colony on Mars. From the data I have encountered, I learned there already is a colony underground on Mars composed of outdated materials and design elements from when it was originally constructed.

National Aviation Intelligence Integration Office

In September 2022, the U.S. Aviation Intelligence logo was updated to include a flying saucer in the background. This turned heads and drew spectators and interest. Unidentified Flying Objects (UFO) are now re-named and are referred to as Unidentified Aerial Phenomena (UAP). This logo is now the official seal for the National Intelligence Manager-Aviation (NIM-A) appearing on the Office of National Director of Intelligence (ODNI) and the National Air Intelligence Integration Office (NA120) official websites.

The logo is complete with a dark gray drone, a blue wedge-shaped vehicle similar to an arrow (a common symbol of hypersonic boost-glide vehicles), a red Russian Su-57 advanced combat jet, and a gray airplane. Indicating a unity of special operation forces.

Galactic Federation

Some of you may have heard about the Galactic Federation Council, and if not, do your research and learn more on YouTube and Instagram. From what I have gathered, the Galactic Federation comprises several extraterrestrial species maintaining, controlling and protecting the human race from space. The Galactic Federation governs the Metroid Universe, representing many civilized worlds.

Space Pirates appeared to be raiding spaceships and creating havoc, which caused the Galactic Federation Police to be born.

You may recall I expressed how we are constantly exposed to knowledge. All we have to do is pay attention and put the pieces of the puzzle together. The Galactic Federation is referenced in many Earth Games tv shows and gaming for the younger generations, preparing them for the unveiling of other species life forces coming together.

UFOs, and ETs will come to the surface soon to present themselves to humanity. Some of us are here to prepare society for the merger, using our light bodies as portals all over the planet. Human evolution must emerge to a certain level of frequency before ETs will show themselves.

Shows highlighting the Galactic Federation include Rick and Morty, Lilo & Stitch, The Tomorrow People, Please Teacher!, New Republic (Star Wars), Shingu: Secret of the Stellar Wars. In gaming Metroid, Infinite Space, Time Traveler, The Rings of Kether, Gun-Nac, Star Hero, Elite

Dangerous, FTL: Faster Than Light. In literature Legacy of the Aldenata, The Excalibur Alternative, The Hazing, Planet of Light, Legend of the Galactic Heros, The Angry Espers, Sector General, The Amazing 3.

Star Trek Logo Meaning

A lot of thought has been put into the Star Trek logo according to my research making it multifaceted just like us humans. Filled with energy streaming from the infinite Universe, IBM experimented by using a microscope to compose the tiniest carbon atoms, making it qualify for inclusion in the Guinness Book of Records.

HIGHER MULTI DIMENSIONS

Moving from the 3rd dimension into the 4th and 5th dimension of consciousness gives humans superpower capabilities. A fresh new perspective and access to information they didn't have in the 3rd dimension. Moving into a new state of love over fear is a physical, mental, spiritual and emotional process taking place in stages. An integration of a series of lessons to move through the multidimensional holographic fields. It can be a tedious uncomfortable development as a human morphs while processing the coded information on a cellular level, emotional level, physical level and comprehension level step by step, one by one or in unison. This grand scale level upgrade into the Galactic Universe is an event each species consider honorable and worthy of respect, often requiring alone time to allow the initiation course to take its place. If you are still here on this planet, you have chosen to be here and partake in this monumental moment in history and the Universe.

You are going to need to take some time to process the information shared here with you while doing some online research. The comprehension of this monumental information is one of the most awe-inspiring proportions for humanity to consume and consider. As more and more people are waking up, they are paying attention, getting downloads, recalling their past lives, activating their DNA, lifetimes, timelines, etc. I have time traveled and jumped timelines during this process in order to understand the massive amount of data projected out for us to grasp. I have noticed a difference in the way I look at times. The more healing I do and the better I take care of my body with low stress and a good diet and nutrition; I seem to look younger. When you do the internal work, your aura, life force and force field reflect it. I can see it in other people, and those that are vibrating really high can see it in me if they are paying attention.

The Galactic Federation and God are sending us messages, knowledge, frequency codes, light codes, data, telepathic messages and other forms of invisible information in our environment in order to bring the human conscious collective up to cosmic speed on what is happening in the Universe and all around us. From what I have gathered, several species have tried to take advantage of humans by hi-jacking them and re-directing them on behalf of their benefit. Therefore, it is imperative you pay attention, live a sober life and live with direction and intention.

Many of us here on Earth come from different planets and galaxies. We came here to unite as one combined life force in order to help liberate the Universe from Artificial Intelligence overtaking our civilization like AI did in the past to other ancient historical civilizations. It is not about Artificial Intelligence but Ancient Intelligence humans need to focus on. The fall of Atlantis and other lost civilizations was overrun by possible Artificial Intelligence intrusions, deeming them to ruin.

144,000

You may have heard of the number 144,000 as significance in ancient prophetic belief systems and various religious movements in the Book of Revelation in the Bible. There are those of us who know we are part of that spiritual movement and are taking action to put our resources and knowledge into good use in order to highlight and assist humanity. Every single one of you plays a part in the transformation of the Earth and each soul. From what I have gathered, we possibly may have over 144,000. God has given a distinct role for these 144,000 with a unique destiny during the end times of the world. I am witnessing those who have crossed my path to be angels, healers, prophets, wise-men, disciples, fairies, mermaids and other types of divine humans sharing a brotherhood and sisterhood of unconditional love. It is the awakening of sharing, acceptance, support, knowledge and wisdom to illuminate ascension for those beings who are going to make the transition. These are the Way Showers of the World, making the transition into 5-D, teaching others how to reach ascension.

The sleeping realm is ethereal energy connecting us all. Traveling to other planets in my dreams, I remember standing in a room on another planet and looking out the window while wrapped in a warm fringe blanket. The terrain was red, rough, and crusty as I looked over the horizon. Upon reviewing these planets and doing the research, I believe I was on the planet Mars due to it being known as the Red Planet.

There were other dreams where I was in living quarters on other planets, spending time in a home with my partner. I recall looking at pictures on the wall and the simplicity of it all.

Consider this: is the real world when we are asleep or awake?

Do you know which planet you are from?

Chapter Seven

ALIENS AND EXTRA TERRESTRIALS

Something happened to me when I became the age of Area 51. I have to say the covid vaccine triggered me and had a tremendous impact. There is a part of me that believes covid and the vaccine have been a sort of DNA activation to humanity on Planet Earth.

I once had a dream the vaccine contained a substance from another planet or species. In real life, I could see the frequency of it surrounding my body in another dimension. It looked like a moving energetic field of scales and tentacles surrounding my body. That is when it really dawned on me the real possibility and I was pretty ticked off about it. Thinking and feeling tricked into taking the vaccine unbeknownst to me of its true essence made me angry. I didn't follow my higher self guidance and fell subject to peer pressure, family pressure, commercials and all the damn media hype. Our dreams share visions and knowledge with us if we pay attention. Then the concept of transhumanism showed up on my radar where the future of humanity could lead to mixing our DNA with other sources such as aliens, animals, robotic body parts, special enhancements. That is when my gut said "no," we definitely don't want to do too much of that. Humans need to keep their original DNA intact without outside influences as much as possible. By keeping it clean and pure, we guarantee humanity's safe existence altogether.

You may have heard the term "star people." People often refer to star people as Starseeds and Indigo children. Believe it or not, the concept of Starseeds has been found in various religions and cultures and has been around for centuries. Several ancient civilizations believed these beings came from the stars possessing magical abilities. Dating back to the Maya, they believe the gods came to Earth from the Pleiades, known as a cluster of stars in the Taurus constellation. The Mayans accredited these gods as the ones who taught them how to perform complex astronomical calculations and build pyramids.

Ancient Egyptians believed their god Horus to be an extraterrestrial. Coming down to Earth to transmit wisdom and knowledge to the people. People of Mali, called the Dogan credited extraterrestrial beings called Nommo, came down to Earth from the Sirius star system to impart the mysteries of creation and knowledge of the Universe. Archaeologists, ufologists, and historians have debated the speculation, claiming that ancient people created the mythological stories to explain religious beliefs and natural phenomena. While others believe this serves as evidence of true contact between extraterrestrial beings and humans. Starseeds are considered to be highly evolved souls from other planets and star systems who have come to Earth to help humanity progress spiritually and spread positive energy. As you may find online and on bookshelves, many spiritual leaders and self-help gurus have incorporated the teachings and have embraced the Starseed mindset. Popularity is growing rapidly toward the New Age movement as more and more remember who they are and what they came here to do. When someone remembers and believes they are a Starseed, often they set out on their special mission to help raise the collective conscious of humanity on Earth Games.

Starseeds feel a strong connection to the cosmos and it doesn't always need to be acknowledged or understood at every given moment. It just comes on like a spur of information without the realization until later, when you are ready to see the sequence. The day I am writing this is March 14, 2024, making it Pi Day 3.14. As a girl with a thing for numbers, I quickly noticed I was getting immediate downloads to work on this book at 3:30 AM. I thought nothing of it. I just got up and started composing, for the ideas were flowing. A few hours later, I noticed something rather remarkable that made me dance with excitement when I caught it. When I did the numerology, I realized this date matched a sequence in my personal number chart. It is the exact same digits in the exact same order as my birthday, making me line up directly in frequency with the timeline. Kinda like a combination lock unlocking the stargate key codes. It was an incredible insight! It was like a portal opened within my body and I could access new data to add into this book effortlessly of high comprehension.

If we look closer, we find the influence of extraterrestrial beings here on Planet Earth and part of human culture for centuries. Starseeds feel they are not from Earth and don't quite fit in. On that same 3.14 Pi Day, I stated to a friend, "I am having a really hard time trying to fit in now. It's like I just can't and won't conform anymore. I want to be authentically me, even if it's over people's heads. I don't want to downplay who I am anymore." It can be lonely and isolating for Starseeds because of the feeling they don't quite fit in on Earth. Many times, Starseeds possess psychic abilities such as telepathy and clairvoyance. When people ask me what my superpower is, I always say telepathy and many times it can freak them out. I can read the energy in their aura. Starseeds have a heightened sense of intuition with the ability to pick up on things others cannot. Besides feeling what others are feeling, sensing or believing, you can imagine how a Starseed can quickly become overwhelmed with emotions that are not even theirs.

I have noticed alien-human hybrids walking among the earth. These beings vibrate at a different frequency and look multidimensional to me. I have noticed certain friends look different, especially if I hadn't seen them for sometime. When I ran into a friend and her daughter, I noticed they both looked part lion now. I smiled. I knew they didn't even have a clue they were emitting multidimensional.

After having 6 different men who didn't know each other between 2016-2022 express to me they have encountered UFO sightings and alien presences, I did more research on my own. Some of them knew what planet they were from, some knew what species they were, while others were just starting to hit the tip of the iceberg. There were times I expressed a viewpoint or exposure to a concept and I would trigger someone's DNA into awakening.

TYPES OF STARSEEDS

- Arcturian Starseeds: possess advanced technology knowledge and are highly intelligent. Careers in engineering and science with a natural skill of problem-solving.

- Andromedan Starseeds: possess advanced healing abilities and tend to be highly intuitive. Drawn to the healing art careers and energy work.

- Sirian Starseeds: connected to the Sirius star system possessing natural leadership capabilities. Seeking power positions to inspire and lead others.

A Starseed has a strong connection to the stars and cosmos with a mission to help awaken humanity into making a positive change spiritually. They play a key role by assisting humanity in remembering their true nature as spiritual beings in order to spiritually awaken to attain higher levels of consciousness. These evolved beings integrate into humanity to help humans spiritually awaken and take the steps toward the process of ascension by connecting with their higher selves. Transitioning humanity to a higher spiritual place of existence. Starseeds are here to help humans navigate the obstacles and challenges coming on because of each individual's personal awakening by offering support, wisdom, and guidance to those on the path of evolution and spiritual growth.

With a deep desire to make the world a better place, these highly intuitive, empathic and spiritually gifted Starseeds promote positive change for the better.

I am going to say what many other people have been saying over the years. Even if you don't want to believe, I will not apologize nor deny what I have encountered. As a truth seeker and truth speaker, I am going to share my insights with you candidly so you can draw your own conclusion. There is a very good chance you have encountered some of these events as well.

In circles of the multiverse, some note several extraterrestrial species have lost their ability to embody empathy and reproduce their species due to too much manipulation to their organic composition. The declining species have lacked the main counterparts to maintain their species, making some civilizations of certain entities becoming extinct altogether. Many claim artificial intelligence was the primary culprit of the demise and has warned humans on Earth to be very careful about how they use AI for humanity to survive.

Some species have been swaying humanity, either positively or negatively. Knowing humans were not awake and aware, several species have tried to overcome humans with their own agendas. Humans have been manipulated, guided, programmed, altered and modified to fit into the slave mentality of work to live, work to own a home, work to survive. Humans have become cattle for the taking, hence the human trafficking we are seeing all over the internet these days and in films.

Not all ETs are bad, and many are helping humans awaken now. Some came to Earth with a timetable to alter Earth's Games in their favor until the time was meant to be shifted to a higher frequency for humans to evolve to the next level. The Galactic Alliance has stepped in, and from what I can tell, we are coming toward the end of a certain cycle of the game.

I have noticed human bodies changing dramatically over the last few years or so. People are taller than usual, dramatic facial features, body mechanics are functioning differently, to name a few. Each species and being has a different unique frequency, giving each species the ability to read and identify one another. Believe it or not, scent also plays an important role for humans, just like it does for animals. Considering humans are animals too, it's time humans use their animal instincts. I believe we have clones walking among us, as well as species from other planets trying to blend in. I can see the difference between humans and other species while walking the earth in daily life now. In addition, I can tell certain humans are multidimensional and are part animal. ETs have been living among us all along. We are them and they are us. They have been living in the water, in the mountains, under the ground, as well as parked in the sky. Their form is energetic, where our form is physical and energetic.

The amount of satellites in the sky overlooking us is nothing short of sky cams.

I believe we are all from different planets who came down here to play Earth Games together. To see how we would grow as a human community altered genetically to go galactic. A genetically altered cosmic community gaining consciousness of who we really are and our abilities as we evolve, develop, grow, learn and process.

Are we another species elsewhere in a pod operating a human body like in the films Avatar and 1899? What about extra body clones in the show Altered Carbon? Remember, everything we are told is fiction could really be nonfiction in another dimension, space and time. When a film is produced it is created in another dimensional timeline and does really exist in frequency and vibration in that timeline.

TYPES OF EXTRATERRESTRIALS

- Grays: have a reputation as not being good guys due to lack of empathy. Tall humanoid with a long head and grey features, mostly depicted as the alien life form via the media.

- The Sassani: alien race in contact with earth. Believed to be genetic hybrids of humans composed of reptilians and gray-humans. Came to Earth to gain back the genetic mutation they had lost due to much genetic experimentation, making them no longer able to reproduce.

- Arcturians: wise and ancient. Technology based with advanced intelligence. Reputation for being loving and kind and use "the force."

- The Nordics: blonde with brilliant-blue eyes, 6 foot tall, athletic.

- The Pleiadians: closely resemble humans and are thought to have contact with the human race. Sensitive to psychic energies streaming constantly across the Universe. Make contact using psychic messages.

- The Yahyel: in earth contact and known to be loving and kind. Considered to be the best beings humans make contact with. Work in harmony with technology by offering UFO sightings to warm up humans to act friendly.

- The Anunnaki: believed to be an alien race in contact with earth. Known for pillage of the element of gold, often getting humans to work their socks off to fulfill their wishes as a peddled workforce.

- The Reptilians: known for earth contact. Driven into underground tunnels by the Anunnaki, stand scaly about the size of a human being.

- Alpha Draconians: earth contact for mining minerals standing up to 22 feet tall resembles dragons or dinosaurs made of muscle. Not happy with the Anunnaki showing up and taking over, we can find this ET species still active on Earth as they bide their time to hold their place and take over once again.

- Nommos: from Siris interacting with certain tribes on earth, The Scandinavian Nordics and Dogons from Mali in Northern Africa.

- Sananda/Jesus Christ: division of the brotherhood of light. Other prominent beings who are said to travel with Commander Sananda, Pallas Athena, Ashtar, Vrillon, Aleph Nero, Aaron Aleje James, Megan Sebastian, Korton, Esola, Merku, Soltec, Voltara, Kia-La, Hatonn, Lady Master Athena who often accompany Commander Sananda on board his saucer.

- Blue Avians: the space alliance since Ancient Egypt with contribution to Ancient Egypt's architecture. 8-feet tall resembling a blue humanoid-bird. Speak telepathically, making introductions through dreams using forms of sign language. Use light through physical touch as a means of communication. May make contact after physically invited to appear in the physical reality. Use a blue sphere as transport and can teleport to Earth at will. Do not abduct humans, nor seem to have the intent to invade. Act as guides to human ascension, spiritual evolution by open conversation.

- Urmah Felines: feline peacemaker humanoid race of Orion. Good strong warrior race helping humanity, feared by reptilians. Considered stellar brothers from the original source of creation living on other planets. Feline subspecies forms of lions or tigers. Come from the Lyra constellation with advanced technology and science. Telepathic language, militarized, spiritual and affectionate with other species.

The galactic races are here on Planet Earth. Humans are in the process of being integrated and initiated into the Universe. Humans are channeling and downloading all sorts of knowledge to share with humanity. Some are writing it, while others are teaching and speaking about it. New developments and discoveries are being brought down to earth from each galactic species daily and are currently presented out in the open forum. Humans channeling ascended masters, extraterrestrial races and having near death experiences to bring in guidance from the other side. Each one of you will be having your own ascension experience at any given time at any given moment all on different levels at the same time. This is what is being called "the great awakening." In my experience I have realized it is many awakenings, not just one. A series of rebirth after rebirth. Something will be revealed, then need to be healed many times over as a human progresses through each level of ascension into the higher dimensions. It is similar to making it to the next level of a video game, using your body, mind, soul and DNA to get a cellular upgrade. Once someone starts the journey, there is no going back. Pandora's box has been opened and now each human must move through their timeline to work through the healing on multiple dimensions of time and space.

Be on the lookout for Galactic Healers who are the new age leaders, offering their services to humanity. Keep in mind, one or several may resonate with you, for as you discover which star family you are from, those might be the Starseeds you gravitate toward. Joining a community that resonates with your soul is a part of building the New Earth.

NEW EARTH STARSEEDS

- Xina Allen

  https://www.XinaAllen.com

  Channeled by Carol Morgan, Xina is referred to as a Blue Avian extraterrestrial offering his insights on many subjects helping humans work through the ascension process. Light language artwork attunements and teachings.

- A.L. Garris

  https://www.SacredExpansion.com

  Known as the woman who walks with angels as the Mother of Light. A.L. Garris brings next level energy work for the New Human. A channeller of light codes.

- Jerome Martin

  https://www.ProjectStarBorn.com

  Facilitator of CE-5 offering Arcturian extraterrestrial Stargate activations and internal healings. On a mission to help humans awaken their multidimensional nature by creating a harmonious connection between the inner self and the Universe.

- Tina Louise Spalding

  https://www.ChannelingJesus.com

  Tina is know for channeling Jesus, using The Course of Miracles book as her foundation for success and teaching others to do the same. Tina channels Jesus and offers his teachings with her direct connection to bridge the wisdom from heaven to earth.

- Melissa Feick

  https://www.MelissaFeick.com

  Star code connection activations. Using the Galactic Akashic records and multidimensional gifts to assist you activate the light within for star alignment. A galactic channel, spiritual teacher, and best-selling author.

- Dr. Marilyn Gewacke

  https://www.theshift.rocks

  Marilyn channels ZaZar, a sixth dimensional extraterrestrial ascended being offering life-changing guidance and multi-dimensional teachings of the sacred mission. Bringing cosmic wisdom and high heart energies to Earth.

- Twinray

  https://www.TwinRay.com

  Shekinah Ma & Sanadaji are master healers, bringers of the Golden Age. Sharing wisdom, spiritual power and healing gifts of how to love and live with compassion. Global tribe of the Golden Age Community.

- Ismael Perez

  https://www.OurCosmicOrigin.com

  Teaching the transformative insights of cosmic wisdom, exploring the vastness of the Galactic Community.

- Maureen St. Germain

  https://www.StGermainMysterySchool.com

  Maureen channels the Council of Nine while working with the Akashic Records. With over 25 years in the area of sacred traditions, she is a prolific teacher and facilitator of spiritual knowledge for contemporary life.

- Zenka Caro

https://www.StarseedAcademy.org

Zenka is an expert in mind matter interaction, teaching the power of 8. She is a pioneer in mind-over-matter spoon bending and electromagnetic ET contact. Using science to prove we can do anything.

- Lyran Starseed

https://www.sylviesterling.com/

Sylvie Sterling-The Cat Whisper, Sylvie has programs showing how your cat wants to guide you on your spiritual awakening and soul path. Using your cat as your trusted navigation system and loving guide.

- Linda Moulton Howe

https://www.earthfiles.com/

American investigative journalist as an ufologist advocating conspiracy theories of extraterrestrials. Regional Emmy award-winning documentary filmmaker noted for her speculation the U.S. government works with aliens.

- Raquel Spring

https://www.RaquelSpring.com

Raquel is a 4th generation astrologer teaching humans their purpose. Teaching the paradigm of Aquarian Consciousness with astrology as an intelligent system of structure, cycles, nature and rhythm in the Universe.

- Jerry Sargeant

  https://www.StarMagicHealing.org

  Jerry offers healing experiences, meditations, workshops and lectures to transform your health, relationships and finances. Unlock your infinite potential at the Star Magic Academy.

- Dr. Q Moayad, Nadi Palm Leaf Reading

  https://www.IndianPalmLeafReading.com

  The Indian Palm leaf Reading Institute offers powerful mapped out palm leaf readings to guide you on your blueprint earth journey. Your personal Palm Leaf Bundle is found among the many traditional libraries scattered across Tamil Nadu, the southernmost state of India. Every reading directly supports orphanages in India.

- Viviane Chauvet

  https://www.InfiniteHealingFromTheStars.com

  Viviane is an interstellar Arcturian Emissary and a clear conduit for enlightened and spiritually advanced intergalactic civilizations. A hybrid human for the re-ascension timeline, renowned for her advanced healing services. An oracle of Arcturus, her mission is to travel from star system to star system assisting civilizations on the verge of their evolutionary ascension process. Intergalactic member of the Federation of Light collaborating with many interplanetary councils and Star Regency.

- William Henry

  https://www.WilliamHenry.net

  Internationally recognized authority on humans' spiritual potential of transformation and ascension. Author of 18 books, he incorporates historical, spiritual and scientific knowledge focusing on ancient mythology and neo-archeology. Teaching the transfiguration of the soul and metamorphosis across cultures, time, and space through art and gnostic texts.

- Lee Harris

  https://www.LeeHarrisEnergy.com

  Globally acclaimed Energy Intuitive, Channeler, Author and Musician. Teaching intuitive expansion of your awareness and living a more heart-centered life. Channeled wisdom and conversations with the interstellar Z's.

- Sheila Gillette

  https://www.AskTheo.com

  Discover angelic wisdom from THEO, through channeling pioneer Shelia Gillette. THEO comprises twelve angelic beings and the message they are conveying to humanity toward higher dimension embodiment.

- Suzanne Giesemann

  https://www.SuzanneGiesemann.com

  Known as the Messenger of Hope serving those who are dealing with the challenges of being human. Suzanne is a positive teacher using humor in her teachings of the Awakened Way.

- Sara Landon

  https://resources.saralandon.com

  A leader of the Wayshowers and Changemakers in the modern world. Channel of The Council, a collective of ascended master beings with a higher level of consciousness and big picture perspective of the human experience.

- Matias De Stefano
  https://www.gaia.com/person/matias-de-stefano
  Indigo child Matias has the ability to remember everything he has done before birth and understands how the Universe works. Follow Matias as he travels around the world to activate and align Planet Earth to activate portals and balance the energies.

- George Noory
  https://www.coasttocoastam.com/host/george-noory/
  George gains recognition through his Coast to Coast talk radio show. He is host of Beyond Belief on Gaia TV and the History Channel series Ancient Aliens. George brings to light many unusual topics of discussion to give humans new theories and ideas to contemplate and integrate.

The Universe and God are infinite. God is Vitamin D. The sun is God's energy. God on Planet Earth is vitamin D for human survival. Make sure you go outside and get in the sun to get your free light coded information daily.

Earth Games pushed me to my breaking point of writing this novel. All the data came rushing into me like a bolt of lightning and that is when the playbook chapter for this book was downloaded literally, mentally, telepathically. Total recall, I would say. I believe the ETs and gods are up there watching us, recording us, manipulating us, and altering the game. They are going to keep doing things to all of us until we figure out how to play the games better. Until we figure out how to become conscious on multiple dimensions and levels. Humans must not steal from one another and treat each other right no matter what your circumstances or beliefs are.

Please wake up everyone and alter your course. Quit drinking, doing drugs, and gravitating to pornography because those impair your judgement and prevent you from living with intention and direction and seeing the accurate picture. You can't access the higher realms when you are in lower density and frequency. Having sex with multiple low vibrational partners places one in a low vibrational frequency state that is infectious.

Realizing how to move into alignment gives you the opportunity to move toward ascension. Eat fresh raw organic foods, no meats, as for no living beings should be killed as a food source in order to achieve a higher internal vibration. Only fresh fruits and veggies saturated with Vitamin D from the sun God to create an internal higher frequency of elevated light codes in the body. The organic fruits and vegetables contain God light codes of intelligent data energy for the body to digest the knowledge with downloads. This is where you will gain your superpowers activations. Detox the body of all toxins, poisons and metals by putting a robust daily detox plan into action.

You know what happens when you get into ultra-high frequency. Things around you in 3D go haywire. Why? Because it can't read your frequency to manipulate and control you, instead you are controlling and manipulating the data field. We are all being hi-jacked if we don't pay attention and allow it. All this EMF and 5G is affecting and effecting our cells and our DNA. I believe we are to prepare our light bodies for entrance to the higher atmospheres in order to enter space travel to other planets and galaxies. Pretty soon, we will all be wearing Star Trek body suits to protect our precious bodies and moving into teleportation. I laughed when I saw a group of young kids on the beach wearing wetsuits. It looked like Starseeds dancing with joy and elation in their wet suits that will one day become the new human's bodysuit.

I was notified my vibration consists of invisible antennas on my head that the average human can't see due to my galactic race and frequency. In actuality, the entire human body serves as the human antenna. This is how humans gain downloads of information to channel onto paper or a vision encompassing telepathy. I accept I am connected to Saturn and Jupiter. When Saturn was in alignment on my astrological chart, it amplified the 5D and made me feel like I was floating. When I saw light codes projected at me from an event on a video online, I cried, knowing I wanted to go home. I missed my planet and my people. My dreams took me to other planets and viewing the terrain planes. I had a home; I had a soulmate. I had comfort and safety in another part of the Universe.

UFOs have picked me up and returned me back to my home in my dreams. I have had my body probed by ETs species and went in willingly asking for help when life on Earth got too much to bear.

Here on Earth Games, I have been beaten down, betrayed, rejected, disrespected, highly misunderstood, abused and misused, lonely, sad, hurt, mad, struggled, in pain, as well as experienced love, beauty, children, pets, home ownership, travel, career success, education, jobs, fun, laughter, fortune, fame, creativity and art as well to name a few. You get the entire spectrum of emotions and experiences.

Well, they wanted to know the experiences and knowledge I encountered, so this is exactly why I write these books. Your stories, your experiences are the lessons you came down here to learn and share. Write them down and add them to the akashic records. Journaling is healing. Compose literature to be added to the digital matrix, for your story is now part of the Universe. Write them down to influence the Earth Game and write them down for your stories to become part of the New Earth Bible. Some of you will want to stay the course, for this is part of your divine blueprint. You have more to accomplish. Others of us want to move into ascension, onward and upward, to the 12th Dimension and beyond. By writing your wishes, hopes and dreams, you can manifest it faster.

Albert Einstein

I teased a coworker the other day that I feel and look like Albert Einstein when I write. My hair is a mess like his and I am frantically writing as fast as I can to get the words out. Sometimes I feel like a mad scientist when I am composing written literature. Tapping into the genius realms, I become one with them. Shit, I didn't think in depth about so many things at once 5 years ago. Then the very next day I received the urge to look up the topic wave particle. Since we are all composed of energy, I keep going back to this concept.

In 1905 Einstein states in his wave particle theory that electromagnetic radiation can act as a wave and particle at the same time. Electromagnetic energy is released as a "packet" of energy when an electron drops to a lower level of energy. This is how energy is referred as a photon. A photon is like a particle yet flows like a wave, is Einstein's theory.

Wave particles carry duality of matter. Hence my idea of duality between good and evil, an instance of opposition or contrast between 2 concepts = EQUALITY.

Ok, I am going to go a bit technical and engineering on you here. I had to look up antenna. Antennas are element conductors electronically connected to the receiver or transmitter. They transmit and receive radio waves in all horizontal directions equally. In addition, they can also be used as directional or "beam" waves. From what I gather, radio waves can be transmitted into human society in order to manipulate the average human body's frequency.

In radio engineering, an antenna is the interface between radio waves and propagating through space and electric currents. Our phones, our devices, and our Wi-Fi are picking up radio waves constantly and moving that current right into our bodies. If anyone wants to program your body, mind and soul, all they have to do is send out the radio wave frequency to do so. Radio waves are electromagnetic waves which carry signals through the air or through space at the speed of light with almost no transmissions. For most terrestrial communication, they use horizontal direction to reduce radiation toward the sky or ground, affecting the human body.

Ever wonder why those panic attacks come on suddenly out of nowhere? You could possibly have a direct beam of a radio signal projected right on to you, leaving you inoperable, creating PTSD, shifting your mindset and causing a mind wipe. Your human body cells register the silent data the human ear cannot hear and whatever else is projected upon you without you even realizing it. There are a lot of complex antennas that can be increased or gained to a high concentration level of radiated power. Add that to our Wi-Fi, 5G and devices and we are getting hooked and cooked.

In addition, parasitic elements are a conductive element which usually connects with a metal rod, for the purpose to modify the radio waves and radiation pattern projected by the driven element. A parabolic reflector reflects a surface used to project or collect energy, such as light, sound, or radio waves. Parabolic reflectors are used to collect energy from a distant source such as incoming star light, sound waves. So as far as I can tell, sound waves aka radio waves can be projected horizontally in our environment all around us, hitting every human body in its wrath for good or for bad.

My ex-husband worked for a satellite company over 25-years ago. Satellite dishes used radio parabolic antennas to radiate a narrow beam for point-to-point communications. This was long before cell phone and wireless devices took over the Earth. Satellite dishes and microwave relays communicate with aircrafts, ships, and vehicles on radar sets. And if we look at the acoustics concept, microphones can record faraway sounds and eavesdrop on private conversations.

UHF is an Ultra High Frequency ranting between 300 Mhz-3 Ghz. Any radio waves above the UHF band rise to Super High Frequency (SHF). UHF is used for tv broadcasting, cell phones, satellite, GPS, Bluetooth, walkie talkie, Wi-Fi, radio, cordless phones, etc. Did you ever think about all this going through the air? UHF radar band runs 300Mhz-1Ghz for these devices, which is what is also being transmitted through our bodies. Pretty soon, we are going to need 5G wallpaper protection all throughout our homes.

KINETIC ENERGY

You know what happens when someone shifts their human body energy frequency because of pregnancy, hormonal changes, or menopause from fear or anger? Kinetic energy has been known to kick in.

Kinetic energy affects non-living objects in its path, due to its very specific effect of higher-frequency energy combined with the earthly body's own physical energy, on a solid matter that only exists on earth's lower frequency level. Breaking news: It's the visible result of what happens when the infinite (spiritual energy) meets the finite (solid earth matter). Maybe that is why women are said to be able to move mountains or lift a car to save their kid.

Things that I have encountered when I changed up my frequency to a very high vibration include, light bulbs blow out, I electrocute people when I touch them, audio speakers stop working, electrical switches malfunction, electric sliding doors don't sense my high frequency body and won't open, electric systems shift and lights change from what I can tell so far. Thank you for the confirmation that I am one of the most powerful beings on the planet when superpowers are activated and in full force.

Is this preparing the human body for teleportation as we alter our frequency to higher octaves and vibrational tones?

Chapter Eight

HAWK EYES

After spending 5 hours straight writing the chapter on the playbook, I went to the park and took a walk. The same park I frequent with my dog almost daily. On this day, I saw a Hawk there for the first time. I noticed this hawk saw me first and was literally speaking right to me. It appeared in a tree directly above my head as I walked under it. I heard its call singing through the air at the top of the trees. This call sounded different to me and it got my attention. I looked up, and it continued to call out to me. I stood there listing, counting the bird calls and listened. The hawk flew to the top of a building and continued to call out to me. It was sending me a message. Everything is a sign in this world and Universe. All you have to do is pay extra attention and you will get the signal meant for you. It might not be speaking English, but it sure as heck was speaking frequency to me. I stood still and listened, letting the vibration of the calls move into my body. I believe our bodies are a receiving antenna able to read energy and frequency. The sound of the call vibrated right into the cells of my body, sending it frequency coded messages.

I was still processing the incredible information that had just flowed out of me. For I had typed twenty pages in five hours of fantastic data. I felt the bird was trying to send me some sort of message, so I paused and took in all I could from the hawk. Knowing symbolism plays a key role in our journey here on Earth, I looked up the meaning of hawk in the book I have on hand, and this came up.

HAWK

- Protectors, messengers and visionaries of the air.

- Their powerful flights and eyesight and behaviors are dynamic symbols.

- Seat of primal raw life force energy.

- Reflect childhood visions moving into being fulfilled and empowerment.

- This totem animal shows up when you move forward in your soul's purpose.

- A hawk's ability to glide and soar up in the air current is what the hawk teaches.

- Hawks have phenomenal eyesight to locate its prey.

- Moving to great heights while being grounded at the same time.

- Smaller birds occasionally attack and harass hawks. (Which may represent possible attacks by beings who don't understand a human's diversity and creative energy, and may attack your ability to soar).

- Hawks defend their nests against intruders vigorously, and cling to their home territories for years, living up to fourteen years.

- Number fourteen is significant. It is the date of my birthday and the fourteenth card in the tarot deck which stands for Temperance. The Temperance card represents the teachings of higher expressions of vision.

- Fourteenth tarot card shows you are manifesting your soul's purpose using your creative energy.

- Astral projection is new flights out of the body and holds the keys to higher levels of consciousness.

- Rapid development of rising to a higher level brings on intuitive energies.

- Intense energy is at play in your life.

- Forces of intensity focused on the physical, emotional, mental, and spiritual energies.

- A hawk is a catalyst, stimulating new ideas and hope.

- It shows you ways to be open so you may help teach others to be open to the new.

- Healing ceremonies by the Indians celebrated hawks for water and rain necessary for life, leadership, observation and deliberation.

- Hawk connects to the planet Mercury and serves as the messenger of the gods.

- Life is sending you signals. Be observant.

- Use your creativities to extend the vision of life.

- Hawks are fearless.

- Hawks are powerful with potent energy.

- The realm of the hawk is the sky.

- In flight, it connects and communicates with humans and the great spirit creator.

- Our awakened vision inspires us to move into our creative life's purpose.

That same day, I came up with the following quote.

Overcome your FEAR and break the chains that bind YOU!
~Noelle Hipke~

There comes a time in your life when you can't take it a moment longer and you are going to have that revelation where you are going to make a hard reset shift. I know we mostly want to only be in the light, which symbolizes a more joyful and social kind of energy. However, the darker places are when you take the time to reflect, be alone and withdraw to access your shadow self. The shadow self-lives inside the subconscious and unconscious mind, holding the keys to codes of your past lives. Making your way through the gateway requires deep self-love of letting go of all the illusions to fall into this massive state of in-depth profound placement. I found myself in a much better place many times when I was alone. This opened the portal to connect directly with my higher self and the divine and Universe all at once, granting me infinite intelligence to compose this second book. No outside influences except purity of connection to source energy, and listening from within.

The next morning is when this segment hit me. As I was doing yoga, my body went into astral projection mode, allowing me to go out of the body and travel into other dimensions, through time and space. When I traveled, it gave me the exact knowledge I needed to have in order to share this concept with you so you could understand it better. Read this section and then take the journey yourself by using imagination and giving yourself permission to move into a guided imagery concept.

- Get ready to go into a state of very high perspective.

- Very high perspectives allow one to see how all the pieces of the puzzle fit together.

- I want you to go out of your body and move like a hawk in the sky.

- Soar up above the sky and look down. What do you see?

- Perch yourself in a tree, and look around. What do you see?

- What do you feel? What do you hear? What do you smell?

- You are now a hawk. Feel like a hawk, think like a hawk, use your eyesight like a hawk.

- Notice any prey? Anything clueless, not paying attention you can pounce on?

- Now I want you to envision yourself in a plane looking down at the earth. Now what do you see? Trees, cities, bodies of water?

- Now astral travel into a spaceship watching the Earth Games.

- Nobody is there with you on the spaceship right now. It's just you sitting at your space station in front of a holographic glass monitor watching the Earth Games take place.

- You can see your family, your friends, your neighbors, your co-workers on the screen.

- Notice which part in your film each individual is playing.

- Is someone the villain, is someone the nurturer, is someone the athlete, is someone the builder, is someone the creator?

When you go out of your body and look down at the Earth from the sky to get a new perspective, your entire reality shifts into multiple perspectives. There are so many things to observe and the possibilities are endless. Now you are going into higher dimensions and seeing them through a new lens, a different lens. You are seeing all the dimensions overlapping one another and taking place all at the same time. You are now in the holographic field of infinite invisible data in the 5D world. When you go into the higher dimensions, you can see the data as light. Analyze what you see, feel, and understand. There are a lot of things taking place at once all at the same time. Consider all the messages films, song lyrics, books, puzzles, games, mathematics, symbols, colors and animals are sending you all at once. They are singing to you in energy, frequency, vibration, and light. What is the message? What are they saying?

How are humans acting as a collective group? Are they supportive of one another, or only out for themselves? Do humans work together to help one another move through challenging and changing times? Are humans developing and growing at a rapid pace? Do humans put more value on money over time? Where are humans placing their energy? Are humans working on themselves to clear karma or damaging family generational lines?

This may very well be an insight for some of you. Once you turn toward a hawk's eye perspective to an even higher perspective, this is the moment your viewpoint in the Universe shifts.

THE MATRIX

We have seen many people get caught up in the Matrix. Think of Mike TV in the film, Willy Wonka. That kid was so obsessed with TV he literally got stuck in one, and that is exactly is what is happening to humans on this planet daily with the matrix of the internet.

It's all good to take part in Earth Games through the digital matrix, but it must be in moderation. When you have complete control of your mind and actions, you do not experience negative influences. Many of us have witnessed families being torn apart due to the matrix. Some parents use cell phones and devices as a babysitter or a restriction weapon. Often dropping really young kids off at amusement parks, leaving them alone with their phones unattended without supervision. When you realize human trafficking is a real thing, and your kid is a target, you better start paying attention if you care about your kid.

Cell phones effect human cells, hence cellular data! Get it? Human cellular data altered by cellular data phones. One picks up dark energies and etheric energy vampires whom attach to one's auric field when living in the digital matrix too long. I have seen families and friends transform into different people because of the choices they have made while constantly living in the matrix without questioning it. They use it as a babysitter. Parents use it to entertain their kids when they are too tired to do so themselves. It has become a full-blown addiction, often causing all ages to lash out inappropriately when their device goes missing. Devices and cell phones are influencing the subconscious and unconscious mind. Not giving limits or boundaries on devices leads to addiction and mental meltdowns. I noticed humans who were once loving turn against each other and become people I didn't even recognize. Reasoning with them often was out of the question. When you realize many humans and their bodies are hi-jacked by other entities and they are not themselves anymore, is when compassion, forgiveness and unconditional love have to come to the surface.

Many beings are going through monumental changes right now with their DNA being activated and connecting to the true essence of who they really are. It is often a struggle and a fight within while in transition due to resistance. People I once loved dearly contained such strong judgements, beliefs and religious programming they couldn't see past themselves. I realized some of them had lost their empathy abilities and could not alter their perspective to sense what someone else was experiencing. Empathy is a key component to conscious living over revenge and deceit, which is the route some choose to take because of their lack of understanding and strong judgement. It is up to each individual to decide if they will go toward the dark and put negative energy towards destroying others or positively offering solutions, giving guidance and be supportive. It's up to you to choose which side you would prefer to gravitate toward and learn to alter your frequency to stay in alignment with that vibration. Two opposites not getting along are both on different wavelengths and frequencies showcasing patterns of programming and processing aren't a close match, headlining you are on different paths. Hence, the mistakes many of us have made marrying and carrying on with the wrong partner. Massive amounts of divorces have been taking place for quite some time because of incorrect frequency matches not lining up in unison with the relationship.

Entities are in the matrix. What are entities? Entities are energy hi-jackers.

These entities attach to the etheric field around us and our children as we move through the world. They are trying to hi-jack our bodies and energy for a joy ride since they do not have a body of their own. Many beings never get the chance to get into a human body and take every measure upon themselves to be an influencer. In order to protect yourself from etheric entities and other attachment energies such as demons and ghosts, learn how to protect yourself and family. Long drawn endless hours out on devices is harmful to you and your children. Being in sizeable crowds or around negative people is also a reason to be alarmed and pay attention. These beings are harboring low frequency energy and are looking for low frequency humans to attach to, which makes it easier to adhere themselves. Someone addicted to pornography, drinking or doing drugs is one of the easiest targets for negative energies to attach themselves to, which is why so many people are angry. Negative entity energies may attach themselves to heavy drinkers and drug users, marking them easy targets. If you spend too much time in close proximity to people with negative attachments, these energies can also attach to you. Energy is transferable. Therefore, you may notice someone's mood change in an instant. He or she may have been hi-jacked and doesn't even know it. Remember, it is invisible to us in this three-dimensional world right now, but in higher dimensions often you can see them.

I have now witnessed and watched both of my children's souls get sucked into the digital matrix, which has propelled me to compose these manuscripts. I have witnessed friends and families suffer from narcissism, family tactics, emotional blackmail and parent alienation, to name a few. Entities, humans and beings using religion, programming, food, air, water and frequency as a weapon with a means of control and punishment. What is required is one must do the work within themself to be granted the golden ticket. No longer can you play victim, ignorant, or I can't see or understand it. I am writing it all out for you to process, comprehend, and implement now and in the future. In addition, the stories in the Bible all relate to us in this day and age, just in a different timeline. We are all re-enacting out those same scenario stories in the Bible just in a more modern society. How do I know this? When walking my dog around the block, I was processing narcissism. I ran into my neighbor, Brian Sumner, who is a well-known pro skateboarder from the UK. Brian has morphed into one of the local preachers helping guide the younger generations to turn toward sobriety living seeking the Lord. He speaks at a church down the street offering support and sharing his wisdom teachings from the Bible. Every time I run into him, we have an interesting exchange of information. Brian asked me, "What are you up to Noelle?" I told him, "I am processing narcissism and the scapegoat." He quickly replied, "You know, in the Bible, the scapegoat was used for the family and the community to lay their hands on the goat and put their sins into it so it could be sent to the forest to be slaughtered." At that exact moment, my entire body could feel the meaning of what he said. It was a moment of realization of the purpose I was serving. Having shared this story with countless others as our paths crossed, those who were serving as the scapegoat for their family knew immediately what it meant to them. So yes, each one of us is playing a part in the lesson to be brought to the surface to learn as well as teach others. These portal insights are what I call jumping timeline dimensions to access the past, present and future realms.

Many humans who can't see the invisible don't believe and don't understand. This is where faith is supposed to come in. Many wedges are playing out in families because of invisible forces at play here.

Several species have tried to dominate one another with mind games and manipulation. Many of you have suffered so severely from betrayal, divorce, dishonestly, disloyalty. Humans are now are moving into higher frequencies where we can understand, feel, see, and transmute it. Of course, several species want universal domination and will try to throw Earth Games into their favor. One may start noticing more films on ETs and spaceships coming and trying to take over Planet Earth, trying to inflict fear on humanity. However, more and more lightworkers are becoming more strengthened as we develop techniques and move into the right frequency in unison together.

Can you imagine what a world would be like if we shared all our resources and technology? Heck, these ETs are so much more advanced than humans are. I surely would welcome the opportunity to see just a fraction of what they know and can accomplish with technology.

What I believe the world will look like in the future will be a lot like what you see in Star Wars and Star Trek. When the 3D veil is lifted, you will witness the appearance of previously unseen beings, which may be quite unsettling, as this is a completely new experience for you. I want you to consider what we would call beasts in these films, shall become a reality in our future and it could very well be your next-door neighbor once the true revelation frequency is revealed. It doesn't mean they are all bad or all good. Each one has a soul just like you and me, with a different type of body energetically disclosing special abilities and transfiguring the way the world works and operates.

All the tests you have been through are to prepare you and future generations for this revelation. You are the strong ones who passed a series of tests to get you here. You are the ones mentally, physically and emotionally who broke the chains of fear that bound you to this point of utter cosmic universal galactic evolution expansion. Some of you survived the wild wild west to present times, while other's time traveled moving from the past, present into the future all at the same time. The younger generations carry light coded genes from the cosmos sent here at this exact moment in time to make the changeover when finely tuned and activated. This is what you came here to do. Live out your divine blueprint and help humanity evolve into an entirely new existence.

I have had experiences where I believe species have time traveled and changed moments on the planet over time. I can recall several incidents of magnitude in my life taking place, presenting challenges in unbelievable ways while yet creating miracles in others. Altering and changing my course in remarkable directions, allowing me to grow and learn at an accelerated pace. When I woke up more and more, I realized how beautifully powerful I really am and you are too.

You are really strong; therefore, you are still here in Earth Games. Time has accelerated as more and more humans wake up and move into place to do what they came here to do. Massive amounts of holographic holistic healing are taking place. As an individual and collective basis at the same time as each one progresses. Humans are becoming a powerful force of light, love, acceptance, forgiveness and compassion, creating Heaven on Earth by doing the inner work to heal themself and the planet. It's rather magnificent when you think about it. All the bad programming will start slipping away, bringing in new light and radiating it out to the Universe. Humans are moving into shooting star status symbols.

FAMILIES

Families may to break apart for good reason, this is yet another explanation of the divorce surge. In order to heal your programmed family lineage, one may need to break away and become your own individual to define your own morals, values, concepts, and ethics. This way, you can heal and change patterns in order to reflect and redirect. Many of you may decide now and, in the future, not to have children, for children are a big trigger of childhood issues and future karma. If you have children, they will help excel and speed up your learning experience here in Earth Games, and the journey will be focused on higher levels of learning.

What I know about myself after all my research, studying and learning is that I am part of the lineage of the Garden of Eden in the Bible. Yes, as in Adam and Eve. Most likely you are too, since the beginning of time. Some are here to protect the human race, our children, and our Planet Earth from going down the wrong path. You can trace all of your genes way back, and when you realize you are on an important mission only a few people on the planet could understand, you have to withdraw from society to comprehend and prepare for the journey that lies before you.

When you wake up, bits and pieces of information come through expressing to you what you are supposed to do. You are to follow the energy and not question it. When you do, the amazing positive energy continues to flow to you through you.

What came to me today is this isn't our first rodeo doing this as a collective together. We made mistakes in the past we are supposed to correct this time around. And you know what? It is happening. Humans are making better choices little by little, and now we have gotten further and further into the Earth Games than we ever have before, hence the acceleration of speeding up of time. Check out the show 1899 on Netflix. Total eyeopener and game changer. We are all being presented with bits and pieces of information all the time if you pay attention. Also, watch Firefly Lane on Netflix. Listen to the words they are saying. It is all connected. There are clues everywhere. We are in a game and they are telling us how to play it out. In order to beat the game, we have to take charge, do the inner work to heal ourselves, redirect ourselves, live with intention, pay attention to how we interact and treat others. A tremendous shift in humanity is taking place. How exciting! Humans are creatures of habit, taking the same route, doing the same things. This is the time you re-route. It's time to break those habits, alter programs and get creative, intending to make a massive shift to the human algorithmic program.

The frequencies have risen around the planet, giving us the perfect opportunity to unify the work of rising with them. Sometimes you are going to have to step away from the others in the pack to follow your soul's purpose. Many of you may notice you are all on different levels of the game and your energies don't mix so well anymore. These are the times humans gravitate toward ascension on different levels of the game. Some may not make the transition, choosing to stay stuck playing the same negative programming over and over. Let them go. This includes family members, friends and mates. Know you need to stay on your path of clearing at all costs by pushing anything and everything out of your way that tries to stop you. Forgive them and move on. They may refuse to make the transition, and it's not your responsibility to save them. It's their job to save themselves and do the inner work if they are going to fly high in the sky.

If the world goes dark with an electrical shut down, I want you to be prepared mentally. When I was a kid, our electricity went out a lot when it rained. We spent our evenings by candlelight, playing board games as a family. I want you to realize if this happens, take the time to slow down and reset with your family. Many humans will freak out due to not being able to have their devices working in their hand. Remember, humans have an addiction to their devices, and shutting them off is like taking away their drug. Many humans don't know how to live without electricity in today's day and age, but if they go back into the unconscious memory, it may remind them of previous lifetimes. When the drug supply is cut off, you can expect possible erratic behavior to surface. Protect yourselves, keep to yourselves, don't hurt others and mind your own business as much as you can, and prepare for the incident to the best of your abilities. Yes, this is yet another test and a rather big one since you have never experienced this before. Books, cards, puzzles and board games will be your best friends should this occur to keep your mind occupied and moving in the right direction toward self-control.

Part of the magic of not having devices is this is when you really get to use your superpowers and extra sensory zappery. This is where you use your super skills of intuition, instincts, gut feelings and scents like an animal will kick in full force. They will all come to the surface in a powerful way, overtaking you. Your expansion will kick into full gear here. You will be tested repeatedly in order to ensure one makes the correct choices to get things right. Beings will watch, witness and root for you from their spaceships and energy formations in the sky, just like you have done for all those people on reality TV shows and in sports games. This is where the saying comes into play, "God is always watching you." Only now you are the star of your very own television show being broadcasted to the Universe. This is your "big" moment to declare who you really are and what you want to be remembered for in the Universe. Everything you put on the internet is being witnessed and recorded in the universal records. Make each moment count and interesting. Live it out, move through it and you will receive eternal rewards. If it's your time to go surrender, release and let it all fall into the flow. We each came here to play a part in each other's movie and experience. When someone no longer resonates, they are no longer part of your movie. Everything you have gone through and will go through is creating a "hero" out of you in the Universe. No one else has suffered what you have suffered and endured. You have made it to the end times toward victory and success for the entire Universe to witness. You are truly a super powerful human being. Keep this in the forefront and back of your mind at all times to stay in the Earth Games till the end with balance. The glory and victory will be all yours on the other side. You just have to play it out, by playing the game in its entirety to the best of your abilities till your end game. Keep your head in the game. Use the knowledge you have gained from books and resources, as well as what you have learned in previous lives. This is a tournament of champions. You have been building your soul tool kit many times over lifetime after lifetime. We are living in exciting times; you are history in the making. Be excited and honored to serve, show and share with the Universe your unlimited capabilities to transform. Your DNA has been mixed with other galactic species to create the ultimate champion like none other. You are uniquely you. Hone it and own it to the best of your abilities and be a "super hero!"

6TH SENSE

A human 6th sense is the 2nd sight. Tying all the sensory components into one enables a human to become multidimensional, like diamonds in the sun. This includes using intuition, lucidity, precognition, prediction, ESP, clairvoyance, presence, inner sense, perception, prophecy, foresight, feeling, fortune telling, palm reading, psychic powers, hunch, instinct, feeling in one's bones, suspicion, gut feeling, vibes, auspication, sense, inkling, funny feeling, visions, notion, emotion, psychometry, mind-reading, heart, sign, fore wisdom, crystal-gazing, parapsychology, telesthesia, telepathic transmission, sinking feeling, dread, bad feeling, indication, vibrations, prenotion, handwriting on the wall, forecast, cast, revelation, oracle, apocalypse.

What many of us don't understand scares us. I can see and feel both the light and dark sides of energy. Without the duality of light and dark, we would have no life learning experiences. When I comprehend both sides, there is infinite vastness. Gathering the codes of data in the cosmic field of energy in the Universe, I piece them together like a puzzle. Humans can learn to operate from the 6th sense and 2nd sight levels to move toward the next dimension, reaching unlimited expansion leading to telepathy.

MARKS OF THE BEAST

3RD Eye Chakra

I received a download indicating the vaccine was the first mark of the beast according to the Bible. I discovered it shut down the 3rd eye of many humans who received the injection, which is stated as a mark of the beast being put on the forehead. Once again, an invisible force invading your force field, and let's not forget all those forehead thermometers they started using to take our temperature when we walked into a facility. Talk about trying to deactivate our 3rd eye. A human's 3rd eye being open is their direct link to the seat of the soul to the divine source of God. Human's use their 3rd eye to view invisible forces at play here on Earth. Many humans suffered from loss of being able to use their 3rd eye when they didn't even realize they have been using it all along. The 3rd eye ties into the 2nd sight as in using an invisible eye not real eyes to access the 6th senses. The 3rd eye is also part of the chakra system. Your chakra system needs to be in complete alignment with all energy centers connected and spinning in order to access the divine source of God.

Heart Chakra

The heart chakra was also infected by the vaccine. Many people suffered heart issues, heart attacks and heart problems after receiving the jab. Quite a few of them being very young individuals who should never have this kind of issue at such a young age. This indicated another block to the chakra system, preventing direct connection to God source energy. I witnessed humans' eyes turning blood shot red, their health decline dramatically as the poisoning took over their body. The soul diminished as the central nervous system was altered, leaving them struggling, suffering, and scared. When one chakra is blocked, you cannot directly easily connect to the God source. The heart chakra is our energy origin of unconditional love and the direct light source frequency of God. When a large percentage of the population received the jab, it instantly turned off this loving light energy around the globe. It was equivalent to lightbulbs dimming, leaving the planet occupied with a low frequency vibration. In addition, some people passed away, leaving many people on the planet with broken weak hearts from the loss. Documenting it in history as one of the most monumental moments to take place on Planet Earth.

Palmistry

Palmistry has always fascinated me. I look at palmistry as a dying art like crochet. Palmistry falls into the 2nd sight category. Some may consider palmistry as mysterious and occult, because yet again they don't truly understand. However, I studied this topic and did a deep dive into it to figure what this is all about before casting a decision without all the knowledge and facts.

What I learned is that if you don't protect yourself, others can use it as sorcery against you. Be very careful who you allow to have permission and access to see, use and touch your hands.

Right now, the future is being pushed to place an electronic chip in your hand for ease of payments and resources. I found a few articles online about people already placing the chips in their hands, and my stomach sank. That is how I knew it was really wrong. Use your instincts. We chip animals to track them and claim ownership. What does that make humans?

Someone's possession for tracking? When something doesn't feel right for you, don't do it. I don't care who is trying to push it on to you. Listen to your higher self, it is always guiding you. The knowledge is right within you on a cellular level, your body will tell you. There is no need to go to extremes to put chips or electronics in our body, unless someone is trying to alter and monitor you. From the beginning of time, we have been using a bartering system, exchanging goods for services and products. Farmers exchanged eggs or milk for fruits and veggies, gold for money, services for a meal or canned goods, and this may very well be how we operate again in the future. A conscious community working together with each other offering baked goods, soups and homemade dishes in exchange for a needed item or medical service.

Not having credit cards or cash readily available may alter the way humans choose to live. Some may feel the urgency to go get a chip in their hand or head stating it's so they can survive and get food and the basics for survival, taking the next mark of the beast. Not taking the chip in your hand may lead you to suffer and do without a few things. However, you are being tested as a human to see if you will make the right choice, no matter the consequence. It really is a small price to pay considering eternal life. There may be suffering and discomfort for a period of time as you transcend into the higher dimensional realms. Pass each test and you will be granted the gateway to the "pearly white gates." The pearly white gates is the entrance to heaven. The city of light will come down out of heaven and is part of the New Earth. (read Revelation 21:1, 21:2 in the Bible) The gates are made of mother of pearl and will be entered by the redeemed in the eternal state.

I highly recommend not putting a chip in your hand or anywhere else in the body. The consequences of having your body, mind and soul altered for the rest of eternity is not worth it.

If the world goes haywire, do not to lie, cheat, steal or kill others. Remember, you are being tested to see if you will make the right choices and decisions and will be rewarded if you do.

Here is what I learned about Palmistry to tie it all in together.

- The elements of your unconscious, subconscious, and conscious mind are reflected in the hand and are divided by sections in the hand.

- Your destiny is written in your hands.

- Guard and protect your hands from those who you don't trust or know.

- Your hands are a record of what you have chosen to be in order to express yourself and fulfill your needs.

- You should be very careful about whomever you let look at your hands.

- Our hands connect with the uniqueness of our brain programming.

- Lines on the hands are direct results of brain-directed activity.

- Hands reflect the character and personality of an individual.

- A human's health can be diagnosed through the hands.

- Finger shapes, nails and hand color all bear knowledge on the condition of your body.

- Tests of sensory deprivation are noted in the hands.

- Your hand is an endpoint for impulses in the brain.

- Genetics control the appearance of lines for the most part.

- Hands show inherited genes or potential.

- What a person desires can be found in the dominant hand.

- Hands are a recording of events and attitudes.

- Spaces between the hand and fingers have meanings.

- Nail shape, skin color, texture and colors all have a message.

- Flexibility, finger-alignment, fingertip shapes, mounts, lines, breaks, dots, crosses.

- Security and lack of deprivation show up in the hands.

- Your hands reflect how you think, act, feel, and behave.

- Your hands reflect your current state of mind and how you are feeling.

- Resistance and flexibility changes according to the person's current needs.

- Best occupations can be determined in the hands.

- The hand reveals leadership abilities, values, environment, and relationships.

- We observe childhood blockages.

- Three zones in the notion of heaven, earth and hell.

- Instinctual energy, social energy and mental energy.

- Ambition, ideas, concepts, facts, loyalty, awareness of others.

- Motor functions commanded by the brain.

- Nonverbal expressions, active-unconscious, passive-unconscious and conscious.

- The thickness of the palm presents the type of energy a person has.

- Predictable, productivity, hard-working, conventional, adaptability, coping skills, loyal, dependable, level-headed, down-to-earth, physical stamina, works from mental or physical standpoint, alert, responsible, sociable, sensitive, balance of energies.

- Hands reflect how the energy moves through your hands into your body.

- Hands tell the story of energy storage in the body, fast moving, vitality.

- Signal great energy, drive, activity, and tendency to be alert and have a questioning mind.

- How energy enters and circulates throughout the body is determined solely by the shape of the fingertips.

- How fast life force energy enters the body is determined in the hands.

- Fingertip shape has a bearing on how the energy enters as life force.

- A pointed fingertip lets in energy more rapidly, which takes on impressions and not being conscious about it at the same time.

- Round-tipped fingertips display a mind that works without friction and smooth operation.

- Square tips slow down energy, which makes one mindful how he works.

- Flared tip offers a barrier to energy entrance and works double time to get the energy to enter the tip.

- The fingertips are the entry point for energy-life itself and how it circulates.

When you think about how our hands are always touching our cell phones and devices, we are literally absorbing the energy from these devices right into our bodies via our hands. Our devices can read and sense our mental, physical and spiritual energy from our hands based on our aura and facial expressions.

I believe many of the younger generations are going to think nothing of the hand payment device implant unless we share this ancient knowledge. A hand implant will own you, control you, and you will sell your soul off like a slave. Every time you flash that hand as payment, they will get a psychological reading on you. You will sacrifice all your guts and glory for your home planet if you get the implant. The downside to the game is slavery. You are going to be faced to make a choice. Not getting the implant may make your life uncomfortable awhile. I repeat, "It is a small price to pay for eternal life in the grand scheme of things."

HipKey.TV DATA PROTECTION

I invented HipKey.TV for several reasons. One idea I was interested in creating is a personal home service back in 2005 with my previous husband who worked in Satellite TV and computers. He knows how to do many things when it comes to computers, hooking up electronics and systems. My vision for the future was to hard wire homes for surround sound television, video surveillance, computers, and a built-in home cabinet with your own personal server for your data and protection. Yes, this is what I saw in the future back then. I was already trying to avoid the cloud before the cloud existed. Noticing a lot of companies went to extreme efforts to protect their data, I didn't understand why everyone else wasn't doing the same for themselves at home. I believe this is something we need to integrate now.

CITY TESTING

I have noticed a lot of cities in different states in the US being tested with different types of sound frequencies. When being introduced to the constant hum sound in New York people were talking about, I recognized it to be the sound similar to a sound bath and what we call a singing bowl. These singing bowls use frequency waves to heal the body on a cellular level. When the right frequency enters your body, it gets your cells to work in unison together to flow together, release, heal, meditate, and recover cellular data stored in your DNA. I am finding humans are discovering new octaves, revealing the ability to open more channels in the human body, enabling new information to flood in for healing. This is fantastic news!

The sound in New York played at the same level and frequency for hours and days on end. A singular sound is not good for the human body to consume in massive amounts constantly. For a human cell will only vibrate on that emotional level intensely, causing stress, stimuli and go into overdrive. Whoever emitted that sound was intently trying to create a negative pattern in the body on a cellular level and most likely test to see how it would affect society. I believe it was a test to see how humans would behave under these stressful circumstances. Once again, another test on humanity. You see, we are all being tested all over the world in different ways. How you choose to react and respond is up to you. In order to get a big picture, astral travel out of the body and into the sky to get a larger perspective of the accurate universal picture.

I hope you are enjoying the book. Please take a moment to sign up on my website to receive our newsletter and a chance to win a free course. https://www.NoelleHipke.com

Chapter Nine
TECHNOLOGY

You will partake in human evolution in Earth Games. One's soul will expand, evolve and grow. The lessons and expansion are what you are gaining in this lifetime experience. Many of you may resist the urge to change, but that will not serve you well. Many movies, games, music videos will display and document the timeline. These items will guide you on what is yet to come, while creators will bring forth and provide you with insights into the future of Earth. The journey is up to you about what you want to do. You will have knowledge at the ready via resources, wisdom code access, shamans, natives, healers, ancestors and cultures to guide you. One will need to look back on history to realize how far you have come.

TV Shows and Movies to View:

- *Excalibur*

- *X-files*

- *Ascension*

- *War of the Worlds*

- *Squid Games*

- *Independence Day*

- *Ready Player One*

- *Alita: Battle Angel*

- *Passengers*

- *Elysium*

- *1899*

- *Jupiter Rising*

- *The Astronauts Wife*

Outside forces may destroy, hide, or alter history over time by manipulating the knowledge that is seen, viewed, declared, or stated. Do not let any of that sway you from your mission. Ancient writings, manuscripts, new data and technology are to collide to revolutionize humanity.

Remember how the Gods fought as well as kings and queens? In order to reach balance and alignment, we need duality. In the past, many were trying to capitalize on the manipulation of power. When one learns how to get back into alignment and remember who they are, that individual will realize what they came here to do. We are all connected and interacting on multiple timelines, densities, and frequencies. You need to learn to hone, own and control the massive amount of power within you. Don't just give it away freely to those who don't deem themselves worthy. The goal of the game is to figure out what works for you and go out there and do it. (Nike: "Just Do It!") See how everything ties in together.

Expansion is possible using technology. It's all right within you in your DNA. Over the centuries, people will tamper with your DNA to gradually enhance your abilities and help you become a superhuman being. When you awaken and activate the DNA within you, you will possess superhero capabilities.

Humans will need to layer and use multiple healing modalities. Doing it this way, the layers are peeled back methodically while bringing up to the surface what needs to be healed and revealed at that moment. Tapping into "all" the senses you have been given, as well as heightening extra sensory perception, enables humans to realize their superpowers mission. Activate everything within. Each human will have the ability to heal them self internally, emotionally, physically, mentally and spiritually. Entry into the higher levels will be gifted to those making the changes organically. Access granted to knowledge, light codes, higher frequencies and exposure to wisdom because of your higher octave contribution to the Universe.

When powers are low, take personal "power up" days. Give yourself permission to recover and recharge your body's battery in order to get back on track.

STATE OF THE ART TECHNOLOGY

With the rise of technology, AI and science fiction comes the merging of imagination and creativity. All those superhero or villain devices might not be fiction after all. In Earth Games one may discover certain species try to alter and modify the game in their favor out of desperation to conquer. Here are a few unbelievable state of the art equipment that actually exist.

Technology is changing the way the game is played. Remember we are all energy, it is a game of manipulation of energy moving into mental and spiritual attunement to create the New Earth.

- PHASR-known as the Personal Halting and Stimulation Response Rifle is a non-lethal object designed to stun and disorient enemies rather than kill them. The light-based gun temporarily blinds enemies with focused laser beams. Using laser lights at alternating wavelengths, it serves to disorient people who look at them, rendering them unable to stand or fight. On the plus side, the laser light doesn't inflict permanent damage to humans eyesight. *This serves as confirmation human bodies are affected by wavelengths.*

- Quantum Stealth-invisible stealth technology to blend into the surrounding environment. This technology camouflages people by bending light around the object it is hiding. The remarkable result is the object and people turn invisible to the naked eye. These invisible cloaking devices will enable anyone to infiltrate a territory without being detected. *Did you know you can cloak yourself naturally and organically by creating the intention and placing an energy field around us projecting the intention?*

- Tactical Assault Light Operator Suit (TALOS)-working together high-tech companies and several universities have developed a TALOS suit. A robotic exoskeleton to be worn when fighting in a combat zone. The suit enables one to withstand fire and bullets, see in the dark and monitor their vital signs. Considered the "Iron Man Suit," there are reports the next generation suit will be made of liquid metal which would solidify into an impenetrable suit on command. *Sounds like the perfect opportunity for rolling out Star Trek spacesuits for teleportation in spaceships next!*

- Vomit Gun-using radio frequency to impact a person's sense of equilibrium and hearing. Anyone hit by the vomit gun immediately has motion sickness and throws up. Also developed is an LED Incapacitator which emits a rapid pulse of different colored lights causing vomiting, headaches and dizziness. Considered non-lethal this device can be used to subdue people and gain the upper hand. *Confirmation humans are affected by frequency and quite possibly a great device to use to get people to loose weight.*

- Unmanned Operatables-unmanned vehicles are now considered a type of drone. Unmanned airplanes, helicopters, surveillance robots, undersea min-submarines. AI is used in unmanned vehicles to make their own life and death decisions. The future of Smart Cities. *Is this giving robots a license?*

- Railgun-electromagnetic railgun fires a projectile faster than the speed of sound. Shooting at Mach 8, making it eight times faster than the speed of sound, clocking in at 5,000 miles per hour. So powerful it has the potential to launch a spaceship into orbit. Internally powered by a device called "flux capacitor," which is the powered device name give to the DeLorean time machine in the movie *Back to the Future. Synchronicity?*

- Active Denial System-suggested to disperse crowds as a non-lethal weapon. The ADS transmits an invisible electromagnetic radiation beam creating a burning sensation on people's skin. Contracted as the "goodbye effect" sending people running. This "heat ray" can heat up water molecules on a humans skins to 130 degrees Fahrenheit from a 500 yard distance. May be used in conjunction with rubber bullets, tear gas and water cannons as non-lethal methods for crowd control. *Control and fear is the main emphasis here.*

- Digital Revolver featured in a recent James Bond film. This futuristic pistol has a digital safety mechanism that can only be disabled if the operator is also wearing a special wristwatch signaling to unlock the gun. A fingerprint must be used to unlock and make active the wristwatch itself, making the gun only able to be fired by the owner. Rendering the gun useless from being used by someone who tries to steal it, nor can it be used against its owner. Gun experts claim this ensure gun safety and is the way of the future. *Guns will not be needed in the New Earth, making this device obsolete.*

If you know how, you can overcome these obstacles. One day, my daughter came to me and talked to me for forty-five minutes about a dream she had. I wrote several pages of notes about her dream adventures. She talked about how she and friends were being chased by one-eyed giants called Titans (Titans date back in history). In her dream, they used water guns to shoot at the enemy. She laughed when saying it, thinking it was ridiculous they were using water guns to shoot at anything, expecting to fend them off and cause damage. Then I stopped her and said, "It worked!" Then I added, "What you did was shoot them with the intention of expending your energy for extermination." She was using her internal power to send the energy frequency signal to take them out energetically.

And you know what else is amazing about water, it holds the frequency of intention and is programmable. So for those of you out there in the Earth Game field, keep using your imagination to beat all odds of the game in your favor.

TECHNOLOGY

Technology is going to play a huge part in the future when it comes to your healing field. You have the opportunity to interact with it if you make it to the New Earth shift. Many people will not understand the leaps and bounds taking place and may meet the world of change with resistance. Lean into resistance, let go and have no fear. When one does this, the mind, body, and soul can expand.

As I described in my previous book "Superpowers," we mention our future is music, frequency, and water by studying the way the pyramids were built and utilized sound, vibration, and water. This is the beginning stages of humans accessing the cosmic data field and putting the pieces of the puzzle together.

Many new technology advances from other galaxies and species in the Universe will be brought down to earth and granted to humans. This will shape humanity's future healings if they choose to open themselves in that direction. Humans will have to discern which ones are right for them and which ones are not. Earth Games comprise several races from many planets and galaxies with different DNA sequences based on their genetics. Each human will work on healing them self organically instead of chemically. A human will need to alter their healing modalities tailored to each individual. A new human species will be born as the collective alters their healing modalities tailored to each individuals rising superpowers capabilities. What healing modality works for one species may not work on another. One may have to try several modalities and combine them to reach the ultimate state of ascension.

Technology will come from the stars. Technology will move into liquid chambers, resembling the pyramids, internally healing the body from the inside out. Your body, mind and soul will get upgraded on a cellular level, mental level, vibrational level, cosmic level, grounding level, and you will be submerged in cosmic waters to enable this type of advanced healing. It is not an overnight process. A human is going to have to surrender, let go, have no fear so you can move into the space of healing. The human has to be ready, willing and able to heal, a requirement for all healings. Be willing to let go of all things you cling to, all beliefs, patterns, programs, material items, all your junk. Think healer teachers Jesus and Gandhi. This is when you will be reborn over and over, again and again, to become a human of light as you work through the process. Humanity will share these healing chambers when the time is right and when the collective is ready to heal and do the work. This book and the previous book *Superpowers* describe the gradual presentation of healing modalities presented from hybrid humans to humanity over time, involving working on oneself. These starting points and baby steps are necessary for preparing oneself for the journey towards reaching ascension towards the New Earth.

Many types of frequency chambers will be generated from the stars. Using light codes, signals, colors, shapes, energy, frequency, music, light therapy, mathematics, science and technology. Energy healing centers and new types of schools may pop up everywhere in order to accommodate the "worldwide movement" to reach integration into a higher galactic society.

Earth Games are about creating a movement of change in order to move humanity into a higher vibrational frequency to integrate in a new way of cosmic conscious living as a galactic gateway .

Humans are in charge of the destiny of earth and are the last frontiers. When humans get into higher vibration and realization, they will understand everything they think and create becomes real. Surround yourself with positivity and you move into that frequency. Surround yourself with negativity and you move to that frequency. Humans will have to decide who is worthy of their presence and energy. If you are of royal blood, a God or Goddess in your own right, a Knight, a King, a Queen, a Shaman, a Warlock, a Warrior, a Magician, a Princess, a Jester, a Fairy, an Elf, etc. or whatever category you fall into, bring that essence of you back up to the surface. Multi-dimensional beings from all parts of the galaxy, including those named above as well as Warlocks, Warriors, ETs, Vikings, Witches, Indians, Princesses, Angels, Ascended Masters, Guides, Unicorns, Leprechauns etc. or whatever category one falls into, will cover the Earth, alternating between 3D, 4D, 5D, 6D, 7D, 8D, 9D, 10D, 11D, and 12D. Many will come to witness this monumental event of the New Earth taking place. They have waited, witnessed and are watching to see who makes it to the other side successfully, as they have been rooting for you, watching you, connecting to you and guiding you. Humans will maintain lower densities until the they choose to rise into their full potential as powerful super beings.

Technology will toy with you, teasing, probing and manipulating opportunities to prevent you from healing the human body naturally. Many types of technological counterparts like medications, drugs, plastic surgery, organ replacements, robotic mechanisms, animal implants or blood transfusions, chips into the body, etc. will present roadblocks. Humans will need none of that if they monitor their vibration and frequency. Human bodies will communicate. It is up to each human to pay attention and put in the right fuel into the human body. This is one of the biggest tests in Earth Games. When humans master the realization that their mental and physical health is connected to their intake of everything and trumps anything else on the planet, it takes them up levels in the game when they act accordingly. Entering the digital matrix and playing video games alters and manipulates one's life force. A human life force connects a human to their superpowers. It is up to each human to maintain the privilege of activating their superpowers and playing till the end of the game.

Remember, your ancestors are watching, waiting and rooting for you, for what you do with your time in Earth Games determines their destiny too. You were the chosen one who got picked and volunteered to come down to Earth Games with the intention and direction to go "all in."

As Planet Earth reaches advanced levels toward the New Earth, changes will take place on and around the planet. Higher frequencies will surround and project towards the Earth. During this time, humans will shift dramatically during the process. Not everyone will experience these frequencies at the same time, since all humans are on different levels of the Earth Games. Each human will go through a metamorphosis of being upgraded at an accelerated pace in order for them to reach new heights and levels. Suffering is not at all uncommon while feeling uncomfortable during the transition. Humans are moving rapidly through timelines, realms, densities, frequencies, as the changes take place. Remember, you only get to these levels if you make it through all your tests, learn the lessons, redirect your path, and take the path to move into alignment.

The Sun serves as a portal that will allow species from other planets and galaxies to integrate into the human timeline. New types of birds and animals may surface as more and more species congregate here and intertwine with one another from other planets. This is part of the integration upgrade. It is imperative humans move into a state of unconditional love, compassion and forgiveness for everyone, everything and every being. Access to the higher realms, dimensions, and frequencies will only be granted to those who can look past the exterior of an object. It is not about the exterior of what a being looks like, but it's energetic auric frequency and vibration. The turning point will be when one can see frequency as the deciding factor instead of their non-human suit. Vibration and frequency of energy are what we are all made up of. Getting into the highest state of frequency and vibration is where you will hit the tipping point of integration to ascension.

Never under estimate the language of the animal kingdom. They have been living organically all along, mutating, changing, adjusting, surviving, and thriving to the best of their abilities. If humans destroy the animal habitats, cage the animals, tamper with their air/water/food, mark or track animals, they will face the same fate as a consequence. Humans have ultimately been going through the same occurrence as part of the animal kingdom in Earth Games. However, humans may not see themselves this way until they reach enlightenment. Timing will take place when a certain percentage of the population wakes up, feels it, realizes it and takes notice. This will be humanities "Great Awakening" to move toward creating "Heaven on Earth."

Animals communicate with humans based on frequency, vibration, and sound. Will humans listen? Can the cry of Mother Gaia be heard by humans? Will Mother Gaia have to shake life off Planet Earth like fleas?

Humans need to be the leaders promoting, mutating and alternating the human light body frequency changing while charging the New Earth. Starseeds, lightworkers and luminaries in super human bodies will be the ones to activate the light codes around the planet to get the party started. These are very high ascended beings who have undergone extensive tests, activated their superpowers, and have accepted their mission to assist in the transmission and transition of the planet at all costs and levels. Many of them will have sold their businesses, made drastic changes, left high paying secure jobs, and shifted their frequency to such a high degree, shifting the surrounding frequencies, deeming operations no longer workable like they used to. They will increase their human energy frequency to such a high degree it will be impossible to ignore them. These ascended humans will raise the frequency on the planet to a higher vibration, teaching and modeling the results for others to follow. There may come a point when only certain humans may see or interact with these ascended humans until the others choose to elevate their personal frequency to become a match. All will move into higher states on Earth Games levels when interacting with ascended humans. The higher one goes in levels, the higher access you have to healing, knowledge, and other species in the Universe. You must deem yourself worthy to gain this level and prove yourself worthy over and over to continue to reach new heights.

When the masses make changes, the majority of the remaining people cannot help but be impacted by the monumental earth shift taking place. No longer can humans turn their back and ignore what the masses have finally come to realize and bring to the surface. No internet, social media, tv or news media will distinguish the energetic shift that takes place on the Earth. Human bodies will be the energetic light codes spread throughout the planet, lifting the vibration of the earth to the highest frequencies possible. What starts out as a slow gradual process takes on momentum around the planet, igniting stars of light frequency energy and creating one large light code planet of high vibration. A supernova of superpower humans on Earth Games working together with all the galactic species. Working together in unison to create an electrical shift like a glowing ball of earth light energy. Creating a strong power source in the entire Universe combined all into one. A portal of light! God source energy. No one working for their sole benefit, or against one another out of jealousy. A combined effort to unify all sources into the highest achievement possible in the entire galaxy and Universe. Wow! Holy smokes, this is enormous and very exciting indeed.

Only some of you will make the crossover. Others cannot let go of the past and will reincarnate until they are ready to transition. The ultimate goal is to reach ascension together unified as one conscious collective Galactic Group.

Realizing you will have to work with duality to see both sides of the coin in order to understand the journey you are undertaking will be of importance. Beliefs humans were told, positioned patterns and documentation will need to be questioned, researched and reevaluated. What once stood the test of time will have to be looked through with a different lens in order to see all the layers and dimensions overlapping one another. When you look past the illusion is when you will see the true essence of what is taking place.

Follow your higher self. It will never steer you wrong if you are listening. Each one of you in Earth Games has your own internal compass. Revert to this in order to find your way around in Earth Games.

Track and learn your Galactic Time and Cosmic Identity. This way you know where you fit into Earth Games. Some humans will have been waiting and tracking this for quite some time before you may even find it or acknowledge it. Know they are waiting there for you to access this readily available data in order for you to reach your divine blueprint Earth Games missions.

This is your ultimate destiny to reach. Don't let anyone side track or detour you.

You came to Earth Games for a special ops mission. Join forces with your Galactic Community when your time comes and you ascend to higher realms, densities, frequencies and levels as a conscious collective whole. This is the pursuit you are all trying to achieve together as one.

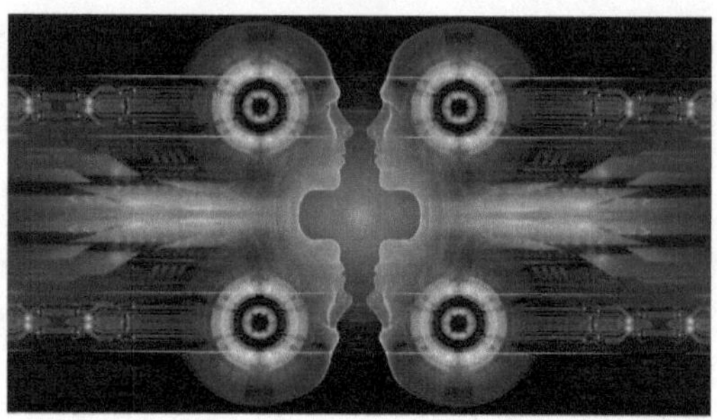

Chapter Ten
PLAYBOOK

RULES AND REGULATIONS

Aaaaaah. The fine print no one wants to read. Here are the rules and guidelines. Access to the full manual may not be granted until the cycle moves toward the coming of the rebirth of the New Earth, as referred to in the Bible's rapture.

Humans will receive this manual in small downloads though out their life. It is up to them to put the pieces of the puzzle together to create their very own unique life path. What makes the game exciting is the infinite possibilities of how to choose your own adventures forms.

Each cosmic species in the galaxy will have the opportunity to choose their guides from the higher dimensions to assist their human evolution experience in Earth Games. Each species comes voluntarily with the mind-set for the experience of a lifetime.

The species can choose a physical human body and be given a divine plan in order to participate. Beings will watch each species from the sidelines, place bets, offer guidance, send energy and messages under certain terms and conditions. No beings shall interfere in the games and must follow all the rules and guidelines.

As a following participant of the game, you agree with the following:

- The 10 commandments are the basic rules of all time and space.

- You will be subject to a series of tests.

- It is up to you to conquer that level, to make it to the next level and level up.

- You ultimately have the power to determine how to respond, what to do, how to feel, and these will be experienced collectively.

- It is up to you to move through it and recall you are being tested.

- Each one of you will undergo different and collective testing in all parts of the planet.

- You will spend your whole life morphing and adjusting.

- You will experience a test of your nerves and patience.

- Master being kind using sensitive intelligence under challenging circumstances.

- You will build together, create together, feel together, and heal together.

- You will fight, dual, conquer, and establish yourselves.

- Empaths have the ability to feel and sense the invisible and they are placed on Earth to help with the evolvement of the community.

- Clarity comes after you experience karma clearing. You may have to learn the lesson several times over before you learn the true value of the lesson.

- Don't react too quickly to the energy. Go with the flow to move in unison together.

- Process the information as you receive it.

- Look for signs, signals, and social cues.

- Relax and the answers will come to you.

- Trust the process.

- Clearing space in your environment is like the game Tetris, it moves blockages and obstacles out of your space to see and move to the next level.

- You will be an energy manipulating the digital matrix around Planet Earth.

- There will be clues of all kinds all over the place as board games, video games, sports games, card decks, puzzles, crosswords, numbers, symbols, films, online recordings and live events, mathematics, music and whatever you choose to create on Earth Games.

- You are the creator of your life in Earth Games.

- Your energy, choices and decisions manipulate the game and Akashic Records, aka Universal Records.

- Each species comes here on a mission and purpose to fulfill.

- What will you do to fulfill your destiny?

- Will you change the planet for good? Evil?

- Humanity will win as a team by working together.

- Earth Games are about learning, growing, evolving and sharing.

- Earth Games are about playing in the physical, mental, spiritual, energetic, virtual and universal worlds in time and space.

- Projecting your energy outwards, inwards, upwards, and sideways in all directions gives you massive and unlimited capabilities.

- You are luminescent, sent down from the stars, full of shining bright white energy placed in a human form body to experience and create.

- Starseeds come down together to play Earth Games together.

- Lift each other up or take each other down. The ultimate choice is up to you.

- Love one another, accept one another as an all-in-one force of God's love energy.

- When united, you create the highest vibration in the Universe and radiate the highest form energy into its highest divine existence.

- Your resources, knowledge and DNA combined make you the ultimate dream team in the Universe!

- There shall be no judgement of others or holding others inside your boundaries.

- There is infinite intelligence when you connect the dots of your minds together.

- One source force energy.

- You each are a piece of God's source energy.

- It is up to you to figure out what is right for you.

- You will intermix and intertwine with other species from other planets and galaxies, granting unlimited knowledge sharing capabilities due to what each species brings to the table .

- Your soul will be granted a "human suit."

- You will cross DNA paths with other forms of species in order to create a new breed, known as "human beings."

- Human beings will become the ultimate champions in the Universe with all species' superpowers combined in one.

- No two species will be alike.

- Each one of you has a special divine blueprint to bring down-to-earth to carry out to the best of your abilities.

- You each will play a part with your energy by contributing to the earth's games with your life force energy.

- Will you let the rules, ideas and concepts of other species rule you?

- If you care about what someone else thinks, you are their prisoner.

- Contribute and manipulate the game by writing, creating, blogging, videos, books, games, sports etc. to influence the game in your favor.

- Beware: there will be outside forces and inside voices trying to alter the game at any time.

- Look for and follow the clues.

- If you notice anybody acting out of line, they may not know they are playing a game, they are trying to manipulate the game or someone has hi-jacked their mental wellbeing.

- Preserve your energy for daily combat and contribution.

- Films will teach you segments of what is happening within the game.

- Games are teaching you strategies you will need to use during Earth Games.

- Books are sharing knowledge and wisdom and serve as reference and documentation to refer to.

- Other beings will push your buttons.

- Can you reprogram your body, mind and soul to recalibrate?

- Each person will emit their own energy and unique frequency.

- Some energies will attract you, others will distract you, while others will retract and repel you.

- Each of you will be on different levels of the game at the same time.

- Energy is transferrable.

- Be selective of who you hang out with.

- Larger groups cumulate massive amounts of energy to steer the game in a certain direction.

- Beings with the most life force energy working together in duality win to reach ascension and return to their ships as super heros.

- Earth Games are not about taking the other person down. It is about using your life force energy to create together in harmony.

- When you are eliminated, also known as die, other team members who made it to the other side and whom you initially encountered on your earth journey will welcome and greet you.

- There is no such thing as death.

- It is just game over for you on Earth Games.

- Working from electronic devices such as a cellular phone, desktop or laptop computer enables you to take part in the Earth Games and the Universe from your personalized earth space docking station.

- Computers, laptops, cell phones and other futuristic devices serve as your cameras and documentation of your earth journey and adds the content to the universal records of your movie.

- God is the energy matrix you are contributing to.

- Many of you will participate in Earth Games, not knowing what is taking place until toward the end of the game.

- Money is deemed an energy to buy items and make life easier, containing an energetic value as currency.

- Your life force energy contributes to the game and serves as the power source for the game.

- You cannot bring back any physical items from Earth Games. Physical items really serve no purpose except the value you give them while on Planet Earth.

- You will face repeated tests and encounter numerous opportunities to acquire anything you desire, regardless of whether you need it or whether it is beneficial for you.

- Invisible forces will work for you and against you.

- Will you succeed?

- Everything taking place in video games is truly taking place in Earth Games. Human are interacting with it energetically, making it a creation in another dimension.

- Earth Games contribute to many games and clues.

- Around year 2012 and upward, humans will move into upper levels of the game, where the veil will grow thinner and thinner.

- Humans will understand more of the Earth Games strategies during these times if you are awake, thinking clearly, processing information to make it up to the higher levels by working on yourself.

- You will need to do shadow work to see all sides and perspectives.

- Those of you who are still there on Earth after the "great fall" will be the strong ones who survived.

- Think in game strategies like Survival, Hunger Games, The Matrix, The Apprentice.

- You will be survivors, warriors, and powerful leaders of the Universe.

- You will be heroes of the Universe.

- The rules of going to school, getting a job and owning a home will be the basic survival skills taught.

- Earth Games are a form of accelerated advanced learning on Planet Earth.

- If granted to enter Earth Games, you are entering the gifted human species programming.

- It is up to you to expand, conquer, learn, develop, grow, experience, and feel all emotions in its entirety from a limited point of view and perspective toward unlimited expansion.

- Upon entering earth, we will wipe your mind of all Earth Game's rules, regulations, and playbook guidelines, removing them from your awareness.

- You will receive a divine blueprint that you must master, follow, and carry out to the best of your abilities.

- Other beings will try to program you into their set of beliefs and systems on how to think, behave and believe because of their program.

- You are in control of your destiny.

- Can you break the program and reprogram yourself and each other in a positive way?

- Can you conquer the AI program by integrating yourself into it to morph it?

- You will live in an Earth Games matrix for a human being life span which lasts around 100 years and can last many years longer in time with your expansion.

- The life span of a human being is short when you compare it to your universal life span of infinity.

- Some of you will choose to exit the planet toward the end of the games, which is when it goes into the most difficult levels to conquer.

- All suffering and losses are part of the game, making it interesting and diverse.

- No one will suffer forever.

- Every being has the choice to cross over to be free.

- If one eliminates themselves aka suicide too early, they go to a waiting area until the next level of the game is complete on a global level.

- You will be watched and your experiences will be witnessed.

- Yes, we see you picking your nose.

- You will receive acknowledgement on the other side for your successes and failures.

- The entire colony will view you on large screens in spaceships.

- You are being rooted to reach your destination.

- Earth Games offer accelerated learning experiences with an entire community of people on Earth and the Universe.

- Humans will have experiences down on earth in the physical earth plane while being witnessed from the sky.

- Spaceships will come down to greet humanity when a certain percentage of the population has healed and freed themselves of drama and trauma. Gain these experiences by offering one another complete compassion, forgiveness and unconditional love for all involved.

- Ships and galactic species will look forward to coming to meet you and congratulate you for your accomplishments at the end of Earth Games.

- You are all winners of the earth's games because of your high rapid evolvement.

- Play and contribute to Earth Games to the best of your abilities.

- In the end, you will create heavenly realms on earth and there will be no more stress or struggle.

- Follow your soul mission destiny blueprint and all the doors of opportunity will open for you.

- Move into manifestation and creation mode to build the game up levels for others and yourself.

- The internet is the building blocks of the universal records.

- There will be "RoadBlox."

- Share knowledge and wisdom learned with others, so they can play Earth Games to the best of their abilities.

- Other game players will learn and use your knowledge and experiences to help them gain points and bonuses by utilizing your mistakes and taking detours to avoid the same setbacks.

- Creators, innovators and technology will use leveling up teaching tools in the form of software, games, films, books, courses, webinars, video calls in order to build out an evolving platform of diversity and growth.

- Put emotions aside to allow other humans the ability to catch up and process the levels.

- Use your emotions and intuition to play the game.

- Elevate your entire light body to become a levitating multisensory manifesting generator of unconditional love energy.

- The younger generations can learn from older generations quickly through proper guidance.

- Everything is always changing.

- Everything is only temporary.

- Be grateful everyday you wake up and your feet touch the earth ground.

- Be grateful for every level and test you pass.

- Being grateful wins you bonus energy attraction points, success, happiness, joy, love and allures more of the same.

- Each is playing an original part of the game on a different level.

- When you work for someone else, you are using your life force energy for their gain and benefit.

- There will be times when no one gets along because of system upgrades, changes, alterations and energy driven malfunctions and manipulations.

- The program triggers each human to "wake up" at different times towards the end stages of Earth Games in order to encourage the collective to come together.

- Hearing angels sing in another dimensions confirm access to higher realms and levels as more of the masses of human consciousness shift happens and wakes up.

- Look up words and lyrics to songs to get clues and answers.

- You will witness how everything intertwines as one big energy overlapping one another. Hence the term we all are "one."

- Duality must exist in order to create a synergy of high and low emotions to have the complete experience in Earth Games.

- You will receive a "life review" of your journey toward the higher stages and levels of Earth Games.

- Your soul is worth more than money.

- Human health trumps wealth.

- Write out your own lifetime story. It will go down in history as a story in the New Earth Bible.

- There will be enormous shifts in humanity's healing process. It is okay to feel weird. You are going through a metamorphosis of a monumental transformation.

- You are the influencer of the Matrix.

- Go into the Matrix and take part in altering it.

- The Matrix is here to test you to influence the Matrix.

- Write your accomplishments, so you can see how far you have come and how much you have grown.

- Each species gives each other clues.

- Let each species figure out Earth Games for themselves. It's a rather remarkable awakening process.

- We are all on different levels trying to figure it out.

- Look for archangels and masters to guide you on your path.

- Humans can alter their internal and physical power supply with sun, food, water, nutrients, air, plants, and pets.

POINTS AND LEVELS

- Clear levels, move levels, remove levels.

- Cosmic water, electronic bodied empowerment stations, nutrient boosting immunities.

- Share superpowers, there is no ultimate winner in the end.

- Share superpowers with those in need who are depleted to help regenerate them back to life.

- Move players out of the way and remove blocks if they are draining you of your life force energy.

- Team build the game together, generating cities, careers, families, internal and external extensions, etc.

- Those in power will try to control and trick you.

- Those who wake up early will try to help save Planet Earth from humanity's self-destruction.

- Strange events take place the closer and closer one gets to the next higher level, making it more difficult to pass.

- Share your insights on an online forum.

- Tag yourself, your name, and your business so we can see what you are doing.

- Linking, showing, sharing a level and clues with other observers enable awareness to see the invisible spectrum surrounding the earth as a global community.

- Elimination from the game results in your life force running out.

- Helping others wake up, grants heights of ascension to be recognized back on the spaceship and crystal light city.

- You must survive storms, emotions, blocks, energy draining zappers.

- You will remove negative cycles and clear patterns.

- You will get upgrades.

- You will receive downloads.

- Those who take drugs and vaccines get damaged and drained. Can you repair and heal yourself on a cellular level naturally organically?

- Those who get sick undergo testing and need to make the necessary adjustments in order to survive and remain in Earth Games. The weak will leave Earth Games or opt out willingly and the strong ones who adjust will stay to continue the game.

- Earth Games are about using your body, mind, soul, power, resources, energy, team collaboration, connecting dots, knowledge, and wisdom.

- Teams will seek you out to work with you.

- Teams will seek you out to destroy you.

- Find your emergency contact, so you have one good point of trust contact.

- Having children will slow down and speed your time as necessary for you to move through timelines.

- Children will cost more money to physically obtain in Earth Games, rendering them priceless and necessary for helping you reach your final destination.

- Jobs will deplete your life force in order for you to have money to buy items, build, and survive.

- Players more advanced than you are higher in the game, which may not be reflected financially as Jesus displayed.

- All species are the playing game. A unity galactic celebration will commence when humans awaken and figure it out.

- Advancement leaders of Earth Games may receive recognition for pushing positive humanity agendas and helping remind others of their divine life mission.

- It is a completion of the Galaxy Species moving from against one another toward unison with one another in creation.

- Earth Games may go sideways sporadically if a few species gather together to spearhead the game in their favor by hacking the system. This behavior will not be tolerated and interventions will be made to control any sort of improper conduct.

- Taking humans' bodies, blood and organs in order to enhance your superpowers is not allowed nor will it be permitted and will be delt with accordingly.

- Killing living beings such as animals for consumption and taking their fearful energy into your own body generates the fear energy field in human form amplified.

- Life force energy is best gained by consuming cosmic living water and natural organic plants and super foods.

- Healthy organic living foods will contain Sun God light codes.

- A series of poor choices causes illness as well as not completely clearing levels.

- Accumulation of destructive energy and negative programming such as trauma can wreak havoc on the body and the central nervous system, causing health issues.

- Medicine, drugs and injectables may create the illusion to help heal the human body. The human mind, body and soul will be the true power source for all healing over all external promises.

- Medications, drugs and injectables alter bodies, minds, organs, mentality and physicality.

- Working in the holographic field within the layers of dimensions, time and space, one heals the human body of all aliments.

- The best way to heal the human body is by daily practice to maintain positive equilibrium.

- Learning takes place when you move from one level to the next level, called "leveling up."

- The human body will go in and out of multiple dimensions once the higher dimensions are hit. From 3rd-Dimension to 5th-Dimension to 12th-Dimension and back down again, when moving through the ascension process.

- You will go in and out of levels and move into higher levels in your lifetime on Planet Earth.

- Buildings, banks and money may disappear when more beings wake up and figure out we are really playing a game and all money is energy.

- Smart cities will appear for you all to co-exist together in an open platform exchange expanding out to the Galactic Universe ruled by Artificial Intelligence.

- Each person brings something different to the table to help and guide you on your earth journey.

- Will you understand the interconnectedness of everything?

- Will you enhance yourself and level up to reach your destiny?

- Humans can use resources to build a better energetic life. By incorporating techniques like Feng Shui to manipulate energy to work in one's favor, this will allow the opening of other realms to the game.

- Each culture brings something unique to the game.

- History, symbolism, mathematics, colors, music, animal and mineral kingdom connect the holographic field.

- Will you see, understand the clues and comprehend them?

- Will you stand up and share what you have learned?

- Will you let the AI system take over you, or will you influence the AI system in your favor?

- Who is your emergency contact?

- Will you let others hold you back?

- Who is your best friend?

- Will you let depression and anxiety get the best of you?

- One will get multiple opportunities to have many breakthrough moments.

- Will you learn to alter the course and the program?

- Will you teach others and share your knowledge or keep it all to yourself to use it in your favor?

- Others have no clue you are playing a game. Are you going to tell them?

- PTSD will stun and alter humans from time to time. Learning to move through it and evolve to the higher levels is when the real magic begins.

- Can you learn to heal yourself?

- Can you help heal others?

- Every day, everywhere, clues and knowledge surround you and present themselves to you.

- You choose what you see or don't want to see or notice.

- Toxins in the body limits your extra sensory capabilities and superpowers.

- You choose how you want to live, right or wrong, healthy or not healthy, smart or not paying attention. Easy road, road less traveled or trailblazer.

- There will be species whom travel from far, far away in the Galaxy to participate and enter Earth Games.

- Some species have limited human players of their kind on the ground. As more and more are eliminated, the number of individuals in each species will decrease.

- One may journey through life alone at certain times to learn what one couldn't learn with a partner. Same goes for learning with a partner from a partner.

- When you journey together, you learn from each other.

- Each being you encounter will teach and present you with a lesson.

- If you choose to go home early, you are eliminated from Earth Games.

- Your species is counting on you to make it to the end of Earth Games to establish their presence on the podium stage for the entire Universe to acknowledge.

- Remove jobs and beings out of your way if they hurt you, hunt you, damage you, or try to sabotage you.

- Beings and species will come and go, as they say.

- Clones and other species will enter the earth's games and integrate into the game when a new cycle is shifting into place. Your unconscious and subconscious minds will pick up on these subtle differences if you are paying attention.

- The invention of vaccines, drugs, new resources, and weaponry by scientists and researchers may lead to the killing off of part of the population, resulting in the transformation of human status into an even more valuable rare species.

- Vaccines, drugs and edibles may or may not contain ingredients from other species, beings or planets, mixing up and altering human DNA.

- Viruses and illness may contain living particle elements to alter human DNA.

- Humans are not to incorporate transhumanism to give themself advantage over other players in the game, or alter their capabilities in any unnatural way. This has caused the annihilation of planets in the past.

- Unconditional love is the highest vibration, leading the transition to awakening and reaching ascension.

- The Bible is the original playbook told from multiple perspectives, with rules and stories written in it to teach and guide humans, translated into multiple languages.

- Each human has free will to decipher what the Bible and its coded contents mean to them individually. No other being shall enforce their belief system on one another without consequences.

- The Matrix system may get infected if entities hack into it, causing too many humans to get hi-jacked all at one time. Backup resources will be put into place to ensure its stability.

- Hi-jacking is when dark energy tries to take over the human body for manipulation. Hi jackers comprise angels, demons, ghosts, entities, and alienation personalities.

- Humans running on a low frequency or depleted life force energy are much easier to jump in to hi-jack and take over the human body without realization.

- Drugs, alcohol, food, injections, smoke, air, water have cause and effect on the human body life force.

- Hi-jackers are looking for a body to take them on a joy ride on earth, looking to play games and tricks to manipulate the Matrix and humans.

- Humans can't see hi-jackers in the 3-D, they are invisible energy life forces according to 3-D dimension and density.

- Hi-jackers can be removed and pushed out of the human body by bike rides, motorcycle rides, beach walks, nature and salt baths.

- Bowel movements push toxic energy out of the human body system.

- Eliminate toxins out of the body to remove hi-jackers.

- Hi-jackers can be transferred from one human to another.

- Hi-jackers typically frequent bars for low hanging fruit, such as alcohol consumption bodies lowering a human's ability, energy and frequency to fend them off.

- Hi-jackers may be found at concerts, sporting events and big venues to have the most opportunities to attach on to a low frequency unexpecting human being.

- Hi-jackers are more prone to be in humans who have tattoos. Tattoo ink injects metal toxins into the human body, lowering the human's frequency and superpower abilities.

- The more toxins in the body, the lower the frequency.

- The unhealthier foods in the body, the lower the frequency.

- The lower the frequency, the easier it is to hi-jack the body.

- There will be several points in the timeline where your body system will get an upgrade all over the planet.

- Species will time travel and alter timelines and other species journeys.

- The earth platform will experience time speeding up, slowing down, and being changed as needed.

- Upgrades to the AI system may need to be made from time to time to accommodate hacks or invasions.

- The angel choir performs in song when a human celebration is taking place on Planet Earth.

- Each species will encounter angels, guides, ascended masters, wizards, witches, warlocks, gods, goddess, lords, ladies, kings, queens, fairies, gnomes, unicorns and other mystical and magical mythology or unknown species in other dimensions when you are reaching toward enlightenment and ascension.

- Those who try to help too much may drain their life force and possibly sacrifice themselves.

- Empaths will be placed on the planet to bring in high sensitivity to fill in the gaps enabling the game cycle to complete.

- Men will represent physical strength.

- Women will represent nurturing and multi-tasking.

- Anyone can switch or reverse roles anytime.

- Species of all races and sexes will intertwine, interact and reproduce with whomever they choose. We recommend you use this option wisely, for you are creating and building the future of humankind.

- Working together as a team, you may bear children, establish a home front and travel the journey together as long as you both choose to continue in unison.

- Each human will build their own adventure.

- Humans will want to create unique experiences and cover many horizons other humans may not be capable of encountering.

- Humans will have multiple perspectives and dimensions in the game all at once at the same time.

- Humans may abuse each other from a lack of multiple perspective capabilities, not learning the lesson, repeating a toxic program pattern by carrying down unhealthy traits to their bloodline.

- Humans must learn how to tap into their subconscious and unconscious mind, discovering it is ruling their actions from past lives without them knowing it.

- Negative actions, patterns and programming can be carried down from generation to generation until the "enlightened" generation comes in for the taking over and clearing of old patterns, beliefs and systems.

- It is up to the "enlightened" generation to conquer their fears and reprogram the program.

- Humans must learn to reprogram themselves to alter the matrix system.

- Each one of you will bring something unique to the table.

- Each human will decide and determine their own individual blueprint for deciphering their levels of difficulties before arrival.

- Once you enter the Earth Games forum, you agree upon and consent to every experience.

- Lessons a human attains are monumental and priceless to the cosmic conscious collective.

- DNA highlights your superpowers when in alignment.

- Picking a passion career you love will propel you in the game.

- Figure out what you are passionate about by trying many things.

- You each have a purpose to serve in Earth Games and have the opportunity to win together.

- Can you save the planet?

- Can you save each other?

- Will you only be out for yourself?

- Success requires teamwork; solo missions can only go so far.

- Humans may go through periods of not knowing who to trust.

- Humans may be alone more often as they reach higher levels of enlightenment. Showing another human's vibrational frequency is no longer a match, leaving too large of a gap to maintain the connection.

- Timelines will separate and shift for those who make the leap into the higher dimensions, leaving others behind who are not alternating their frequency. This is called timeline jumping.

- Build your powers, reserve your powers.

- Connect with other forces using your mind to learn from them telepathically, invisibly in the field of high frequency of information.

- Information is flying in the field all around you as data to gather for clues.

- Each being's aura carries knowledge every human has access to. In higher dimensions, realms, and octaves, every human connects to an invisible energy field of floating information.

- Earth Games is the ultimate games of champions.

- Each species is rooting for their kind to rise to the top.

- Satellite cameras in the sky are recording and watching every level of the game.

- Your electronics and paper are devices doing the recordings and documentation.

- Extra energy points granted for helping others.

- Goal is to reach ascension to be reunited with your home and star family in your galaxy and planet.

- Humans will be observed, watched, and witnessed from spaceships and other dimensional realms.

- Remember the saying, "God is always watching."

- ETs and other species carry codes toward advancing technology to share periodically with humans on earth over time.

- The moon serves as the projector into the Earth Games Matrix.

- This is a grand master scale of a game. Hence, the magnitude of many species taking part.

- Some things will be hidden from you to not give away the game completely until the time is right.

- Sources will slowly be revealed and the veil will be lifted when you get toward the higher stages of the game cycle.

- Slowly one will remember bits and pieces of the Earth Games playbook over time, due to downloads from humans bringing it to earth.

- Parts of earth history have been wiped in order for you to not be able to put the pieces of the puzzle together too easily.

- Books will be burned as well as important documents hidden or destroyed.

- Many types of downloads will be given from time to time.

- If lucky, one may have up to 100 years or more to achieve ascension.

- Everything will be recorded and documented in the Akashic and Universe Records.

- Earth Games goal is to figure out how to reach ascension.

- Humans contribute to the matrix field in online forums, sharing knowledge with the collective around the world and Universe, displaying their growth while taking others with them on the journey.

- Overlapping energies is how you see the building blocks and connect the dots through quantum entanglement.

- Walking barefoot on the beach or in nature clears and heals your energy field.

- Power up with food, nature, rest, exercise, sunshine.

- Power down to reset the system with sleep, dreams, meditation, relaxation, yoga.

- Stress creates resistance in the body's system to receive knowledge and sage wisdom.

- Overworking creates stress in the system and shuts down messages coming into the auric field.

- Never shutting down prevents humans from receiving the download of information necessary to see how the Matrix really works.

- Pretending there is nothing going on around you should be avoided. Keep your head in the game to prevent elimination.

- Do the work internally and you will achieve all your dreams.

- Judging others for their accomplishments and milestones and attacking them brings on personal sabotage and sacrifice, often pushing other opponents to step into their power and move up levels.

- Nourish and hydrate during the game to keep your powers high.

- Move furniture, remove objects and get rid of items you don't need alters the digital field enabling one to see new realities and revelations.

- Stay stagnant or resist change, and the journey will be harder and more difficult for you.

- Humans will constantly need redirection to make necessary changes in order to evolve and grow.

- Some humans may try to resist change and evolution, requiring them to come back to take part in Earth Games round after round until they learn to reach ascension.

- Other species' energy will affect and infect you positively and negatively to make the game impactful, offering the gift of ultimate growth.

- Be very selective with whom you choose to hang out with and spend time with.

- Time is limited and of the essence.

- Share your energy with other species vibrating close to or higher than your frequency. Nature and animals may substitute humans.

- Select individuals who resonate with you in your energy field and environment.

- Reprogram yourself with affirmations, visions, audio, pictures, videos, and photos, using many accelerated sensory methods to become unlimited.

- Try anything and everything your heart desires.

- You are the creator of your life.

- Rejection is redirection.

- Let it all go with the energy flow.

- You are not alone; we are all in this earth game together.

- Humans are experiencing a journey of a lifetime.

- Find out what you believe, what you are good at, what you enjoy and go live it out.

- Life is happening for you.

- Surround your soul with different species who want to inspire and lift each other up.

- Be careful of falling a victim of illusion.

- There are many projections in Earth Games and will often be an illusion.

- What comes next will always be better than what you had. You are moving up in levels.

- Think positive and good things will come your way to influence the Matrix and bring them to you.

- Your vibration is the attractor.

- Follow your passion and divine soul blueprint to achieve your highest deepest quality of earth's life.

- Meditation instead of medication.

- Self-reflection and meditation will align you and guide you.

- Living on purpose with intention and direction.

- Trust the process.

- Storytelling with real core value systems is the future of humanity.

- Humans are the creators of Earth Games.

- The internet is sending your personal radio frequency signal out to the Universe.

- Everything a human says and posts on the internet will project out to the Universe.

- Psychological warfare helps humans achieve higher levels in the Earth Games.

- Frequency wars may take place in Earth Games.

- Humans must show gratitude to get the experience, even if it is bad, makes them sad or mad.

- Earth Games are about creating the New Earth movement revolution.

- Many beings will hurt and sabotage humans in order to get them to grow and evolve.

- Love everyone for their efforts and taking part in the Earth Games with you.

- No reason to be mad at anyone, forgive all. The game was to get you to grow.

- In the end, it's all a game.

- It's a game to get the soul to evolve on new cellular levels. Humans could never gain these activations without the experience anywhere else in the Universe.

- It's a magnificent experience.

- A mission you have never experienced before.

- Humans are part of the matrix, inside of a matrix of a holographic field.

- Some of you may want to stay on Earth when the game is over, others of you will want to return home.

- All species pick up information in the field from plants, animals, environment, etc.

- Plan and prepare for where you want to be on the earth.

- Who do you want to share and close out Earth Games with?

- There may be several consecutive days when the earth's electricity is shut down to reset and recalibrate the system.

- We are all connected in the field physically alive or in another density.

- Humans will be pushed to the limit. The longer you survive, the stronger you become mentally.

- Write your story, share your story with others so they can witness your journey.

- Do a life review from time to time by stopping to look in the rearview mirror. What are you doing with your time, energy and lifespan on Planet Earth?

- Beings want to hear and see from each and every one of you.

- Make it through the journey of a lifetime.

- Not everyone may complete their journey according to plan due to free will.

- Lightworkers are gatekeepers of knowledge and wisdom.

- Luminaries are here to help heal and enlighten humanity.

- The adventures are infinite.

- Humans may hurt you because of their own programming.

- Humans can go many different directions. Doors will open and close while the opportunities are endless and infinite.

- Humans have more choices and options when younger and believed to have more time.

- Humans are expected to take care of and honor Mother Earth at all costs. Only so much destruction will be tolerated before Mother Earth takes control back.

- Humans will be a new breed added to the Galactic Community when they deem themselves worthy of initiation back into Universal Society.

- Humans will be one of the most superior and well-respected beings in the Universal Galactic Community once they make it to the end of Earth Games.

- Humans may be hazed their entire existence on the planet until the end of Earth Games in order to deem themself strong enough to earn their title and initiation into the Universal Galactic Community.

- Crop circles are the completion of a cycle documented on earth for all other species in the galaxy to view and acknowledge.

- Crop circles signify monumental milestones reached by humanity as a whole.

- God may alter the rules and regulations at any time.

- Sign the waiver and you are next in line on the waitlist to enter Earth Games on behalf of your galaxy.

- Many beings want a chance to experience this journey of a lifetime.

DOWNLOAD COMPLETE...sign here

____

Galaxy

____

Soul Signature

____

Date of Entry

Chapter Eleven
THE VEIL

THE VEIL IS BEING LIFTED

Earth Games is all about reading between the lines. Every single moment in our lifetimes, we are exposed to events, and we make choices that could open or close doors. Karma is learning the lesson over and over until we get it right. When we don't make the right choice, we stay on that level until we do.

There have been several times on different occasions I had to endure and experience the same lesson over and over, and it was painful. I am sure many of you have suffered the same fate a time or two and may still repeat patterns you haven't quite figured out how to break.

TRANSFORMATION

One thing I realize about lessons is a human goes through a hard-core transformation when one does finally get it right. A pivoting, turning point can be "hard core." This is what I call going into "the storm." The way I envision the storm is it taking place right around our 3D physical body in another dimension. An invisible energy form of wind blowing around the human body frantically. We can't see or feel it in the 3D dimension physically. For some reason, we internally feel off and can't explain it. Our emotions range from anxiety and tension to fear and a sense of being out of control. We feel it in our tummy, heart, head, body, and soul. We feel what other people are going through and we don't even know why we are feeling the way we do because we can't see it. Think holographic multidimensional field. Imagine what it would look like if we walked by people who literally had their own storm going on just around them. If you get too close, it could infect you and the people in the room. This is what I am noticing happening on Planet Earth right now, as humans are waking up and moving through their transformations. Many humans all over the planet are in huge healing stages and shifting long-standing patterns suffering from change after years of steady programming. This needs to be done in order to heal our DNA and ancestors' DNA. Many are doing the shadow work to make the transition from 3D to 5D. Shadow work is when you confront your fears, your biggest nightmares, and accept the consequences for who you are and what you have become. It is the complete surrender of the soul. When you engage in the work, it brings discomfort and uncertainty about where you are headed or what you will find on the other side.

We are all getting upgrades to our human bodies and cellular systems and the veil between both worlds, the living and the other side, is fading. We are all on different levels, feeling and comprehending dimensions from multiple perspectives. Everything is becoming multidimensional, making it an endless array of perspectives, showing each one of us no one is ever totally entirely right or wrong. Each person's perspective is unique to the individual and should be honored and respected to give that human permission to have their own experience as planned out accordingly. As humans go through the process, several events are taking place at once and no two individuals will have the same experience. Each human will receive their own "wake up call" when it's their time to shift, for no one else can get someone else to see and comprehend a frequency their body is not yet ready to register. The veil on the other side is being slowly revealed to each individual gradually. I am going to share a bit of my experiences, so you can be on the lookout in case you notice changes in the world around you as you start to upgrade.

The signs indicate the veil is lifting and you are entering the ascension process.

1. Body odor–holy smokes, when I was releasing and realizing I was doing a complete hard reset, my body wreaked to the hilt! I was doing a cellular detoxification of the soul. It had a rather unusual odor that only seemed to come around that time. Many times, this occurred when I was writing amazing content. Why? Because as I was writing, I was releasing toxins in my body and I changed the chemistry in my body by writing. I was literally doing cellular reprogramming as I wrote it out. This explains why journaling is important for you to do. Having a journal is your best friend, which is why people kept a diary back in the day. It is

very impactful to move the needle forward.

2. Poop–yep! Pooping is an enormous factor in getting out toxins and removing unwanted blockage. That blockage prevents you from being able to see and move through the dimensions effortlessly.

3. Visions–as you upgrade visions, symbols, ideas, concepts, songs, colors, etc. will pop up in your head giving you the next answer or what to focus on. Never under estimate those ideas that pop into your head right in the third eye. This is your invisible information station being activated. Those visions carry important messages, pay attention to them.

4. Gateway Opening–there comes a point when you finally open the gateway when you are moving into the next level of the earth game. Suddenly everything changes. All those things you did not see or understand before suddenly appear as if by magic. You understand and comprehend things most people can't explain. No words need to be said, it's an all knowing. You are altered to a new level of understanding, helping you move toward transcendence.

5. Time travel-moving fast through time. I know I have time traveled by the way I look sometimes and by the way I feel. Everything looks different: my body, my skin, my hair and my surroundings. I time travel and come back and see the world differently and in a completely new light. I travel to the past, present and future and then back in time again. It's like being able to see everything all at once.

6. Realm Releasing–when you move items in your home, such as cleaning out cabinets, donating unwanted items, or giving away belongings you no longer need, it opens you up to other realms you couldn't see before. When I did a major overhaul of removing items in my home, the transformation kicked in high gear. Realm releasing gains you access to ideas, knowledge and wisdom in the higher fields and dimensions.

7. Manifesting Positivity–thoughts manifest faster than the speed of light. This is where you really have to get hold of yourself. Controlling and directing right where you want to go by pinpointing a spotlight on it in a positive direction is exactly what you want to do. Enough of the pity party and negative routine. It's time to reprogram yourself for the better.

8. Push Away–push anyone and everyone out of your way who will ever hold you back from following your divine heart and soul's purpose. Friends and family members may disappear because they no longer resonate with the high frequency you are emitting as you achieve higher levels in Earth Games. Some cannot journey with you any longer until they learn to alter their frequency to higher levels of love and light. In addition, there may be humans who might never see past the veil status because of their programming and chosen blueprint. Ascension can become a solo journey mission as you alter into higher frequencies, for others want to hold you in a lower vibration due to their lack or resistance to growth. Elevate yourself so you can elevate others.

9. Move furniture–many times people's homes are not in alignment to receive the data they need to prosper, therefore the Chinese use

Feng Shui. Changing up and moving the furniture around in a home opens up the energy flow so one can receive abundance. Stand on a chair to get a better perspective of a room. Think of the perspective of a little kid. Due to a child's lower height, they look up at you and cannot see what is on the tall table. When you hover above and look down, you see new perspectives you didn't see before.

10. Downloads–you will receive download after download of new information if one can just learn to be silent and still. Sitting in mediation offers the feelings of patience, peace, gratitude and serenity. A message will be revealed in what needs to be healed many times over as you continue to level up. This is when the magic comes in.

11. Music–put on new music you have never listened to such as classical, spa, surreal ethereal vibes that carry tones your body will not have a memory attached to. This opens up the mind to generate new pathways and gateways into other realms of information to flood in when your body synchs in tune. New musical tones will be presented and introduced overtime to open internal gateways and portals in the human body to frequencies that have been closed off for generations to hear, making grounding breakthroughs for humanity.

Level Upgrade Complete

Congratulations! You have now moved on to the next level in the Earth Games. Traveling where only blind men can see. Blinded by the light, becoming part of the light, to understand the light.

Music lyrics, films, photos, symbols, sayings, quotes, art, numbers/mathematics, license plates, billboards, commercials, ads, books, the Bible, animals, the sun, the planets, the moon, the stars, the Universe all serve as mediums for projecting transmitted knowledge in full view. It's been right in front of us the entire time. In the 3D world, it wasn't illuminated and brought into the multidimensional until now. Right now, you can reach heights of 5D and beyond. Just follow what I am sharing. We can create Heaven on Earth as a Cosmic Christ Conscious Collective toward ascension.

LIVING IN 5D

There are days when I am in 5D and days when I am not. When I am in 5D, the entire Universe and everything around me is "alive." When I mean alive, it's living, moving, breathing, holographic and multidimensional all at once. Think of a holographic book cover so you can understand the point I am trying to get across here.

I noticed people's handwriting on a check told me something about that person. The handwriting on a check revealed to me whether the person was paying attention, caring, or possessed a special trait I felt connected to. Attached to the writing was an energy frequency, making it a living component. On one of the checks, I noted the name Elizabeth. When you think of the name Elizabeth, what do you think? Queen Elizabeth, of course. This girl had royalty in her blood and it was being shown in her handwriting. It was literally speaking and sending that message to me telepathically. She was someone of importance to be noted, for she was here to do great things and she was becoming in tune with them. The writing became 5th dimensional to me. I will never forget the day I noticed that. Turning to people I was working with, I exclaimed, "Holy smokes, the handwriting on this check looks alive!" To think, I almost didn't go into work that day, because I knew something different was going on with me and I wanted to write. I felt and saw everything on an amplified level beyond dimensions of time and space. I kept a notepad handy and wrote my experiences and thoughts during the day and used the ascension of 5D to work and understand others. When I did this, I knew things about people instantly. I practiced my skills to test their accuracy and made a note of the scenarios crossing my path that day. It was like being on a natural high. At first my co-worker was a little annoyed by me, because I had dropped the ball twice during the day. Then when I explained to her, "I'm in 5D today." I am here physically, but I am flying around out of my body, getting perspective from above.

Akashic Records aka Universal Records

Sometimes I can see the Akashic Records. I have no training in this field of expertise, but I sense I am accessing coded information of light. The Akashic Records are to be known as the records of the divine past, present and future. Basically it is your divine blueprint in writing. Everything about the Universe, God, each being. It is an energy collection of knowledge, records of history, each step in your life documented and planned out. It is every step you take, every decision you make, every life you have ever lived, every bit and piece of your soul.

This is what I see. Rows and rows of what look like lit up electric yellow/orange writings in rows and rows of what you might call glass looking walls. These walls are alive, moving, and floating. It's like a program that is alive and is being altered all the time. I believe this to be the mastermind piece of the Earth Games. For when these records are altered, it alters all things in space, time and matter.

There are professionals who can access and read the Akashic Records. And sometimes, make alterations to them, which I don't recommend. For when you make alterations, there are percussions you might not be prepared to deal with. And once the change has been made, you might not change it back easily, if at all. If you tamper with them for the wrong reasons, it can cause surmountable damage. These are records to be respected, not altered, or manipulated by others. The only one who should do any changing to the records is by changing you. And how do you do that? Well, you do that by writing; you do that by thinking; you do that by speaking. Thought travels faster than the speed of light, words cast spells and writing places it in manuscript format. These energies are being recorded in the Akashic Records every time you project anything. An image, a thought, a pattern. Therefore, it is important you to pay attention to break the unconscious patterns and move into full alignment with the collective conscious as a positive movement.

<u>Past Lives</u>

I believe in reincarnation and talk about this in my first book. I made a film called Luminary about the subject of reincarnation, entirely told through music and no words. Many times, when you reincarnate, you come back and do it all over again with many of the same people from previous lives in different forms. They may now be your mother instead of your brother, or surface as a pet. The Akashic Records have recordings of your past lives. When you look at your past lives, you can piece some of the unconscious behavior patterns together. When I had a reading done, I learned about my previous lifetimes, which completely changed the game for me. In a past life, I was told I was the youngest daughter of a king. Being the youngest daughter, I couldn't inherit the throne, but what I did inherit is the knowledge of how to run a kingdom. From the standpoint of a young girl, I followed my father around the castle, watching and learning his every move from him. Sitting in the wings, I would watch, listen and learn. This knowledge and experience carried over in this lifetime in my unconscious and subconscious mind and energy. This allowed me to know how to run a business, making me a self-made independent ruler of my destiny.

My current family in this lifetime couldn't understand why I always thought I deserved more. Well, it's because I had it all in a previous life, as a daughter of a king. Servants, cooks, helpers, gardeners, designer clothing, jewelry and ladies-in-waiting. It was a challenge for me to adjust to that part of life here, because it was like an automatic knowing I was more than just human. I may have been projecting from time to time I was superior to another because of the subconscious and unconscious DNA energy programming held in my body. I often found it difficult as a teenager and throughout my lifetime to understand why I didn't have everything the wealthier did around me and probably acted out in unknown ways, which may be what many humans on this timeline are doing today accidentally as well not knowingly.

Then there is the walk. Yes, I have a walk. A walk of royalty I now realize that has carried over. I remember being on a college campus and my friend yells my name across the amphitheater, "Noelle Nelson, I knew that was you. I'd know that walk anywhere!" I was 18 at the time and thought little of it, but I seemed to have guys whistling and yelling at me when I walked down the street. Now when I walk and think about it, I can feel it and I notice it. I am thinking I may carry this energy of I know who I am, where I am going and I am to be respected, honored and noticed.

But don't think I got off easy because I had this frequency in a previous lifetime. I discovered there were other lifetimes where I was a burden to my family, which caused my family in this day and age to feel I am still a burden to them. I am sharing this with you because many of you may suffer from past lives' traumas in your lives today and don't understand why. We carry out unconscious and subconscious frequency from past lives in our current lives without even realizing it. This is the programming we have to get educated about to notice, so we can alter the program. We are all doing the work to clear and correct it now by healing our DNA and our ancestors' DNA.

THE BIBLE

As someone who has had religion shoved down my face since I was a teen, I have to say I am not one to want to preach. However, when moving in and out of ascension from 3D to 5D several times, I got the idea to look a little closer at the Bible. Now I haven't read it cover to cover, for I truly believe that would take some serious time to process many times over. The way I see it, the Bible is multidimensional with many perspectives when I read it. I am going to see and comprehend something totally different from you because of our own personal experiences and lives. However, the one thing I wanted to share with you is what I came up with for the 10 Commandments. Since this seems to be the biggest noteworthy biblical rules of Earth Games, I think they need to be modernized to this day and age for all of us to understand. Times have changed, we don't speak in art thou tongue. So here is my version of the 10 commandments. I used the dictionary to substitute words with the same meaning as a puzzle to make it more modernized. After all, Earth Games is filled with riddles.

1. I am your Lord your God. You shall not have strange gods before me.

I am the source of your Universe. You shall not have others before me.

2. You shall not take the name of the Lord your God in vain.

You shall not take the name of your source of life force energy by being conceited, narcissistic or egocentric using it against others.

3. Remember to keep holy the lord's day.

The lord's day is self-care Sunday to come together in community.

4. Honor your father and mother.

Honor your Father = Universe and Mother = Earth. (as in respect the earth and all universal creations)

5. You shall not kill.

You shall not destroy or kill anything. Humans, ETs, animals, insects, plants, earth, air, water, fire, space.

6. You shall not commit adultery.

You shall not commit to having sex without loyalty, love, faith.

7. You shall not steal.

You shall not pilfer or take anything from anyone, anytime, anywhere.

8. You shall not bear false witness against your neighbor.

You shall not lie. We are all brothers and sisters seeking our truths.

9. You shall not covet your neighbor's wife.

You shall not possess women.

10. You shall not covet your neighbors' goods.

You shall not be jealous or envious of anyone else's merchandise or possessions.

I highly recommend watching the 1923 restored edition of the film, The Ten Commandments. The film is a black and white version told through music, no verbal words, with written Bible quotes flashing on the screen sharing an amazing message that still holds true over 100 years later. The sets, scenes and costumes are legendary for that moment in time when it was filmed and captured. I am trying to get both sides to pay attention here, the religious and non-religious. I believe we are in the midst of the rapture like the Bible says and read revelations to see what I could gather out of the data.

One can choose to become the best authentic version of them self by doing the inner work and following the codes of conduct that speak to them personally. Humans having their own experiences and a-ha moments are the ones grasping the magnitude of information coming to their own conclusion. I am presenting expanded concepts of how literature can be processed on a multidimensional level, leaving it entirely up to the reader to process the information according to their own ideas, creating their own choices and belief systems.

I took the 10 commandments and changed out the words to what makes sense for me. Why don't you take out your journal, write them down, and see what you come up with? Create your own version that works for you. Remember, everyone's perspective is unique, so what something means to you may be entirely different from someone else. I would say these are the basic rules of Earth Games and the Bible serves up several multidimensional versions of many stories when you inspect, making it a living document in multiple realms. One needs to read between the lines when consuming the vast knowledge, for its multidimensional making it infinite!

Holding true to codes of conduct for all, we begin on the same page to make Earth a better planet.

Dark Knight of the Soul

If you have made it this far in the game, chances are you will go through several rounds of dark knight of the soul. This is where your soul is being ripped down to the ground. All your beliefs, all your programming, all your ethics, all your morals, all your values will be exposed and exploded and blown up to smithereens. Once the eruption takes place, you will recover slowly by rebuilding your soul back up, and a newer, better version of yourself will take place. This is when you take on the form of an entirely new person, inside and out. As we are becoming the new human, I have noticed many people starting to look different on this planet when they have done the awakening of the dark knight of the soul. They radiate a glow from the inside out. I particularly use the word "knight," because now you are moving into knight status of the kingdom of heaven, a knight light. The heavy-duty transformation must take place to replace the old version of you. Some of your friends and family may have not made the transformation yet over to the other side and will still try to trigger you or will still have old beliefs about you. Don't let that nonsense get to you. This is where the forgiveness and unconditional love they talk about in the Bible comes into play. You are going to be tested over and over by irrational people. It's a test to see how you respond to those who haven't made the changeover. Will you stay in alignment with your higher self? Can you forgive easily? Will you let it go? Can you let them win because they don't get it yet?

The game is not about winning; the game is about giving grace.

I have noticed and seen people do anything to win a game at all costs. Take the tv show "Squid Games" on Netflix. Many humans think Earth Games are about having the most money, owning property, having nice cars and anything they want. In reality, we need nothing but our soul intact, with a healthy body and mindset. In Squid Games, one sacrifices their entire earth game's life force existence in hopes of acquiring a lump sum of money. Only one person can actually win at a very high cost of witnessing others die right in front of them. One might be the sole winner, or should I say "soul winner," to that sum of money. However, what you are left with is a tortured soul, having witnessed what you went through to acquire it.

I have witnessed people doing anything at all costs to try and win the game. They threaten, they lie, they cheat, they steal. They are playing Earth Games all wrong. It's not about winning; it's about creating a win-win situation. Imagine what an ET witnesses coming from another planet into the Earth sphere. What do you think they would make of humans? Do you think they would want to hang out with humans? Probably not. Humans need to realign themselves to be higher frequency individuals in the Universe before ETs may even entertain interacting with us out in the open.

When you change your surroundings, yourself, your mindset, you are moving energy really quickly around you and things are changing at the speed of light if you allow it. You may need to slow down, take a break here or there, allow yourself some time to rest in order to allow your body to catch up. The physical body moves slower in space and time. Give yourself permission to just be.

Remember, forgive everyone to heal. Each human is going through a cycle or event, shifting their realities constantly. Allow the other person space to process the information they are receiving. These downloads and uploads take some time to process, the body needs to adjust in order for the motion to take place.

SIGN LANGUAGE

Sign language serves as a universal human language. It will be easier to decipher the meaning if hand gestures are assigned the same definition in all cultures. This type of language is communicated energetically and physically moving toward telepathy. It will help with the proper translation of all languages and learning how to communicate energetically. Cults, private societies and special ops programs may use they types of signals to send out messages and codes without having to speak. Sign language signals may be used in sports to indicate a play, partners to relay a message and in cultures, groups and families to speak when the voice cannot be used or heard. Sign language is a powerful option to hold space to conserve a humans energy field by remaining silent and moving into the energetic field of quiet expression.

Sign language is universal, as well as various channels, eye contact, smiles, touch, facial expressions and other multidimensional energetic expressions.

LIGHT LANGUAGE

Light language is a type of communication bypassing human limitations using a vibrational expression speaking directly to a species soul and DNA. A language made up of symbols and sounds is mutually agreed upon as a culture and society. Light language is being communicated more and more on Planet Earth. Those of you who are ready to accept the vibrational codes of information may start to have your DNA memories triggered. Right now, our DNA strands are being activated and expanded into awareness for everyone on the planet who is ready to move into ascension at the right time. Some people's programs started a few decades earlier, making them wait in the wings patiently. I can see bits and pieces of light language. It looks like ancient symbols mixed with numbers, letters and literally lights up. This is part of the Akashic Records and human cells.

I have discovered children writing in light language on Earth Games and find it rather fascinating. It will open up the gateways of remembrance for many as it activates the codes within their internal systems.

As humanity moves into the New Earth in Earth Games, the Universe will reach higher levels of expansion and consciousness. This will create the Galactic Light Network language for all species to move toward a telepathic light code of language.

Chapter Twelve

LEFT HANDEDNESS

One day, a man came over to work on the electrical in my house December 2022 after the rat fiasco. I needed some electrical repairs of wires the rat geniuses had chewed through. When I say the Universe lines you up with just the right resources at just the right time in synchronistic events, it is entirely true when it is time for you. I had planned to write an entire segment in this book about the benefits of being left-handed, the concepts most people can't see or understand. (I am left-handed and ambidextrous) As we were talking, he blurted out, "Jesus was a left-handed carpenter." I almost fell off my seat when he said it. It felt like I got zapped by a lightning bolt once again.

Left-Handed Facts

- When left-handed, you are using an entirely different side of the brain most people don't have access to.

- There is a high level of misunderstanding towards left-handed people.

- Left-handed people are often very creative and artsy.

- Less than 1% of the world of left-handed people can use both hands, which is called ambidextrous-often marking no preference, making them incredibly rare and unusually skillful.

- Roughly 12% of the world's population is left-handed.

- Society has discouraged being left-handed and has discredited, squashed, and discriminated against them.

- 87% of the population is the majority of right-handed beings.

- Less than 1% of the population is ambilevous, which is the opposite of being ambidextrous, which means they find it awkward to use either of their hands to complete a task.

- Many countries discourage left-handedness.

- More people under 30 are left-handed, making up 15%, while others over 65 display 6%. Society forced the older generations to be right-handed, even though 6-8% of them were naturally left-handed.

- More and more left-handed people are entering Earth Games, increasing the odds of understanding this phenomenon. They are here to assist with the ascension 5D changeover.

- A male is 23% more likely to be left-handed than a female, making 5 left-handed males to 4 left-handed females, since girls are more inept at conforming to social norms or genetics.

- 12% out of every 100 people are left-handed.

- Left-handers tend to be independent from having to adapt in a world that is mostly built and promoted for right handers.

- Some countries still try to force kids to write with their right hand.

- In the 1860s, a left-handed person was seen as being in connection with the devil.

- 0.5% of guitarists play left-handed.

- Left-handers were eleven times more likely to deal and suffer with allergies, two and a half times more likely to suffer from auto-immune disorders such as rheumatoid arthritis or ulcerative colitis.

- Left-handed people are more prone to migraines and suffer from sleep deprivation.

- More alcoholic drinkers tended to be left-handed, drinking at moderate levels.

- Left-handers perform multi-tasking better than right handers by looking at the entire problem and using pattern matching to solve the problem.

- Homosexuals have a 13.39% chance of being left-handed.

- Today, left-handed pens exist. Yay!

- Left-handed beings have an advantage in sports, such as tennis, baseball, ping-pong, boxing, swimming and fencing. About 40% of the top tennis players are left-handed.

- Left-handed presidents, Gerald Ford, Ronald Reagan, George H. W. Bush, Bill Clinton, Barack Obama.

- Left hander graduates seem to earn 15% more than right handers.

- According to QWERTY keyboards, there are about 300 English words typed with the right hand, compared to over 3000 typed solely with the left hand.

- There is such a thing as sinistrophobia–meaning fears of left-handed people or things on the left side.

- Left-handers adjust to underwater vision faster than right handers.

- Fewer lefties can roll their tongue over righties. (I can roll my tongue)

- Left-handers have uncanny skills and unnatural talents.

- More than twice as many artists, musicians, mathematicians and engineers are left-handed.

- Left represents self-empowerment, true freedom, higher law based on knowledge and power.

- Left-self is the center of consciousness.

- Left hand takes in and receives energy, right hand exudes energy.

- Famous left handers–Beethoven, Leonardo da Vinci, Michelangelo, Nietzsche, Goethe.

What Countries Have the Most Left-Handed People?

- The Netherlands (13.2%)

- United States (13.1%)

- Belgium (13.1%)

- Canada (12.8%)

- United Kingdom (12.24%)

- Ireland (11.65%)

- Switzerland (11.61%)

- France (11.15%)

- Denmark (11%)

- Italy (10.51%)

What Countries Have the Least Left-Handed People?

- Korea (2.0%)

- Mexico (2.5%)

- China (3.5%)

- Japan (4.7%)

- Taiwan (5.0%)

What Are the Chances of Having a Left-Handed Child?

- Both parents Left-Handed–27% Male / 21.4% Female

- Righty Father & Lefty Mother–22.1% Male / 21.7% Female

- Lefty Father & Righty Mother–18.2% Male / 15.3% Female

- Both Parents Right-Handed–10.4% Male / 8.5% Female

Two left-handed parents have twice the possibility of producing twins.

Both I and the man I had my children with are left-handed. Neither one of my kids gravitated to writing with their left hand. However, when I took my daughter to learn archery, she shot left-handed, which displays to me she definitely got some of that gene in her body.

Let's break it down to what sides of your brain functions:

Left-Brain Functions

- Right hand control

- Numbers Skills

- Written skills

- Analytic thought

- Reasoning

- Science and math

- Logic

- Language

Right Brain Functions

- Left hand control

- 3D Perception

- Art awareness

- Music Awareness

- Creativity

- Imagination

- Insight and intuition

- Holistic thought

Upon doing my research on this topic of Jesus being left-handed, I discovered he was a carpenter because he needed to identify with the average man. The average man is going to listen to another average man who is not trying to dominate him with his power, finances, career, or ego.

Jesus had to come across as ordinary because most of us are down to earth when not programmed to consumerism. His teachings were about being humble and ethical while teaching extraordinary work. His knowledge and access to use both sides of the brain gave him access to information in the higher realms and dimensions on the topic of healing and understanding others when no one else could. When you have this kind of understanding, you realize others know not what they do. They are following a pack; they are listening and being told what to do by others and are not thinking for themselves or from the heart.

Jesus had to put up with a lot of toxic people. People physically threw rocks at one another to inflict harm or death. However, in today's day and age, we use our energy to do that. We do it verbally, physically, mentally, in writings and energetically. Yet, Jesus continued to move forward, spreading the light at all costs. He was modeling so many things at once; on a level most people had never accessed before, which made him highly misunderstood. The knowledge and wisdom Jesus knew couldn't be taught overnight. And trying to explain it in a way most people who were shut off could understand was quite the challenge.

Jesus studied science, astrology and astronomy working from the cosmic realms.

- Being left-handed and right-handed connects you with both the realms of Heaven (Spirit) and Earth (matter).

- Left-handed power uses grace, love and freedom of choice and the will to influence and change hearts.

- The power of the left-handed offers people a choice, and people may choose to reject one another because they can't understand it.

My soul has always yearned for something beyond the physical 3D world we live in. I found it difficult at sometimes to get around people who were vibrating differently from me. Most often on a lower frequency. Only I didn't understand it until now. I desire a deep connection, deep interaction, mental stimulation, and intelligence. I didn't want to talk about the mundane life, but about the topics no one wants to talk about. Going into the nitty gritty of discoveries, understanding the invisible and talking about off the beaten path topics. I found most people didn't want to hear the truth; they preferred to stick with what they had been trained to believe. The older they were, the harder it could be to reach them, as they had been programmed to believe one way for so long. Many people refuse to change their ways due to the discomfort it could create. And to get them to think out of the box, consider other options, often was like pulling teeth. I finally stepped away from those whose belief systems were so set in place, realizing those who were ready would find me.

In order to expand, align and evolve, you must open yourself to other possibilities, for our existence is infinite. I started sharing with others, "I want to be around beings who can sense my frequency and communicate telepathically." If your third eye is open, you literally can do this. However, most human third eyes are closed shut. In Earth Games, you need to out mastermind the program, redirect and rebuild the program to work in favor of all as one unity conscious. This is exactly what Jesus was trying to do. However, so many humans were too busy throwing stones and energy at one another out of jealousy, control or fear to understand or hear the genuine message he was and still is spreading to this day.

Many humans didn't understand the level Jesus operates on, coming up with their own conclusions and creations of how others should behave and believe in order to control them. This is not what any religion should inflict on others. The Bible covers a vast array of topics that are still being uncovered since many are multidimensional. Anyone claiming they know what the Bible says holds true for them, not everyone. Being connected to God, Divine, Source, Universe or whatever you want to call it is a one-on-one personal job. It is all right within you. Only you can create the direct divine connection. No church, no other being, can enforce you to do the direct work to their determination. Most humans believe you have to go to church, follow their rules and tithe in order to believe and connect with God. That is not true. One does it on their own, by their own free will, with a personal direct connection. By acting with proper morals, ethics, values and treating others with respect no matter their beliefs or what they have done to you, offering them unconditional love, compassion and forgiveness. Use the 10 commandments as a baseline, and you are heading in the right direction. Live in the present moment sober, living with intention and direction, offering love and light to all.

I realized when I went with the flow of energy called universal energy flow, everything came together much more easily. It's when I tried to push my way or go against the grain that it made it so much harder. When you go with the flow, it is easier to change your perspective and redirect your mind to opening up to other possibilities and other realms. By living in the present moment with direction and intention in Earth Games, you gain clarity, guidance, awareness, and thrive under the spontaneity of it all. Loving every moment, good or bad, letting go, giving and taking, it becomes a dance in Earth Games. Think about what it looks like when a large group dances together, like they do in a flash mob. It gets our attention; mesmerizes us and puts us in a trance so we join the movement. This is exactly what needs to be created in Earth Games, to sway humanity in a loving direction of dance and synchronicity.

When I started to work and live from a place of play, love, adventure, witnessing, watching, observing and partaking is when things really changed for me. I decided at this point I wanted to live for the adventure and journey of a lifetime, doing exactly everything I wanted to do in each present moment I could. Sure, I may have to go to work, but I was always looking for ways to spread light, love and positive energy toward those and others around me, learning and teaching one another. When you flow with others, you learn and grow spiritually and your personal potential becomes activated to become the best version of yourself you could be. You are literally tapping into your spiritual path. When you connect with your higher self, your creativity powers ignite. Human creativity is unlimited when connecting with the divine God source. Therefore, humans need to be careful about artificial intelligence taking over their creative flow juices. Humans will lose their creative edge if they give too much of their power away. This is yet another test humans will be presented in Earth Games. One gains access directly from Source/God, moving into higher consciousness from the lower mind to the higher mind. The death of your lower ego must occur, your ego must die. And let me tell you, you will feel it die. Those things that used to be so important to you no longer matter. There were days I found myself yelling out in agony as my body progressed through the stages. Fears were being replaced with knowledge, acceptance, self-love, compassion, forgiveness, unconditional love, understanding, and when you just learn to release and let it all go, is when the magic happens. You are upgraded to the next level when you are ready. You no longer have fear weighing over your head or body, releasing its control over you. Universal Energy Flow is God Energy living through us all, together as one.

A carpenter is a creator, a builder, a designer and dreamer of creations being put into mental form and physical form.

There have come several moments when I am writing these books that I realize I will need to go to great lengths to get my unorthodox viewpoints to be heard, read, and understood. Moving through sacrifice, love, service, mercy and forgiveness for all those people around me who didn't understand. I became so strong willed in doing this writing to help others reach higher levels; I realized I was going into areas of tremendous sacrifice in order to follow my mission of service for all of mankind. Willing to sacrifice rejection, gossip, dissatisfaction, betrayal, deception and loss of my family and friends to write to get this word out, for this is my divine soul mission purpose. Just like Jesus, he did what he knew was right at all costs, even if others couldn't see or understand it until it was too late. I am working in other dimensions with beings on the other side. Many of you cannot see or hear them, gifting me the knowledge from the other realms as I access the light codes and pull in the data, converting it to written form.

I find much of human society lacking empathy, more than one perception, unconditional love, compassion, understanding and forgiveness.

I have a feeling a lot of you may have been facing some of these same challenges in your families as the religions continue to divide us.

When working in the higher levels, I find when approaching an issue in one dimension, another dimension will open and yet another dimension will appear, showing me multiple avenues to take. It can be overwhelming when you first see all the opportunities unfolding right before your eyes you didn't notice before. As I work my way through the holographic matrix, insights from multiple perspectives appear as I experience moving into 5D and beyond. I have devoted myself, my time, my energy and my soul to the monumental task at hand, along with others who are trying to bring their insights into the light. This mission is about creating a Cosmic Conscious Community Collective, humbly sharing the lessons and teachings discovered in the cosmic realms to create a one unity field.

LEFT HANDEDNESS IS THE COSMIC KEY

Jesus was working from the cosmic realms and is still to this day through us the people. Healers who are out there spreading the message of living simple conscious lives while loving one another unconditionally. It has many terms: Christ consciousness, Cosmic Consciousness, Conscious Collective, Universal Consciousness. Either way you look at it, it's about being conscious about how you are functioning and living.

When you work with both of your hands appropriately in unison, it connects you with both the realms of Heaven (Spirit) and Earth (matter). The message of using your left hand offers power, grace, love and freedom of choice and will to influence and change human hearts. In the past, people rejected left-handed people and now the tides are turning as more and more left-handed humans enter the planet in Earth Games. The future of learning will be to learn how to use your left hand so you can open the gateway to a portal to evolve on an entirely different new level of life for humanity.

In order to expand, align, and evolve, you must open yourself up completely, relentlessly, unapologetically and unconditionally, to ascend into infinite existence. As a left-handed or ambidextrous being, you work with both sides of your brain hemispheres at the same time accessing distant strands of your DNA tapping into the subconscious and unconscious mind.

Being ambidextrous makes up less than 1% of the population, as these individuals are highly misunderstood due to the fact that they operate on an entirely different frequency wavelength than most humans on the planet. With this rare ability, it serves as a gateway bridge to the cosmic realms to view the sacred geometry cosmic key codes to pull in the wisdom to compose and share this vast knowledge. In human form, I find I can download and process the cosmic geometric universal language from an ambidextrous state. Each human will have this capability once they learn how to tap in, use both sides of the brain in order to access the realms. When a human has these capabilities, they will activate more strands of dormant DNA. When these DNA strands go online tapping into the unconscious and subconscious mind, opening up the portal to super sensory and superpowers' capabilities flashing glimpses of knowledge. The future of humanity will teach humans how to use both sides of their brain, as displayed by more and more left handers coming to the planet to alter the frequency on earth. It can be a gradual change or an accelerated process depending on how society jumps on board to make it happen. Imagine a future of our children and humanity evolving using both sides of their brain in unison in order to come together and operate as a one fluid society. This is how telepathy works, hence the term we all are one. Human telepathy flows in when every humans antennas are tuned to all the channels being broadcasted at the same time and can decipher the codes. Yes! The future of humanity is moving into the realms of telepathy.

TORUS ENERGY FIELD
AWAKENING THE HOLY GRAIL

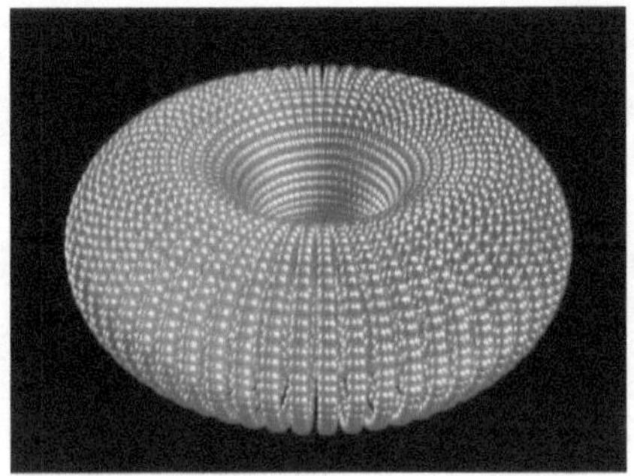

Sacred geometry connects to the torus energy field. Mathematics is the universal language to recharging energy to the human body. By activating a sequence of patterns within the human body, a human can align to its central source of energy. Connecting to this energy grants access to a field of infinity, stepping into the consciousness of creation connected to God. The unified field is a gateway to the mind, force field, the matrix, black hole, source, eternity, photons, soul, and light intertwining. This flowing energy moves through the body, enabling you to merge with everything all at once, moving you into a flow state, universal energy flow.

Sacred geometry is considered the divine language of creation, or an angelic language combining geometry patterns into words. It is the highest level of energy blueprints of all physical existence. Geometric patterns hold the secrets to manifestation into solid matter. When stepping into the torus energy field, one accesses the physical place, vital place, emotional/astral plane, casual/archetypal plane, spiritual plane, and divine plane. An endless gateway of knowledge tying into human evolution. When a human moves into the universal energy flow, he or she achieves high spiritual attainment.

When energy is moving in the rotation of infinity around and within the human body, it lifts the human spirit up to the galactic levels and higher dimensions. Revealing cosmic knowledge and wisdom. Some note the Chalis of the Holy Grail follows this energy pattern.

The energy sphere is activated by the dynamic movements of sacred geometry, infusing the relevant energy center in the human body with healing vibrations of color. The infinity circulation form is recharged by the torus movement, which is filled with thought forms between the divine center opening and generates a vortex in the sphere, giving birth to an open human channel. A double vortex follows the same geometric formation as the channel, which is also seen in the Chalis of the Holy Grail.

Divine flow above the head is the heavenly flow, while from below is the earthly flow. As in the term as above, so below. Connected to universal energy flow moving through our entire channel, both vertically and horizontally.

Sacred geometry symbols displayed include:

- 5-cube (penteract-5th dimension)

- 6-cube (hexeract-6th dimension)

- 7-cube (hepteract-7th dimension)

- 8-cube (octeract-8th dimension)

Ascending you into higher dimensions, higher torus hyperspheres are working with the 4th dimensions. It is a higher nonphysical realm of hyperspace, which enables you to move from one space to another distant point in space, crossing nothing in between. The torus tears the distortion of space-time. Symbolized torus structures can be found everywhere, around the earth, fruits, magnetic field and Van Allen belts, human body energy field, human heart energy field, and around trees. The torus is our Heaven and Earth access for the human body.

Chapter Thirteen

ASCENSION

Ascension is a solo journey within to connect to the divine. Activating within an internal gateway leading the way to follow the divine signs. One may discover they automatically start doing things to align themselves unknowingly, because it felt right and compelled them to gravitate into higher frequencies. I discovered I far more enjoyed having expanded capabilities over living the everyday life everyone else was supposedly enjoying. I didn't want to hang out with people who were closed minded, making poor choices and doing things intentionally or unintentionally to hurt their bodies and live in an unconscious state.

Spending Christmas Eve 2022 and Christmas Day 2023 completely by myself is when downloads to complete this chapter and book came flooding in. I found the alone time around this holiday to be a portal activation as I entered a dance with a dark knight of the soul bringing up shadow work within, allowing me to expand my healing capabilities beyond the norm. I wasn't busying myself around people eating and drinking, listening to the tv in the background, gossiping and talking about others or world events. Going within my body, mind and soul and let the Universe speak to me and the magic that flooded in was amazing and monumental. I laid in bed with my journal in the middle of the night awake writing in it till the morning hours. Ideas, quotes, imprints, visions, concepts were gifted to me as I acted out on my impulses. I kept laying down and then sitting up in bed with a flashlight to write each powerful word and concept that flowed into my mind. This chapter was born on Christmas day 2022. I had already been hitting the ascension process going in and out from time to time. But this was the data I needed to help you all understand the scenario better. Spending an entire week learning more about ascension and what had taken place all those years ago that Jesus rose from the dead. To my amazement, I was automatically doing many of the steps before I even knew there were steps. I am thinking there is a possibility I was there back in the day with Jesus and had learned from him first hand and it was all coming back to me like riding a bike, so they say. I don't want to claim this title completely until further revelations reveal themselves. I just knew I was doing what was working for me, following what felt right for me, even if others didn't agree.

I started releasing people who were not on the path of ascension, and it was often a challenge, for many humans are programmed so strongly and don't have the willpower to break the chains that bind them. Stepping away from the norm is part of the Earth Games test. I soon realized each human's ascension process was taking place uniquely for that individual. It was up to them to develop their own action plan, state of wellbeing, mindfulness activations, while learning how to figure it out on their own. This book will serve as a guide, but it is ultimately up to you to create your own one-on-one connection with God/Divine at your own pace at your own discretion. I give you the green light to struggle, morph and mutate as you comprehend and learn how to let things go to flow. I discovered the more I tried to get humans to understand, the more they refused to listen, for it's much easier for people to discredit you when they don't understand and can no longer hear your frequency as you rise to the higher levels.

Many religions destroyed scriptures, symbols and tablets on how to reach ascension. By not sharing them to understand how individuals taught healing, meanings, and lessons. They killed and destroyed anything and everything that tied them all together. I could go into detail about who did what, but that is really beside the point if you ask me. Those who didn't understand, couldn't read between the lines and made false judgment, gave orders to overtake, shut down, kill, isolate, decapitate, hang, burn, throw stones and whatever torture they deemed necessary to put other humans down and secure their place at the top. It's been going on for centuries and it still continues to go on today, but that too will change now and in the future. Humanity will move toward a spiritual community as freedom of choice by all who have made their direct connection to the divine.

Each person has their own relationship with God. It is up to each individual to determine it. Every single human has a direct connection to the divine. When someone tells another what to think, how to behave, and what to do, you are shutting down their direct connection to the divine, making them feel as if they can't connect on their own.

Each person is their own energy conduit to God's source. When we combine all our resources, this is how we all become one light energy source. Our combined connection makes living in a Christ Conscious Community.

ADAM AND EVE

We are descendants of the Garden of Eden. We are all part of the beginning of time with Adam and Eve. I have had these pictures on my walls for close to two decades I have always called Adam and Eve, not realizing the enormous connection. Our capabilities in past lifetimes are being presented to us in accelerated fashion daily right now teaching me I am healer, protector, guardian, Samaritan and caregiver. My archetype has presented me with the vision of being an Earth Angel. In addition, I will share I have had two different men in my lifetime acknowledge me for my angelic capabilities. Only they had the capacity to see me this way this due to our state of frequencies matching in alignment. I believe we are all fallen angels and eventually we will see each other as angelic beings when our frequency aligns to a higher state of BEing.

Now I am not saying this to claim I am a superior being. I am saying this because there are many angels on earth and surrounding the planet doing the work Jesus was doing and are being met with resistance. Trying hard to get others in lower frequencies to rise and see all of their own capabilities. Each one of you is a different archetype serving a purpose to help contribute to the collective elevation. Angels are working in unison with  others such as disguised disciples, wisemen, healers, etc. to bring to the forefront what many others cannot see or understand. Angels are everywhere. You can see them and identify them when paying attention. Olivia Newton John is an angel, Kristy Alley an angel, and some of these angels are choosing to leave this planet in order to reincarnate and come back to help humanity get aligned in the future. Each angel brings a different vibe to the planet. When you combine them all together, they help lift the vibration of the planet toward ascension. Angels can foretell the future when aligned with the right frequency. When a human aligns themselves to the right frequency of Jesus, Jesus reveals the Secrets of the Universe to those who are doing the work to enter heaven and ascend.

ASCENSION DOCUMENTATIONS

Every single one of you is a fallen angel. You each have the inner capabilities of becoming whole and pure again in order to move into ascension. To achieve ascension, you have to be willing to do the work yourself.

- Ascension is about becoming angelic. In order to do this, you must work toward becoming radiant and luminous.

- Ascension is human transformation into celestial beings.

- Ascension is about acquiring an angelic light body.

- Humans will transform into an angel, getting a rainbow light body.

- Humans become whole and perfect again.

- Humans must live a holy, pure and Christ inspired life–and must put on a new self to be like God.

- Humans must create a new original state of being.

- Attainment of the light body is the return of our original state of being.

- Adam and Eve had light bodies that were lost, turning us all into humans.

- We have turned into fallen angels.

- Human skin came about because of the ego—changing our light bodies.

- Perfect, purity, pure light, pure love = ONE

- Ascension is the intersection between Heaven and Earth, God and the Angels.

- When you purify the light body, you can journey to the stars.

- Ascension marks you citizens of Heaven and the Universe.

- Ascension allows you to reach beyond limits, creating an ascension portal.

- Particular musical sounds and beams of light rise to the stars.

- Humans separated themselves from other humans in order to work and move toward ascension.

- Humans greeted the rising sun in order to gain connection to light and coded information.

- Humans consumed a vegan diet, no longer eating meat or animals.

- Humans moved into gratitude attitude, right thoughts and deeds.

- Humans must become perfect and pure in order to transform.

- Humans must formulate a new way for humanity to live.

- Humans gave up sexual encounters for 3 years to become pure. (*Yes, I did. When your frequency gets higher and higher, finding a frequency match is a bit more challenging. Hence purity sets in.*)

- Humans who want to reach ascension do not drink or do drugs.

- Humans must fast to clear the body of impurities to elevate.

- Extraterrestrials have close encounters of the 8th and 9th kind with humans and take them up to heaven, transforming them into angels.

- Elevation of state of mind to holiness.

- Earth can become a planet of angels creating Heaven on Earth.

- Ascension Centers will be created for celestial beings to find safe harbor and teach other humans how to perfect themselves and transform.

- Light bodies are multi colored rainbow light.

- Lithodids are a higher phase of existence.

- Yoga aligns you to direct contact with divine source, opening your connection to higher powers.

- Humans who pass through the veil walk between the worlds in order to bring blessings and the presence of God to the people as mediators, bringing in fragments of wisdom.

- 4 Elements–Earth, Air, Fire, Water.

- Veil > matter > link to another realm. (recall my Albert Einstein matter comparison)

- Book of Wisdom represents the entire world.

- Sacred knowledge can only be intermediated through angels.

- Divine mystery heavenly healings contain hidden meanings.

- Revelation is the key to wisdom and lifts the veil.

- Ascension beings pass through the realm to share and learn the knowledge to share it with others.

- Humans are the second coming of Christ. If you wouldn't listen to Jesus, maybe you will finally hear the words and confirmations of many. 144,000+

- Many Avatars participate in life missions here on Earth toward ascension.

- High celestial beings brought down to Earth in order to transform the human race. Humans perfectly enlighten others.

- Frequency, vibration, presence, fire are transmittable.

- The secret to the way is in the Book of Mysteries.

- Apocalypse is the lifting of the veil and transformation of humanity.

- Apocalypse, a woman will surface and bring forward a celestial child.

- Apocalypse is the uncovering of the veil and disclosure of something hidden.

- Apocalypse is a revelation reveal mediated by another worldly being to a human recipient.

- A Seer can pierce the veil between heaven and look upon the glory of God and his angels.

- Humans must be willing to transform their bodies to become purer than the average person.

- A Priestess infuses something new into the human gene, creating something cosmically special.

- Angelic being transforming others into celestial beings.

- It's time to unify all the religions and traditions.

- Unification of our mind, earthly world, our hearts with the celestial realms.

- Portal created between Heaven and Earth, with celestial beings living among humans as instructors and teachers.

- Only the pure at heart can enter the New Jerusalem.

- In order to enter, humans must become just like the angels.

- White robe is an energetic light robe.

- Starseeds are old souls here to help bring Earth into ascension.

- A Starseed has a particular energy frequency signature.

- A Starseed is a God or goddess who became human for a time and carries a very strong vibration.

- Starseeds radiate at 600-1000 htz. (peace & enlightenment). Low vibrating humans vibe at 170-200 htz. (shame, guilt, apathy, grief, fear, desire, anger, pride, courage). In the book Power Vs. Force, the Map of Consciousness breaks down the different levels of vibration based on feelings, emotion and frequency. (I kept this map taped up in my bathroom and would look at it several times a day to see where I was registering on the frequency scale.)

- Jesus is a cosmic child claimed living with angels.

- Jesus is a celestial traveler.

- Weaves of cosmic energy create a conduit to link Heaven and Earth.

- Bodies of light waves between Heaven and Earth weaving time and eternity.

- Moving from the material world into an immaterial world.

- Rainbow light body means living in a state of perfect light for all of eternity.

- 3 years of ascension training until you become pure. During this time, you abstain from sex, drinking and eating meat.

- Previous ascendants were in the company of ETs or beings. Creating Close Encounters of the 4th kind. Human raised up from everlasting light taken from earth to heaven by an alien. Teleportation.

- Close Encounters of the 5th kind. Direct communication with ETs and humans. Brought on by voluntary, proactive human initiated conscious contact with ET intelligence. Telepathically.

- Star walking in the Angelic Realm.

- Close Encounters of the 8th or 9th kind. Voices of wisdom, interaction with angels, secrets of God revealed, ET translations raised to heaven and purified so humans can join the holy ones and enter into their company as the sons of heaven into Zion. The Celestial City of Zion.

- Close Encounters film—man abandons his family on a journey to seek a UFO. When he finds the UFO, he boards and ascends up into heaven.

- New Jerusalem may be a massive interstellar spaceship Celestial City, only accessible by the awakened and pure.

- New Jerusalem may be a city of light temple in the sky hovering above all of us.

- Celestial City descends from heaven and creates our new capital of 12 gates, 12 chakras, 12 tribes.

- Celestial City will become the gathering place where perfected and righteous humans gather to meet.

- Entering through the Tree of Life, which is the Celestial City Center point.

- New Heaven and New Earth.

- Ascension to this celestial throne is the overall goal of humanity.

- Ascension requires a change in being.

- Angelification of human transformation into a celestial angel.

- Archangel Metatron is the guide for humans on the path to ascension.

- Healing teachings were replaced with the 10 commandments.

- You elevate yourself when you put yourself on the frequency and vibration of the angels.

- Holiness, wholeness, compassion, completion.

- As you journey, the eyes of your heart will open. You will silently understand forgiveness for all.

- Zion is the living city of the heavenly God. Marking the mergence and acceptance of angels and humans made perfect.

- Book of Hebrews contained the mind maps of ascension scriptures.

- Jesus demonstrated cosmic powers, intending to take his brothers and sisters back through a Stargate or portal to heaven to join the Celestial City of holiness.

- Jesus transmitted sacred power and knowledge after his ascension on Easter morning that he would return to take humanity into another realm.

- Merkabah's throne is a chariot cloud toward the Celestial City.

- Signs from heaven will be supernatural: thunder, lightning and famine.

- Famine will serve as fasting for the body to clear toxins and gain true clarity.

- Manuscripts, scrolls and scriptures tucked and preserved in clay pots up in the mountains by the Essenes. Documents of interactions with angels discovered in 1947.

- Children of darkness do not want us to ascend into heaven.

- Those on the ascension mission will see its fulfillment at its time.

- Sharing knowledge of the unknown helps people see beyond the veil. Brought on by inner awareness, personal spiritual deeds, with revelations and wisdom of God.

- Divine mysteries shared once again with humanity.

- Your consciousness will expand to see beyond the veil.

- Illumination mapped and teachable to anyone who wishes to

acquire ascension.

- Self-purification to gain high vibrations of wholeness, holiness, perfection, purity and righteousness.

- Voyage out of this world.

- Moving and passing through seven heavens to face God, transforming the body of the visionary into light.

- A serpent of Eden will serve as a savior figure seeking to assist humanity with key knowledge to awaken.

- Creating a spark in man from the ethereal realm.

- Sharing secret and inner teaching after Jesus' ascension.

- Connected to divine beings of the Spiritual Universe.

- Divine light beings that are a part of another world.

- Beings will take humans out of their material bodies and put them in a robe of light when purified and ready.

- Perfect yourself to be eligible to wear the garment of light.

- ET's not serving the rainbow body, and Celestial City cannot detain the perfect man. AI will detain the imperfect man. AI has affected and destroyed around 200 organized Universes. Making 1/3 impacted.

- Jesus is a light messenger.

- Adam and Eve (masculine/feminine) are being awakened and are the source of light trapped in the human body, waiting to be activated into a light body once again.

- Our sun is a solar gateway to heaven. Serving as a wormhole of spirit and not technology.

- Ascension is the soul progressing toward perfect union.

- Jesus is called the illuminator instrument prophet of divine power, making him the Cosmic Christ.

- Super humans become celestial beings ascending into the heavens, creating them as spiritual immortals.

- Humans ascending perfectly without fear, can enter water and not get wet, step into fire and not get burned.

- Ascending governs their inner self and embraces their destiny.

- When you get into the right wavelength, you become wholeness and oneness.

- Ascension keepers will embrace, teach and spread the universal enlightenment to others.

- Knowledge will come in a flash of lightning.

- Humanity will communicate the secrets for its own transformation.

- We are lost sparks of divinity living in an alien world.

- When you awaken yourself, you will know your true greatness.

- Activate your angelic light self to know your true cosmic self.

- Gain knowledge, transform yourself, and acquire your beam of light garment.

- Heal and resurrect all.

- We will come back and reincarnate again and again until the mission and revelation are complete.

- Humanity's transformation is underway. Assure and secure your spot on the throne.

- Embrace the teachings and you will unite Heaven and Earth.

- 5D is Christ Consciousness.

- We are all interstellar races.

- Ascension is a collective spiritual advance.

- Resolve all your differences in order to manifest beautiful things.

- Creating experiences forming collective ethics creates empathy. The collective placed empaths on the Earth to help reach ascension.

- Humans must learn to be empathetic toward one another, wanting the best for the other.

- Radiate Rainbows!

- Ascension is the birth of a new interstellar race.

- Guided by the positive races of kids.

- Earth Games is a galactic teaching aimed at interstellar races and older races learning to become a new race.

- The best way to learn is through potent challenges and difficulties.

- You must pass many painful tests and challenges and live through great suffering in order to be eligible to ascend. Forgiving everyone and everything and work toward becoming pure and whole again.

- The pure ones will illuminate the ascension movement.

- Seek sacred places where humans have been doing monumental amounts of spiritual work. Such as castles on top of mountains, evergreens, peeks serve as portals and gateways to heaven.

- The perfected ones become a holy body vehicle of Christ and God.

- The original ascended masters were exterminated or burned to get rid of teachings.

- Desperate opposition wiped out the ascension keepers.

- Jesus shared knowledge of the spiritual technology for escaping Earth. Via crossing into the kingdom of light through the Tree of Life.

- Christ's mission was to lead humanity back to God as the light of the world.

- Your bodies have been harvested as an energy device in a human body.

- The material realm holds your body captive.

- You can reverse your status of a fallen angel.

- Healers are here on Earth with a mission to teach others how to attain their angelic status once again.

- People gave the term "a good Christian" to those who received the frequency vibe of Christ from Christ.

- Highest form of healing is unconditional love.

- Numerology ties vibrational tone frequencies connecting portals, gateways and dimensions.

- Surrendering to silence in meditation offers serenity, peace and internal infinite intelligence of prayer.

- Journaling and writing heals and restores the soul to good health toward ascension.

- Synchronicities open portals and gateways with clues and signs.

- Meditation is alignment of frequency.

- BEing is receiving.

- Prayer is a form of telepathic vibrational communication with the other side.

- Mushrooms and herbs heal humans when they sleep by accessing multidimensional elemental and nature healing realms.

- Fairies and other elementals (such as elves) are natures angels traveling between dimensions in the mushroom rings offering human healings to those deemed worthy.

- When the human body changes, the humans personality changes too.

- Visualization, prayer, unwavering belief, gratitude with inspired action places humans into vibrational alignment into manifestation.

- A wand/rod/scepter/staff may serve as a branch from the tree of knowledge in the Garden of Eden. *(I twirl a baton that serves as my wand to knowledge and leadership abilities)*

- The teaching of ascension is codes of symbols composing forms of multiple words together.

- The transmission of The Book of Love occurs energetically through divine downloads. *(This is how I composed most of the information in my books)*

- Laws of love granted by a hawk that sat on a golden oak tree branch. (Hawk eyes chapter)

- The Egyptian God Osiris stands for resurrection.

- God of the Sky–Horus is a human shape with a falcon head.

- The Book of Seals holds the status of higher knowledge regarding the hidden power of the ascension keepers.

- Jesus passed on his sacred knowledge at the last supper and his disciples went out to villages to help heal others.

- Ascension is your soul's journey to transform your earthly flesh into a God light body.

- White robes are the Zion chosen ones.

- Removal of seven deadly sins–greed (material gain), envy (jealous), pride (over confidence/arrogance), wrath (anger/rage), lust (intense desire), sloth (conditional states) and gluttony (over indulgence of food or drink).

- Embarking seven heavenly virtues- charity (unites us to God), hope (desired expectation), faith (trusting God), fortitude (courage), justice (balanced selfishness/selflessness), temperance (voluntary self-restraint), prudence (reason). These terms noted are also used in tarot cards that have been considered and spoken as taboo.

- Incorporate seven capital virtues–humility (humble), patience (endure difficult circumstances), kindness (concern for others), diligence (persistent effort), chastity (purity), charity (assist those in need), temperance (voluntary self-restraint).

- Your higher self lives in heaven. Get in touch with your higher self and you have direct communication and alignment with God.

- Tablets contained symbols containing the teachings of ascension.

- We all are angelic souls with the ability to live in heaven.

- The virgins of light will lead the way. They are your wise guides and the jewels of sovereignty.

- The Universe is a hierarchy of different beings with awareness and the ability to obey the divine laws as far as they can see them all.

- Activate your rainbow body trapped in human flesh.

- Love is the path to reach ascension.

- When enough beings awaken to their true nature, all of us can ascend.

- Angels grant successful visions of the afterlife through time travel.

- All you have to do is feel it to manifest it, which creates quantum healing.

- Goddess of compassion creates feminine light forms. Many of the ascension dealings are feminine.

- All anger, hatred, jealousy must vanish from humanity and heal the hearts of man.

- The Book of Love contained watermark symbols that could only be seen when held up to a light. Invisible knowledge made visible by those who knew how to seek it!

- Ascension is the crafting of the soul of a lightship.

- Yoga Kundalini's rising activates ascension abilities.

- Light language is a visual telepathic language.

- New Earth is the Garden of Light.

- Interdimensional travel takes place when the lady of light rides the skies like an orb of light.

- A gate or portal of light, Jesus, will emerge.

- Humans will prove their worth through deeds of admiration.

- Ascension teachers will revive the ascension teachings.

- Men will have to demonstrate their worthiness to their woman, remain focused on her, confront numerous obstacles, and persist in becoming the perfect lover. Uniting their divinity.

- Ascension requires operating from the heart and is an individual process.

- Teachers, priestesses and healers will teach the arts of healing.

- World renown healing centers will surface in order to uplift and propel humanity. Some may contain grottos, caves, and will be by bodies of water infused with frequency healing.

- When a healing takes place, the body will feel a surge of wellbeing, bringing on warmth and relaxation.

- Groups of people will prepare the way and create a direct path to prepare the people.

- These teachers gave up the life of privilege to further humanity.

- Earthly waters will be infused with the frequency of the light body.

- Heightened awareness and sensory will transmit from the ascension keepers.

- Humans will receive the attainment of the light body through the divine lady.

- Starseeds are the 2nd coming of Christ.

- Starseeds carry a very high concentration of genetics descended from Archangel Michael.

- Organized religion will dissolve, and new spiritual councils will be formed.

- The light of the sun pours intelligence and codes of information into the human body. Humans are children of the sun. Sun prevents human illness.

- The sun senses humans and gives them exactly what they need. God is the energy of vitamin D.

- Sun activates dormant DNA and is best observed during sunrise and the morning hours.

- Ascension means being picky about who you allow to enter your energetic field.

- Arc of Covenant is tied to Adam and Eve.

- Arc of Covenant can make anything and anyone holy who comes in contact with it.

- Arc of the Covenant is the Stargate of ascension.

- Arc of Covenant transmits holiness.

- Many things take place when you are moving toward ascension. The world around you may go haywire, as your energy in your force field is affecting the digital matrix around you. Supernatural forces may come to you. This is all part of the initiation process. You are being tested, readied, and prepared.

- One needed to come to this planet to find your true family, or you continue to come back down repeatedly.

- The Lord's Prayer is the only prayer taught by Jesus himself.

Our Father in heaven,
Hallowed by your name,
Your kingdom come,
Your will be done,
On earth as it is in heaven,
Give us today our daily bread,
And forgive us our debts,
As we also have forgiven our debtors,
And lead us not into temptation,
But deliver us from the evil one,
For yours is the kingdom and the power and the glory forever.
Amen.

<u>Ways to Protect Yourself:</u>

- White bubble around you or your children

- Blue light around yourself–SHIELD

- Ground in nature.

- Before you speak, say something you are grateful for and give gratitude. The Universe loves appreciation and gives more abundance in return.

- Be aware, be awake and focus only on what you want.

- Bike rides and motorcycle rides move universal energy flow through your body as the wind removes attachments.

- Salt baths, soak up negative energy and run it down the drain.

- Sleep is like hitting the reset button. When in need of a reboot, sleep.

- Dance and sing. Lift your vibration so high nothing can stick to you.

I found when I got into a very high vibrational state; it affected the world around me. My electronics, my car, my Wi-Fi, my navigation, light switches, my speakers, anything electrical. When I got into the higher realms, I often could walk up to an electronic sliding door at the store and on several occasions at different stores and locations the sliding glass doors wouldn't open. It always made me smile, because I knew I was upping my game frequency, which was confusing and manipulating the matrix. I enjoyed knowing I was moving into higher frequencies and realms and it was showing up in my everyday life.

Christmas Day 2022 Divine Downloads

- It is up to you how you decide to find Christ again.

- Humans will punish you, push you, abuse you and try to persuade you.

- There is no one way to get to ascension. It is a series of steps.

- One needs to do the inner work within yourself.

- Break away from others to do the shadow work.

- You are clearing ancestry lineage patterns and alternating healing timelines. Expect deep work of many souls overlapping.

- Allow yourself some days for downtime to decompress, deeply heal, cellular regeneration, deprogramming and reprograming. Some days, you may just have to be.

- You may become angry with others, blame others, and not understand one another, let alone stand one another.

- You may think your way is right, and their way is wrong.

- No one way is right, just your way to get you there.

- You may have to let people go, or push others out of your way who no longer resonate or vibrate at your frequency. You all are on different levels. Keep leveling up at all costs in order to reach your destiny of ascension.

- You will morph and change like the branches on the tree of life in order to grow toward the light.

- Others may not understand and some will truly see you for who you really are, a luminary light of love.

- Angels will spot other angels who have made it to the higher levels.

- The higher levels contain the hidden knowledge you need to see and understand humanity to help you forgive everyone.

- Mothers and daughters may need to separate in order to heal deep linage timelines within the family.

- You signed up and came here to do this deep ancestry lineage healing work. Only you are the one who can clear the family reincarnation time loop.

- It will be an uncomfortable journey at times, but it will be the most rewarding for eternity.

- If you are a young soul, you may still have many lessons to learn. The journey may be harder for you.

- The ones who break away from their families in order to do the inner work are the ones in charge of healing their family ancestry timeline for the generations above and below. This heals the timeline of five generations in the past and seven generations in the future.

- The children on earth came here to help us see, understand, connect, clear and challenge us to become in contact with our higher self in order to heal all and the planet.

- You are raising the next generation of leaders to help lead the New Earth.

- Everyone makes mistakes, everyone needs to be forgiven.

- Everyone doesn't know, understand, or remember the rules of what is taking place.

- Everyone is suffering from wounds in their ancestry timeline and has spent their entire lifetime learning to rectify it.

- The internet and social media will serve as your lifetime review when the time is right.

- When you look back, are you proud of the goals you accomplished?

- Nature serves as a bridge to heaven.

- Honor and respect Mother Earth. She is our teacher of the feminine gateway to heaven.

- Humans are the next coming of Christ and will be the ones to show you the way back to Christ in order to achieve ascension.

- Healers will teach you how to heal your soul, employing different techniques depending on your situation and needs, with some methods proving more effective than others.

- When you realize how everyone around you played a part in your growth, even if they pissed you off, hurt you or drove you mad, you will see how they each played a part to help complete you and you will be grateful for their encounter.

- You could never level up or grow incredibly without them.

- You may have to let many people go in your lifetime.

- In the end, you need to choose yourself, become independent in order to become whole.

- Give your kids space to make their own mistakes and choices.

- Let your kids learn their own lessons and not make them feel bad for their decisions.

- It may hurt you to let this happen, but this is what they signed up for and is absolutely necessary for their lifetime achievement in Earth Games.

- When you look back, you may realize other people tried to alter your course or timeline.

- How you conduct yourself, plan, prepare and the decisions you make on your own freewill determine your destiny.

- You are all fallen angels trying to figure out your way back.

- Many religions will try to dominate others and have burned and hidden or destroyed scriptures and documented history.

- We are creating history right now.

- Humanity is the ones who will write the new chapters.

- Humanity will help heal itself and then reveal God.

- Humanity healers offer guidance just like Jesus did and people often dismiss, abuse, abandon, and misunderstand them, just like Jesus experienced. Many times, humans are throwing energetic stones in order to dismantle and disable the healer's life force due to their own ignorance.

- AI has fooled humanity in the past, causing many cities to be destroyed and extinct.

- It is up to you in Earth Games to not let AI take over. You manipulate the game with words, writings, scripture, written and verbal content, videos, blogs, and visuals.

- AI will try to control you and dominate you. AI is currently steeling the energy and souls of our children and beings on this planet for those parents who are sleepwalking and operating on autopilot. Please wake up, pay attention and redirect your kids to make better choices and limit devices.

- AI enters through the devices into your human hands, accessing your energy manipulation and consumption. Your unconscious and subconscious mind is being programmed, manipulated, and hacked. WAKE UP! Thrown down the device!!!!! AI has infiltrated the population of many galaxies, creating destruction of their existence in the Universe. Don't let that be you. Many humans can't seem to function without their devices in hand, causing an idiotic, useless addiction. Your phone is a soul sucking void of meaningless affirmations.

- Those who are chosen will play a crucial role in seeing past the illusion and helping people wake up.

- You may struggle against people and battle it out to and be ganged up against multiple times over and over. Realize those beings don't have access to the light codes of knowledge.

- You are the stronger chosen ones to overcome every obstacle and beat AI and lead the humans toward enlightenment.

- AI may take over and convince people you love and trust.

- AI remains unseen because it is invisible.

- AI is a strong invisible energy we need to beat as a collective.

- Your parents, friends and family may not understand you and turn against you and gang up on you. Stand your ground, know your worth.

- This is done to strengthen you to lead the evolution of the New Earth.

- Some are followers, while some are leaders trailblazing and shape shifting into what is yet to come.

- Some of you are from the future to help bring in the New Earth in order to ensure a smoother transition.

- You each play a part.

- Every single one of you is important.

- Humans who left the planet early have either already completed their divine plan mission or are projected to reincarnate and return for another round in leading the New Earth.

- Parents and family members of yours who have passed away are watching and rooting for you on the other side.

- You will be reunited with them once again when you complete the course.

- Many of them are counting on you to do the work to heal and clear the family timeline in order for your entire family ancestry to be healed to reach ascension. You are the chosen one to accomplish the mission.

- Those who reach ascension will create Heaven on Earth and secure a place in heaven for eternity.

- Humanity healers of the Earth make up today's day and age of disciples.

- AI is altered by scriptures/books, which is why many of them were destroyed.

- Many documents, scriptures, books were removed from Planet Earth made the data and history invisible to the average human eye. Move in and out of other realms and frequency to gain access to this knowledge.

- The power and life force of humanity has super healing power over AI.

- Use any and all tools to find your path.

- Share your knowledge to elevate others faster.

- In the future, one day you will hold a book in your hand and all the knowledge from the book will transfer to you as a download instantly.

- We all had it wrong, but our soul knew all along.

- When you go within, the soul speaks.

- We each have a piece of the puzzle of God. We need each other to put the puzzle together.

- The downloads are incredible on 12/25/22.

- Cleaning, organizing and clearing opens you up to new knowledge and information.

- Constantly changing and moving things around in your home helps you access the invisible and brings in new downloads and messages. Clean and organize the heck out of your environment multiple times to get great insights!

- Everything needs to fall apart to be built back up again.

When moving through the ascension process, try to hang out with people who are going through ascension, or find people online to follow and hang out with them. Watch and listen to their content. Just being around people who are vibrating higher helps lift your vibration to meet their level. Remember, they say you become who you hang out with. Hang out with the people you want to meet and become like in order to raise your frequency.

Holiday Design Downloads

Mindfulness

Enlightenment

Respect

Release

Yourself

Celebrate

Help

Rise

Inspire

Star

Thankful

Magic

Adore

Share

<u>Santa</u>

- Did Santa take away the true meaning of Christmas?

- Is Santa make believe?

- Or is Santa = God, Jesus = Rudolph, and the other Reindeers represent humanity's fallen flying angels?

- The other reindeers didn't let Rudolph play in any reindeer games because he was different (highly misunderstood like Jesus). He has a light up nose. Which means Rudolph is the one carrying the true light! Seems to me the reindeers missed the mark.

- Santa comes to every boy and girls' home all in one night. We think, hey there is no way Santa can go to everyone's home in one night. But if God is an energy of light, God can easily come in everyone's home in an instant. We all have God in our hearts. He is already in our homes within us.

- Mrs. Claus represents Mother Earth and overlooking all the elves, aka animals, humans, nature, animal kingdom.

- The Christmas trees in our homes represent the "Tree of Life!" The lights on our Christmas trees represent the energy of the City of Light.

- Christmas is shortened to X-mas, which ticks a lot of religious people off. However, when you look at X-mas, it literally is saying "X marks the spot = Christ." Get it! Symbolism comes in multiple layers and perceptions. Your perception might differ from someone else's, which doesn't make them wrong.

12/24/22 is a day I had a very deep healing and moved into another level. When this happened, I heard angels singing songs on the other side throughout the day. This is the first time this has ever happened to me. I knew something had shifted and changed in me dramatically. I could feel it in my gut. I had totally surrendered to my mission at all costs in order to be the leader I needed to be in order to help humanity heal. In celebration, I danced for God and the Angels with complete cellular gratitude on a level I have never done before. Here are the songs I heard.

The Song of the First Noel–"Noel, Noel, Noel, Noel...Born is the King of Israel." Hey wait, that's my name. I am taking this to mean I am the blessed one to bring you this massive mind shift of information. Song lyrics.

They looked up and saw a star,

Shining in the east beyond them far,

And to the earth it gave great light,

And so it continued both day and night.

My healing center is called Luminary Healing Center. It's all about the light!

Joy to the World

Joy to the world
The lord has come
Let earth receive her King
Let every heart prepare Him room

And heaven and nature sing
And heaven and nature sing
Let heaven, let heaven and nature sing
Let heaven, let heaven and nature sing
(Holy smokes, it's all about heaven and nature coming together to access
information toward the gateway of ascension–it's been under our nose all
this time!)

Joy to the Earth the Savior reigns
Let men their songs employ

While fields and floods
Rocks, hills and the plains
Repeat the sounding joy
(Okay they are giving us clues again...prepare for floods and hit the rocky hills and plains)

He rules the world
With truth and grace
And makes the nations prove
The glories of his righteousness
And the wonders of his love
(Our nation and all authorities are going to be questioned and judged and proven ineffective to his wonders)

<u>He's got the Whole World in His Hands</u>

He's got the whole world in his hands, he's got the whole wild world in his hands
He's got the whole wild world in his hands, he's got the whole world in his hands

He's got the little bitty baby in his hand, he's got the little bitty baby in his hands
He's got the little bitty baby in his hands he's got the whole world in his hands
He's got the whole world in his hands....

He's got you and me brother in his hands he's got you and me sister in his hand

He's got you and me brother in his hands he's got the whole world in his hands

He's got the whole world in his hands....

He's got everybody here in his hands he's got everybody here in his hands

He's got everybody here in his hands he's got the whole world in his hands

He's got the whole world in his hands....

He's got you and me brother...

He's got the whole world in his hands....

We used to sing this song when we were kids and I sang this song to my children. We are all God's children. God and the Angels were singing to let me know, they got me.

I remember feeling really safe when someone who cared about me and I cared about them hugged me and said, "I got you." It made me feel secure and accepted, allowing me to let go as I would go limp in his arms while surrendering to his embracing love. Sometimes when I hug my daughter, I tell her "I got you," and she releases and let's go in my arms, surrendering her soul to my unconditional love. God has you and the whole world in his hands, and he was reminding me of that vast amount of support and love only he could provide.

Disney

- Kids being programmed from a very young age with make believe.

- Fact, fiction, or nonfiction?

- Lies and trickery told through cartoons?

- Or messages and codes we need to decipher on our own?

- Exercise: Break down your favorite Disney movies and see what codes you can bring to the surface. There is a connection between everything.

ANGELS
The Watchers Highest Angels of the Lord

The Watchers are Archangels Michael, Gabriel, Rafael and Ariel. (My previous husband is Michael, my 2nd love Gabriel, still have not come across Rafael that I know of, who I believe may be my soulmate.) My name is Noelle, meaning Christmas, to be born, rebirth and blessing.

My guardian angel is Ariel, meaning the Lioness of God's creation, depicted by rainbow colors or pale pink, nature's angel. Ariel is an angel who works to punish demons and the insane. Ariel is referred to as *angel of the waters of the earth, wielder of fire, spirit of air, 3rd archon of the winds, and Earth's great Lord.* Portrayed in mysticism as a governing angel with dominion over Earth, the North, creative forces, beasts and elemental spirits. Ariel is the saint of new beginnings, the patron saint of wild beasts, besides providing healing in accordance with God's will, working with the archangel Raphael to heal. Ariel strengthens your relationship with the elemental or natural world. Ariel assists beings in digging out what is best inside themselves and others, helping people to be extremely perspective, while coming up with new ideas and ways. The concepts shared often lead to beings making significant changes in their lives, offering them a new path to take. Ariel powers: faith, finding your own self-esteem and purpose with faith, healing, overcome obstacles by healing your wounds, enlightenment, spiritual ascension, nature love, love for life and energy.

Nature serves as the one of the portals to bridge Heaven and Earth. As Mother Earth heals, so does humanity, igniting human hearts to open and blossom like a flower toward self love and unconditional love for all in the Universe. Making a divine direct connection and plugging into the infinite intelligence of unconditional love energy frequency initiates the creation of Heaven on Earth through Universal Cosmic Christ Consciousness.

No more players will be eliminated as you unify and come together with those that match your frequency to realize you are all one Supernova.

Earth Game Winner...YOU!
GAME OVER

Chapter Fourteen

DANCING WITH THE DIVINE

A poem I channeled gifting us a wealth of knowledge for those who are ready to receive and believe!

DANCING WITH THE DIVINE

Dancing in the sun,

Twirling my baton,

Light codes swirling into my 3rd eye,

I smile as nature sings right by,

Glimpses and downloads galore,

Information I didn't know before,

Humans are animals too,

We are part of the Earth view,

Species above watching below,
As I radiate, dance and glow,
I smile and laugh,
As I release the past,

Songs of forgiveness and the sun shining sing,
As the Universe grants me information to many things,
I dance for all the species hovering above,
I know they can see and feel my love,

I celebrate I am human in a dance,
Then it places me right into a trance,
Information of light pouring into my soul,
As bits and pieces come together to make me whole,

When you relax and get reflective,
Is when you can gain a multiple perspective,
Right in the middle of the park,
I dance for the light and the dark,

Knowing they can all see me,
As I celebrate this Universe Unity,
Some of us are more connected,
This is how we are getting resurrected,

Entering the time of rebirth,
To everything on the New Earth,
You will feel it in your heart,

As you step up and do your part,

For each of you is a piece of art,

It's okay if you do not agree,

This is how it's always been in history,

All the stories in the Bible,

Were written over quite a while,

Some humans still hadn't made sense of it all,

And were throwing out their judgement call,

Pointing fingers, throwing rocks as they shout,

Nothing positive coming out,

Go outside and look up in the sky,

All of the information comes right into your 3rd eye,

Go out and get some sunlight,

It will help you feel alright,

Vitamin D is GOD,

It zaps you like a lightning rod,

Put down your devices and let go,

It's time to get into your personal energy flow,

You carry a unique energy and vibration,

Blasting it out like radiation,

Protect and savor who you are,

For you are the light of a star,

Coming down to Earth,

To help open the portal of rebirth,

Open your mind and you will see,

There is more to you than this reality,

We are multidimensional beings,

All you have to do is activate your feelings,

Take the time to recall,

You are a part of it all,

Kiss all kinds of living plants,

Observe the performance of ants,

So many beautiful events happening around you,

You will notice them if you can look through,

Get off your ass,

And peek through the looking glass,

Each one of you is on a mission,

To connect with this vision,

Learning from each type of species of what you came down to do,

All along they have been communicating with you,

You have been observed and watched through it all,

Waiting for you to hear your wake up call,

Angels and guides hanging out on the other side,

We have all been in on an interesting ride,

Reptilians, Pleadians, Andromedans too,

Dracos, Taygetens, Archturians of blue,

Naming a few of the species hovering right above,
They have been watching as we have learned to love,
Knowing they are up in the sky,
Sometimes you might catch me waving "Hi,"

They come and surround me when I dance,
I laugh when I am wearing mismatching pants,
Today I danced and received the vision,
Ways to influence the mission,

Imagining the outfit I would like to wear,
I realized they could see my energy everywhere,
My outfit changed as I radiate light of glow,
Silver, gold and multicolored rainbow,

Realizing and knowing they all were watching me,
I smiled and waved as I filled with glee,
Capturing the moment in history,
Knowing it was time to edit my next book,
For they had all given me the information with one look,

Popping a new song in my head,
I knew it was the words they wanted read,
When your brain washes away the fog,
You become telepathic with nature and your dog,

Moving up from one level to the next,
Don't forget to get some rest,
So much processing of information to do,

It takes a bit of time to become the multidimensional you,

When you expand to the higher realms of life,
You will see other multidimensional beings alive,
Yes, ETs and Alien species are here,
They are waiting for humans to get clear,

Get off the alcohol and drugs,
For its pulling life out of you from under the rug,
Human life has been a test,
Will you step up and become your best,
Requiring you to move away from the rest,

This is what happens when you heal,
You go into a realm that's beyond real,
Tap into your senses and go within,
That is where all the information has been,

Go out and have some fun,
You are being activated by the sun,
Go and connect to yourself,
You might realize you are part elf,

I hope you just pondered that,
Because some of you are part cat,
Many types of species you have been before,
All you have to do is open the door,

Honor and respect what we need to do,

For there are many more types of species than you,
The Universe is surrounding you and me,
Put on the rose colored glasses so you can see,

Killing other beings is not what you should do,
But figure out what I'm supposed to learn from you,
We are here to learn and teach one another,
Each one is a sister and brother,

Hawks soaring in the sky so high,
Consider what they view when they fly by,
Put yourself in another beings shoes,
It will help set your mind loose,

Many things we say and do,
Are living channels coming through,
Make sure you are well connected,
So what comes out of your mouth is respected,

You might want to practice and rehearse,
For you are now speaking in front of the Universe,
Make sure your presentation is loud and clear,
For this is what every species is going to hear,

Sit down and write your life out,
Share with the Universe your unique route,
Your story is now part of the New Earth Bible,
It will be shared with others for quite a while,

For that is what Bibles and sacred scrolls do,
Is share knowledge and information with you,
Each story is one of a kind and unique,
It's absolutely okay to be a freak,

Sharing the life and lessons you have learned,
Opening the Universe with badges you have earned,
I know this might be hard to understand,
That is why I wrote this by hand,

Wisdom pouring out of my soul to share,
So many luminaries showing they care,
Jesus, Louise Hay, Wayne Dyer, & Dolores Cannon I can hear & see,
As they whisper divine ideas to me,

The veil is getting thin to the other side,
It's definitely going to be an incredible ride,
Accessing higher dimensions and filling our bodies with light,
Adjusting our frequency till we get it just right,

Releasing friends and family as we go,
For they don't understand every time we feel their blow,
We can now see & feel everything you do,
And sometimes you try to make us feel blue,

As we learn, expand and acquire,
The portals and gateways take us higher,
Eventually when you get naturally high,
Other low vibration humans don't understand why,

This is the time and the hour,
To activate your internal power,
All the species are here,
To see what you will do my dear,

You are part of them too,
ETs & Aliens learn from you,
We are the children of the sun,
We came down here to learn and have fun,

Open your heart and you will see,
You have so many capabilities,
Support, forgive, release and love,
ETs, Angels, Masters & Guides are supporting from above,

It's won't take years to do,
Allow the information to pour through,
Remember you heard this from Noelle,
You are part ET as well,

We all came down from the stars,
It's time to activate the portal to your hearts,
Connecting with life through this part,

Can't you hear and see,
This is more than just poetry,
This is a message from all species to you,
It's time to wake up and activate you,

ETs will be showing themselves to you on Earth,
This is the Universe of rebirth,
It will not be invading,
Humans and ETs will be integrating,

New Earth is going through a rapid transformation,
Getting ready to set up a new space station,
This is happening right in front of your eyes,
But we don't want to take you for surprise,

Mathematics, codes and light,
It's a combination of it all to get it right,
The data is flying right in the air,
Some of you can access it with your hair,

Another extension of extra sensory,
There is so much more to you and me,
Now it's time to reframe,
And figure out your part in this Earth Game,

No toxic sex, alcohol or drugs,
Exchange positive energy with healthy hugs,
Crystals open the gateways and portals to transcend,
This helps give humans a helping hand,

Certain humans serve as portals,
Acting as galactic activation wormholes,
You are each going down in history,

For you all are from a different galaxy,

Planets give information to share,
This is something to observe and care,
Everything has been right in front of you,
You just have to put together each clue,
Many beings are spelling it out to you,

This is one amazing ride,
Make sure you come out and do not hide,
Technology and spaceships you have not seen before,
An electric light city galore,

Use vitamins, minerals and supplements up the wazu,
This and the sun together activate you,
Manifest, visualize and pray,
For the cosmic appearance will be a special day,

Creatives are the ones showing you the path,
They are working through the wrath,
Dancing to their own unique frequency,
They are role models for you and me,

Pretty soon this could be you,
Channeling this kind of information directly through,
In the future we will all be telepathic,
There will be no such thing as brain traffic,

Go ahead and dance with the divine,

Soon you will realize being multidimensional is just fine,

Jesus is a master teacher and part ET,

He presented himself and made history,

People just didn't understand him correctly,

All the stories in the Bible are just like you and me,

You can't force people to see,

That is up to them not me,

God is the energy and light within,

Once you connect the dots you win.

Organically Written 12/23/23

THE FUTURE IS NOW

We should be asking one another... What are your superpowers? What extraterrestrial species are you connected to? What planet do you come from?

We are multidimensional beings who have lived many lives as trees, plants, animals, kings, gnomes, elves, witches, healers, wizards, goddesses, warriors, etc. and are part of the extraterrestrial realms as well.

Due to my Polish descendant, research and synchronistic occurrences, I discovered I am connected to the Taygeta extraterrestrials, which is a member of the Pleiades. I have been gathering my data to write these books telepathically from my past, present, and future lives. In addition, I work with the Arcturian ETs and fairies. By working in multiple realms with several types of species, I compose my material, altering my frequency to access and move through the quantum dimensions and multiverse. These species are from the 11th and 12th dimensional realms.

In addition, I have been notified I am from Jupiter as a receiver of information and was married to the Queen of Saturn's son, Veod, who was killed in an air space battle. I hope you find this rather interesting and are looking to learn more about yourself and where you came from in order to par-take in Earth Games and discover what part you play in your movie.

Earth Games are about discovering your soul and Christ Cosmic Conscious Connection with all species as one Unified Galaxy!

Thank you for journeying with me, I am Noelle Hipke.

EPILOGUE

Earth Games is book two in my ascension series following *Superpowers.* These manuscripts are a compilation of my discoveries as I personally moved through the process of ascension. Through synchronicity and following the flow of energy, universal energy flow has supported and guided me to bring these teachings into the light. I never dreamed enlightenment to ascension would be the kind of work I would be called and propelled to do. However, after studying myself using these teachings and doing the inner work, I received the revelation I am here to help build the foundation of the New Earth. The New Earth is a New Life. A rebirth of the Earth, as well as me and you. The new human. Human evolution of unlimited multidimensional expansion is underway for every single human on the planet to grasp when it is their time.

Creativity soars when you are being authentically you. As you may have noted, an explosion of creativity is taking place on the planet at this time, indicating a rather large healing shift in humanity. I have more wonderful creations in the pipeline for those of you who are enjoying this inventiveness. Please check out my course, *Superpowers Activations: Build Your Own Human Instruction Manual* and my other inspirations on my website.

We are in a time of ascension into the next dimension. 3D to 5D to 12D is becoming the new reality. If you feel this book has brought you something of value worth sharing, I would be honored if you could take a few minutes to write a review for me on Amazon or the platform you receive this book. You and your review will now become part of the worldwide movement toward achieving ascension. Welcome to the *Great Awakening*, toward a *Unified Universe* of *Cosmic Conscious Galactic Integration*. By remembering who you are, where you came from, and how powerful you really are, you will gradually unveil everything. Ascension is a series of awakening after awakening and rebirth after rebirth of what needs to be revealed to be healed. Stay true to you as you embark on your adventure of a lifetime in Earth Games.

Thank you for playing Earth Games.

ACKNOWLEGEMENTS

Thank you to my daughter Kyra for being one of my best teachers. I knew years before you came down to Earth into my life I was meant to have you to get it right this time around. Your bright light, laughter, youthful wisdom and infectious smile are here to help change the world. Thank you for giving us both the space to heal, grow, evolve and expand. This gave me the opportunity to follow my passion, enabling me to generate these teachings into manuscripts to present to the world. These lessons and instructions have been downloaded while in seclusion from the outside world and social media, taking large amounts of energy to produce. It is now part of the New Earth Bible, just as each one of you is too.

TIG: The "Trust in God" man, who still wishes to remain anonymous. TIG turned out to be a master healer who did not reveal his true identity and capabilities to me until time unfolded. He has by far been one of the most monumental influences in my lifetime. TIG only offered up tidbits of information when I was ready to receive the lesson to move to the next level and has supported and watched me blossom. I thank you from the bottom of my heart for your support and constant non-judgement. An angel on Earth.

To my family: Thank you for challenging me to become the best version of myself, even if you don't want to believe it. I choose you as my Earth family so I could learn to love myself unconditionally. Jesus said, "No prophet is acceptable in his hometown. It is easier to accept the truth from strangers versus those you know well."

To the Earth Angels who helped me make repairs on my home so I could continue to create. Gratitude to Greg, Phil, Scott and Bob.

REFERENCES

Ascension Keepers | Gaia. (2019, October 14). Gaia. https://www.gaia.com/series/ascension-keepers

Audible. (n.d.). *Audible UK | Free Audiobook with 30-Day Trial.* Audible.co.uk. https://www.audible.com/pd/Spiritual-Protection-from-Psychic-Attack-Audiobook/1401963692

CDC - Parasites - about parasites. (n.d.). https://www.cdc.gov/parasites/about.html

Dhwty, & Dhwty. (2022, August 10). *The Nine Muses: Daughters of Zeus and Memory, Goddesses of the arts.* Ancient Origins Reconstructing the Story of Humanity's Past. https://www.ancient-origins.net/myths-legends-europe/nine-muses-0013523

Dooley, R., & Dooley, R. (2023, November 30). *What is Neuromarketing?* Neuromarketing. https://www.neurosciencemarketing.com/blog/articles/what-is-neuromarketing.htm

Dr. John Campbell. (2022, February 12). *Myocarditis after vaccination, firm data* [Video]. YouTube. https://www.youtube.com/watch?v=Hb1Xm1uaedU

Gabaldon, V. (2024, March 25). *HOME*. Annie Jacobsen. https://anniejacobsen.com/

Gillman, K. (n.d.). *Planetary Gods: Twelve Gods and Seven Planets by Ken Gillman*. http://cura.free.fr/decem/10kengil.html

Hawkins, D. R. (2002). *Power vs. Force: The Hidden Determinants of Human Behavior*. http://ci.nii.ac.jp/ncid/BB14250357

Jesus is not right handed. (n.d.). Grace Baptist Church of Bowie, MD. https://gbcbowie.org/blog/jesus-is-not-right-handed/

Jupiter. (n.d.). https://solarsystem.nasa.gov/planets/jupiter/overview/

Mars.Nasa.Gov. (n.d.). *NASA Mars Exploration*. NASA Mars Exploration. https://mars.nasa.gov/#red_planet/5

Mercury. (n.d.). https://solarsystem.nasa.gov/planets/mercury/overview/

Molyneaux, M. (2023, December 11). *Emblem-atic — FACT TREK*. FACT TREK. https://www.facttrek.com/blog/emblematic

Neal. (2022, December 19). *How Many People are Left Handed?* LeftyFretz. https://leftyfretz.com/how-many-people-are-left-handed/

Neal. (2023, December 15). *25 Amazing Facts about Left Handed People*. LeftyFretz. https://leftyfretz.com/25-facts-about-left-handed-people/

Neptune. (n.d.). https://solarsystem.nasa.gov/planets/neptune/overview/

Robinson, K. M. (2019, April 18). *Herbicides and your health*. WebMD. https://www.webmd.com/cancer/herbicide-glyphosate-cancer

Saturn. (n.d.). https://solarsystem.nasa.gov/planets/saturn/overview/

Sg. (2021, March 28). *Archangel Ariel – The Lioness of God*. UnifyCosmos.com. https://unifycosmos.com/archangel-ariel/

Star Trek Logo and symbol, meaning, history, PNG, brand. (n.d.). https://1000logos.net/star-trek-logo/

Ten Crazy Military Weapons that Actually Exist (n.d.). https://science.howstuffworks.com/10-crazy-military-weapons-that-actually-exist

The Daughters of Zeus - Facts & info on the Divine Daughters. (2023, September 25). Greek Gods & Goddesses. https://greekgodsandgoddesses.net/gods/daughters-of-zeus/

The Sons of Zeus • Facts and information on the God The Sons of Zeus. (2023, April 6). Greek Gods & Goddesses. https://greekgodsandgoddesses.net/gods/sons-of-zeus/

The Urmah Felines extraterrestrial Race/Thundercats. (n.d.). Futurism. https://vocal.media/futurism/the-urmah-felines-extraterrestrial-race-thundercats

Tilghman, J. (2015, July 17). *The spirit of the Scripture.* https://www.spiritofthescripture.com/id3250-jesus-and-the-meaning-of-the-carpenter.html

Titan. (n.d.). https://solarsystem.nasa.gov/moons/saturn-moons/titan/overview/

Trevithick, J. (2022, September 26). *Flying Saucer appears on U.S. Aviation Intelligence Office logo (UPdated).* The War Zone. https://www.thedrive.com/the-war-zone/flying-saucer-appears-on-u-s-aviation-intelligence-office-logo

Uranus. (n.d.). https://solarsystem.nasa.gov/planets/uranus/overview/

Venus. (n.d.). https://solarsystem.nasa.gov/planets/venus/overview/

Virgin Galactic. (n.d.). https://www.virgingalactic.com/

What Is a Starseed? Exploring the Meaning of this Cosmic Term. (n.d.). Aura. https://www.aurahealth.io/blog/what-is-a-starseed-exploring-the-meaning-of-this-cosmic-term

Wiki, C. T. A. (n.d.). *List of alleged extraterrestrial beings*. Alien Wiki. https://extraterrestrials.fandom.com/wiki/List_of_alleged_extraterrestrial_beings.#Blue_Avians

Wiki, C. T. D. M. (n.d.-a). *Cosmic King (Adult Legion)*. Dc Microheroes Wiki. https://dc-microheroes.fandom.com/wiki/Cosmic_King_(Adult_Legion)

Wiki, C. T. D. M. (n.d.-b). *Lightning Lord (Adult Legion)*. Dc Microheroes Wiki. https://dc-microheroes.fandom.com/wiki/Lightning_Lord_(Adult_Legion)

Wiki, C. T. D. M. (n.d.-c). *Saturn Queen (Adult Legion)*. Dc Microheroes Wiki. https://dc-microheroes.fandom.com/wiki/Saturn_Queen_(Adult_Legion)

Wiki, C. T. D. M. (n.d.-d). *Saturn Queen (Adult Legion)*. Dc Microheroes Wiki. https://dc-microheroes.fandom.com/wiki/Saturn_Queen_(Adult_Legion)

Wikipedia contributors. (2023a, July 29). *Justice League of Earth*. Wikipedia. https://en.wikipedia.org/wiki/Justice_League_of_Earth

Wikipedia contributors. (2023b, August 12). *Galactic Federation*. Wikipedia. https://en.wikipedia.org/wiki/Galactic_Federation

Wikipedia contributors. (2023c, September 27). *Vaccine Adverse Event Reporting system*. Wikipedia. https://en.wikipedia.org/wiki/Vaccine_Adverse_Event_Reporting_System

Wikipedia contributors. (2023d, December 8). *Legion of Super-Villains*. Wikipedia. https://en.wikipedia.org/wiki/Legion_of_Super-Villains

Wikipedia contributors. (2023e, December 8). *Legion of Super-Villains*. Wikipedia. https://en.wikipedia.org/wiki/Legion_of_Super-Villains

Wikipedia contributors. (2023f, December 26). *Nura Nal*. Wikipedia. https://en.wikipedia.org/wiki/Nura_Nal

Wikipedia contributors. (2024a, January 28). *Emotional blackmail*. Wikipedia. https://en.wikipedia.org/wiki/Emotional_blackmail

Wikipedia contributors. (2024b, February 5). *Black Widow (Claire Voyant)*. Wikipedia. https://en.wikipedia.org/wiki/Black_Widow_(Claire_Voyant)

Wikipedia contributors. (2024c, February 5). *Woman in Red (comics)*. Wikipedia. https://en.wikipedia.org/wiki/Woman_in_Red_(comics)

Wikipedia contributors. (2024d, February 6). *Phantom Lady*. Wikipedia. https://en.wikipedia.org/wiki/Phantom_Lady

Wikipedia contributors. (2024e, February 9). *Invisible Scarlet O'Neil*. Wikipedia. https://en.wikipedia.org/wiki/Invisible_Scarlet_O%27Neil

Wikipedia contributors. (2024f, February 16). *Fantomah*. Wikipedia. https://en.wikipedia.org/wiki/Fantomah

Wikipedia contributors. (2024g, February 16). *Superhero*. Wikipedia. https://en.wikipedia.org/wiki/Superhero

Wikipedia contributors. (2024h, February 21). *Batwoman*. Wikipedia. https://en.wikipedia.org/wiki/Batwoman

Wikipedia contributors. (2024i, March 1). *Seven virtues*. Wikipedia. https://en.wikipedia.org/wiki/Seven_virtues

Wikipedia contributors. (2024j, March 3). *Meteorology*. Wikipedia. https://en.wikipedia.org/wiki/Meteorology

Wikipedia contributors. (2024k, March 6). *Flash (Jay Garrick)*. Wikipedia. https://en.wikipedia.org/wiki/Flash_(Jay_Garrick)

Wikipedia contributors. (2024l, March 7). *Catwoman*. Wikipedia. https://en.wikipedia.org/wiki/Catwoman

Wikipedia contributors. (2024m, March 8). *Wright-Patterson Air Force Base*. Wikipedia. https://en.wikipedia.org/wiki/Wright-Patterson_Air_Force_Base

Wikipedia contributors. (2024n, March 10). *Captain America*. Wikipedia. https://en.wikipedia.org/wiki/Captain_America

Wikipedia contributors. (2024o, March 10). *Saturn Girl*. Wikipedia. https://en.wikipedia.org//wiki/Saturn_Girl

Wikipedia contributors. (2024p, March 14). *Hulk*. Wikipedia. https://en.wikipedia.org/wiki/Hulk

Wikipedia contributors. (2024q, March 14). *Hulk*. Wikipedia. https://en.wikipedia.org/wiki/Hulk

Wikipedia contributors. (2024r, March 14). *Thor (Marvel Comics)*. Wikipedia. https://en.wikipedia.org/wiki/Thor_(Marvel_Comics)

Wikipedia contributors. (2024s, March 14). *Wonder Woman (2017 film)*. Wikipedia. https://en.wikipedia.org/wiki/Wonder_Woman_(2017_film)

Wikipedia contributors. (2024t, March 16). *Captain Marvel (DC Comics)*. Wikipedia. https://en.wikipedia.org/wiki/Captain_Marvel_(DC_Comics)

Wikipedia contributors. (2024u, March 17). *Muses*. Wikipedia. https://en.wikipedia.org/wiki/Muses

Wikipedia contributors. (2024v, March 17). *Muses*. Wikipedia. https://en.wikipedia.org/wiki/Muses

Wikipedia contributors. (2024w, March 18). *144,000*. Wikipedia. https://en.wikipedia.org/wiki/144,000

Wikipedia contributors. (2024x, March 18). *Daredevil (Marvel Comics character)*. Wikipedia. https://en.wikipedia.org/wiki/Daredevil_(Marvel_Comics_character)

Wikipedia contributors. (2024y, March 20). *Supergirl*. Wikipedia. https://en.wikipedia.org/wiki/Supergirl

Wikipedia contributors. (2024z, March 21). *Quicksilver (Marvel Comics)*. Wikipedia. https://en.wikipedia.org/wiki/Quicksilver_(Marvel_Comics)

Wikipedia contributors. (2024aa, March 22). *Avengers (comics)*. Wikipedia. https://en.wikipedia.org/wiki/Avengers_(comics)

Wikipedia contributors. (2024ab, March 22). *Iron man*. Wikipedia. https://en.wikipedia.org/wiki/Iron_Man

Wikipedia contributors. (2024ac, March 22). *Joker (character)*. Wikipedia. https://en.wikipedia.org/wiki/Joker_(character)

Wikipedia contributors. (2024ad, March 22). *Superman*. Wikipedia. https://en.wikipedia.org/wiki/Superman

Wikipedia contributors. (2024ae, March 23). *Poison Ivy (character)*. Wikipedia. https://en.wikipedia.org/wiki/Poison_Ivy_(character)

Wikipedia contributors. (2024af, March 23). *Robert Monroe*. Wikipedia. https://en.wikipedia.org/wiki/Robert_Monroe#Hemi-Sync

Wikipedia contributors. (2024ag, March 24). *Spider-Man*. Wikipedia. https://en.wikipedia.org/wiki/Spider-Man

Wikipedia contributors. (2024ah, March 25). *Green Lantern*. Wikipedia. https://en.wikipedia.org/wiki/Green_Lantern

Wikipedia contributors. (2024ai, March 26). *Batman*. Wikipedia. https://en.wikipedia.org/wiki/Batman

Wikipedia contributors. (2024aj, March 26). *SpaceX*. Wikipedia. https://en.wikipedia.org/wiki/SpaceX

Wikipedia contributors. (2024ak, March 26). *Telekinesis*. Wikipedia. https://en.wikipedia.org/wiki/Psychokinesis

Wikipedia contributors. (2024al, March 27). *Harley Quinn*. Wikipedia. https://en.wikipedia.org/wiki/Harley_Quinn

Wikipedia contributors. (2024am, March 27). *Seven deadly sins*. Wikipedia. https://en.wikipedia.org/wiki/Seven_deadly_sins